PENNSYLVANIA COLLEGE OF TECHNOLOGY LIBR

506080
Soble, Ronald L/Th
HV6698 .Z9 E657 19

GW01337377

HV
6698   Soble, Ronald L.
.Z9
E657   The impossible
1975   dream: the Equity
           Funding story,
DATE DUE   the fraud of...

NOV 16 1987			

The Impossible Dream

**THE EQUITY FUNDING STORY:
THE FRAUD OF THE CENTURY**

EDITORIAL CARTOON BY PAUL CONRAD

Copyright, Los Angeles *Times*
Reprinted with permission.

The Impossible Dream

THE EQUITY FUNDING STORY:
THE FRAUD OF THE CENTURY

by Ronald L. Soble
and
Robert E. Dallos

G. P. Putnam's Sons   New York

Copyright © 1975 by Ronald L. Soble
and Robert E. Dallos

All rights reserved. This book, or parts thereof, must not be reproduced in any form without permission. Published simultaneously in Canada by Longman Canada Limited, Toronto.

HV
6698
.Z9
E657
1975
40437

SBN: 399-11378-9
Library of Congress Catalog
Card Number: 74-79643

PRINTED IN THE UNITED STATES OF AMERICA

To Mark Soble and to Lisa, Jeffrey, and Andrew Dallos

CONTENTS

FOREWORD 9

PROLOGUE 12

An intriguing group of characters is indicted in what is believed to be the biggest business fraud ever.

I THE IMPOSSIBLE DREAM 25

Mike Riordan, the chairman of the board of Equity Funding Corporation of America, is killed. Wall Street, the affable Irishman's playground, is shaken. But EFCA and the financial community take it in stride as his colleague, Stanley Goldblum, assumes command.

II IN THE BEGINNING 37

We look back and meet Gordon C. McCormick, who had a good idea and then got caught in a trap play between Riordan and Goldblum.

III THE EARLY YEARS 43

Inflated assets, a bribery conviction, and separate inquiries by two government agencies highlight the history. A new subsidiary emerges, the Equity Funding Life Insurance Company.

IV GOLDBLUM 54

The policies, politics, and personality of the chairman are examined. Goldblum really wanted to be a doctor. We tour his Beverly Hills home and visit his custom-built $100,000 gymnasium. An insight into an inscrutable corporate character.

V SAM AND FRED 74

Here we meet Sam Lowell and Fred Levin, the two top EFCA officers under Goldblum. Lowell would rather play bridge. Levin enjoys company games.

VI   INTERNATIONAL OPERATIONS—
TOO MUCH SPAGHETTI   92

    Equity Funding gets into the spaghetti business in Italy and finds it has bitten off more than it can chew.

VII   INTERNATIONAL OPERATIONS—
THE MAZE   103

    An attractive redhead becomes the target of a secret investigation by the Internal Revenue Service attempting to learn whether there are secret funds abroad. Joseph Golan's international adventures. Who is the mysterious Dr. Heinrich Wangerhof? An endless maze through shell corporations.

VIII   THE ATMOSPHERE, OR, WHAT IT'S LIKE TO WORK FOR A WINNER IN GLAMOROUS CENTURY CITY   125

    A go-go company in an exciting location. A discussion of the "borrowing" theory.

IX   THE COMPUTER GAME (AND THE MAPLE DRIVE GANG)   133

    Stealing the modern-day way. An EFCA programmer tells us how he did it. And a look at the Maple Drive office where there were plenty of pills, champagne—and phony insurance policies.

X   STORM CLOUDS   151

    A flimflam game with $25.3 million in bonds.

XI   HOLES IN THE DIKE   157

    A computer manager observes some weird happenings. Ron Secrist and Pat Hopper decide that they have an unbelievable story to tell to Ray Dirks, a Wall Street insurance-stock analyst.

XII   DIRKS   166

    We meet the bohemian Dirks, an atypical securities analyst if there ever was one.

XIII	**THE IDES OF MARCH**	172
	A blow by blow account of the fall of a financial empire.	
XIV	**THE BANKER AND MR. LEVIN**	230
	A sophisticated New York banker learns that Barnum was right.	
XV	**THE LAST SUPPER**	238
	A dramatic confrontation at an EFCA board meeting during which there is a palace coup ousting Goldblum, Levin, and Lowell.	
XVI	**APRIL**	257
	The Wall Street Journal breaks the story, followed by chaos and plenty of lawsuits.	
XVII	**THE INSIDER ISSUE: A STUDY IN OBFUSCATION**	265
	Wall Street is up in arms over the age-old problem of insider trading. Dirks has stirred up a storm in which two of the nation's biggest institutions find themselves on a collision course.	
XVIII	**THE REAL LOSERS**	275
	The plight of the shareholders. An analysis of the scandal's impact.	
XIX	**GOLDBLUM SPEAKS OUT**	279
	The chairman, in an interview with the authors, expounds on his views of the case.	

EPILOGUE   285

APPENDIX   289

INDEX   307

Illustrations will be found following page 158.

Foreword

THIS book is the result of a painstaking investigation into the odd world of Equity Funding Corporation of America. Dozens upon dozens of present and former employees, investigators, Wall Streeters, persons close to the company, and individuals who were personal friends of the principals in this book were interviewed in an effort to sort out a complex and massive business fraud.

The crimes charged by the Federal Grand Jury sitting in Los Angeles and the county grand jury in Illinois were committed by human beings, not by the computers and other gimmickry the defendants used. Therefore the authors endeavored to humanize the Equity Funding story wherever possible without distorting the facts. Indeed, Equity Funding had a fascinating cast of characters who would lend themselves well to a work of fiction—were it not all true!

As with most major works of investigative reporting, it was a day and night task, mostly sandwiched around the authors' regular jobs as financial writers for the Los Angeles *Times*. That, of course, meant endless interviews in person and by telephone. Many of them took place at Equity Funding's Century City headquarters. Others took place in New York and Washington. Some were easily conducted in the comfortable surroundings of an executive's office. Others were more difficult, involving secret rendezvous with those who either did not wish to be identified or were reticent about being seen talking to the authors. Additionally, countless interviews were conducted in several U.S. cities and in such foreign capitals as London, Paris, and Rome.

At this writing, the full story of the Equity Funding scandal was still being sought by federal and state investigators. Most—but not all—of Equity Funding's domestic activities had been pieced together. But it appeared that much still could be learned from a further probe of the financial conglomerate's foreign activities, and that is where the authorities were concentrating much of their work.

In putting together this type of book, extensive cooperation is required from many sources who, for personal and legal reasons, cannot be identified here. The authors are indebted to these individuals for their own personal sacrifice in spending hours recalling what must have been for many a very painful experience.

Heartfelt thanks also is extended to Anne Soble, the wife of one of the authors, and editor of the Malibu *Surfside News*, for doing some of the research, transcribing many of the tapes, helping with the editing, and with the arduous task of constructing the index. Gratitude also is extended to Mrs. Arthur Dallos for her help in researching the chapter on computer technology.

The authors also wish to thank Herbert K. Schnall, president of the New American Library, and Ward M. Mohrfeld, of NAL, for proposing this book.

Appreciation also is extended to Harry Anderson, the Los Angeles *Times* reporter who followed the day-to-day Equity Funding story, who offered constructive suggestions; and to Michael Chaplin, a Los Angeles *Times* financial news editor, who wielded a deft copy pencil over the final draft.

And finally, both authors are deeply thankful to their wives, Anne and Carol, for their encouragement during the many months of preparation of this book.

Publicly Held Companies Do Not Lose Money.
—STANLEY GOLDBLUM*

*Goldblum's instructions to Fred Levin in February, 1969, as alleged on page 19 of the Federal Grand Jury indictment returned to United States District Court for the Central District of California.

Prologue

ON April 2, 1973, the United States Securities and Exchange Commission charged that Equity Funding Corporation of America (EFCA), acting through certain of its officers and employees, engaged in a massive scheme to manipulate the price of the company's stock. The charges turned on the inflation of the company's earnings by reporting business that simply did not exist.

The Wall Street Journal, which broke the story to the public that day, called the case "one of the biggest scandals in the history of the insurance industry. . . . " That was certainly a correct assessment as far as it went.

Further investigation, however, by the United States Attorney's office, the Federal Bureau of Investigation, the SEC, the United States Postal Service, and the California and Illinois Insurance departments discovered much more cn the ensuing months, leading authorities to conclude that the Equity Funding case may be the most colossal business fraud ever.

Investigators were astonished to find that of the 99,052 life insurance policies worth $3,531,432,871 on the books of the Equity Funding Life Insurance Company (EFLIC), an EFCA subsidiary, approximately 56,000 policies, representing some $2 billion worth of insurance, were phony.

In addition, of approximately $117 million in loan receivables on the books of the company which was alleged to have financed the bogus policies, some $62.3 million was found to be nonexistent.

Thousands of small shareholders lost millions of dollars.

Hundreds of banks and other institutions were stuck with worthless stock.

Wall Street was knocked for a loop when it could least afford it.

The normally staid world of insurance was suddenly turned into an almost unbelievable tale of misadventure, deceit, and fraud.

As unlikely a cast of characters as ever appeared in any of nearby Hollywood's detective films turned up in the Equity Funding saga:

The late chairman of the board, a swinging Irishman who had more friends on Wall Street than he could count, and whose fun-loving ways almost got him rubbed out by the mob.

His partner, an inscrutable weight-lifting fanatic, who had Wall Street hypnotized with a financial empire he put together almost overnight.

A roly-poly insurance-stock analyst from New York's Greenwich Village who couldn't believe what he had heard and then proceeded to break the case wide open after first fearing for his life.

The head of the insurance operations, a young executive with a brilliant mind who was ruled by his own ruthless ambition.

The company's top moneyman, who thought he someday might be president, realized it wasn't to be, and spent his last months with EFCA more interested in tournament bridge than in insurance and mutual funds.

The international contact woman whom the Internal Revenue Service couldn't nail, but who may be the ultimate key to millions of dollars of funds secreted in foreign banks.

The spaghetti-factory fiasco in which the Vatican was almost swindled and which turned into a financial disaster and a confrontation with the Italian government.

The girls of the Maple Drive office who didn't know they were manufacturing fraud, but who celebrated with champagne after each crooked project.

The petty thieves who took for their own pockets, and the bigger ones who inflated the company's stock to feed their own bank accounts.

The sophisticated New York banker who was conned into returning the company's collateral on a big loan at a time when its collapse was imminent.

And last, but hardly least, there were the investigators who weren't sure whether they had enough evidence to crack what they believed to be a massive fraud case, but displayed rare courage and seized the company anyway, to protect the policyholders.

Much—but not all—of this unfolded before a Federal Grand Jury sitting in Los Angeles which, after seven arduous months of investigation, indicted twenty-two men on November 1, 1973, in connection with the case.

They were charged in a 105-count indictment with securities fraud, mail fraud, bank fraud, filing of false documents with the SEC, interstate transportation of counterfeit securities and other securities obtained by fraud, and electronic eavesdropping.

United States Attorney William D. Keller declared:

"This type of crime is epidemic in this community, as the individual feels shielded by the complexity of the enterprise. We intend to dispel this notion and our office will continue to devote all necessary manpower to the investigation and prosecution of such activities."

Meanwhile the DuPage County, Illinois, grand jury made public twenty-three indictments against twenty-two individuals. All were charged with conspiracy to enter false information on the books of the Equity Funding Life Insurance Company in order to deceive the Illinois insurance director, who had regulatory power over the insurance subsidiary which was still chartered in that state, but had moved its offices to its parent's headquarters in Los

Angeles. Other Illinois counts charged the individuals with making false entries in the company's general ledger and annual statement regarding the amount of insurance it had in force.

Jerry Nemer, a partner in the Los Angeles law firm of Buchalter, Nemer, Fields & Savitch, Inc., who had thirty-seven years of legal experience and who had handled countless bankruptcies, said he was astounded by the company's almost instant collapse. Declared Nemer before Judge Harry Pregerson on June 4, 1973, in a United States District Court reorganization hearing on EFCA:

"I have never seen an insolvency—a collapse of a firm in a shorter space of time and with more dramatic impact. On Monday, March 26, [1973], this was a vital, vibrant, operating company controlling seven to eight hundred millions. The following Monday, one week later, it was like a bleeding animal on the ground, which was literally dying because its blood was seeping out of it."

The following Los Angeles area individuals were charged by the Federal Grand Jury:

Stanley Goldblum, forty-six, president and chairman of the board of EFCA.

Samuel B. Lowell, thirty-four, executive vice-president of EFCA and the company's chief financial and investment officer. Lowell was one of EFCA's three top officers.

Fred Levin, thirty-six, executive vice-president of EFCA and head of insurance operations. Levin was the third of EFCA's three top officers.

Jerome H. Evans, fifty-nine, a senior administrative vice-president of EFCA, who resigned from the corporation in January, 1969.

Michael E. Sultan, thirty, EFCA's comptroller, who reported to Lowell.

James Cyrus Smith, Jr., thirty-five, executive vice-president of EFLIC and vice-president of insurance operations for EFCA.

Arthur Stanley Lewis, thirty, EFLIC's chief actuary.

David Jack Capo, twenty-nine, assistant to Sultan.

Lloyd Douglas Edens, thirty-one, EFCA vice-president for financial services, who was responsible for accounting in the insurance subsidiaries.

Lawrence Grey Collins, thirty-three, vice-president of EFLIC.

James Howard Banks, thirty-five, corporate counsel for EFLIC.

William Mercado, thirty-two, EFLIC's former comptroller and executive assistant to Lowell, who was dismissed in 1971.

Donald McClellan, thirty-two, assistant to Capo.

William Edward Symonds, thirty-four, EFLIC reinsurance department manager.

Lester M. Keller, thirty-two, former director of the reinsurance program, who left in 1970.

Alan Lewis Green, twenty-five, a computer programmer.

Julian S. H. Weiner, fifty, a partner in EFCA's independent accounting firm of Seidman and Seidman (formerly Wolfson, Weiner, Ratoff & Lapin).

Solomon Block, forty-four, the Seidman and Seidman audit manager on the EFCA account.

Marvin Al Lichtig, forty-five, a former Wolfson, Weiner employee and EFCA treasurer and an executive vice-president.

Gary Stanley Beckerman, thirty-three, president of Advertising Communications, Inc., an EFCA subsidiary.

Mark Charles Lewis, twenty-five, the brother of Art Lewis, who helped supervise the office at 341 North Maple Drive, where phony insurance policies are alleged to have been manufactured. His title was "project manager."

Richard Gardinier, twenty-seven, EFLIC purification supervisor (one who makes sure that policy details are in order).

In addition, the Federal Grand Jury indictment named as unindicted coconspirators:

Ronald Secrist, thirty-seven, vice-president at Bankers National Life Insurance Company of Parsippany, New

PROLOGUE

Jersey, an EFCA subsidiary, dismissed in February, 1973.

Francis D. Majerus, former comptroller of EFLIC.

William Gootnick, thirty-six, head of EFCA's computer programming.

Aaron Venouziou, who worked with Keller and Gardinier.

The Illinois county grand jury indictment didn't name Evans, McClellan, and Weiner, but it did indict three men not on the Federal Grand Jury list: Frank Majerus, William Gootnick, and Robert Ochoa, twenty-eight, supervisor of EFCA's Santa Monica printshop.*

The felonies charged in the federal indictment carry penalties ranging from two to ten years' imprisonment and fines ranging from $1,000 to $10,000 per count. Additionally, the Illinois charge of filing a false annual report is punishable by a maximum $5,000 fine on each count. Goldblum is named in forty-five Federal counts; Levin in thirty-three federal counts; and Lowell in twenty-two federal counts. All twenty-two defendants initially pleaded innocent.

At the time the galleys for this book were locked up, Levin, Evans, Beckerman, the Lewis brothers, Banks, Edens, Collins, Keller, Sultan, McClellan, Gardenier, Green, Smith, Mercado, Symonds, Capo, and Lowell had changed their pleas to guilty.

Levin pleaded guilty on January 18, 1974, to four counts of the federal indictment charging him with criminal conspiracy, wiretapping, and fraud. Levin told United States District Court Judge Jesse W. Curtis that he decided to change his earlier plea of innocent to guilty "to expedite and accelerate the conclusion of this affair."

Levin's sentencing was put off for several months. He faced penalties of up to seventeen years in prison and fines of $31,000. Some thirty-nine other counts against Levin were dropped by the government.

---

*Later, the State of New Jersey indicted Goldblum, Lowell, Levin, Smith, Edens, Lewis, Sultan, and Banks on charges they conspired to misrepresent the financial condition of Equity Funding in order to induce Bankers and other firms to merge with Equity.

That Levin would eventually plead guilty was suggested by one of his lawyers, former California Governor Edmund G. "Pat" Brown, who told newsmen in June, 1973, that his client was voluntarily cooperating with the prosecution of the Equity Funding case—a big break for the government.

Evans, a former senior vice-president of EFCA, admitted conspiring to doctor company books in the mid-1960's on orders of his superiors to show inflated assets and profits. He left the company in January, 1969, after suffering a heart attack.

The prosecution noted that its investigation had turned up instances of alleged personal embezzlement by defendants Arthur Lewis, Banks, and Edens, and of payment of a personal bill with funds by Mark Lewis. But no charges were filed as part of the bargaining for guilty pleas to the federal charges, which included criminal conspiracy.

For the Equity Funding defendants who had not pleaded guilty, trial date was set for October 1, 1974.

According to the federal indictment, Goldblum would set periodic standards for growth in income, assets, and earnings of EFCA, growth he did not expect to achieve, and growth which was not achieved through legitimate business operations. The indictment charged that Goldblum directed Lowell, Levin, and other EFCA officers to make fictitious entries on the company's books to make these projections come true.

This included the complex phony reinsurance scheme.

Insurance companies legitimately raise cash by selling blocks of new insurance to other companies—the reinsurers or coinsurers—which have enough cash but want more insurance in force.

In EFLIC's case, for every $1.00 in insurance premiums turned over by EFLIC to the reinsurer, EFLIC got $1.80 to $1.98 back from the buyer who got subsequent-year premiums. This high resale price took into account heavy first-year commissions which EFLIC paid its salesmen and, of course, gave EFLIC a nice first-year profit.

Prologue

EFLIC guaranteed its reinsurers that no more than 15 percent of its policies would lapse in their second year. In succeeding years the reinsurer would get $.90 on every premium dollar, and EFLIC $.10 to cover the administrative costs of policy accounts and claims.

The trouble was that two-thirds of EFLIC's insurance was contrived and the pyramid never stopped growing. It was almost like a number constantly squaring itself. The more reinsurance EFLIC sold, the deeper it got in and the more policies it had to create to pay off other reinsurers and, of course, to make money for its parent.*

The indictment spelled out the rigging of computer printouts and records, the forgery of death claims and policy files, the counterfeiting of bank documents, bank stationery, securities purchase confirmations and bonds, and the preparation of falsified financial data.

All this chicanery, of course, had the desired effect of keeping EFCA's stock artificially inflated, which, in turn, made it easy for EFCA to get bank loans and float securities offerings and allowed it to buy other companies by using its bloated stock. It also enabled some of the defendants to sell off their artificially inflated stock at various times at a fat profit.

At the same time, the auditors charged in the indictment

---

*Of the twenty-three reinsurers listed in its 1972 convention report on file with the California Insurance Commission which were carrying $1,756,533,169 worth of coinsurance, Ranger National Life Insurance Company of Dallas, Texas, carried the most—$835,628,424.

Ultimately, suggested an accountant's calculation for *Fortune*, the pyramid would have had to collapse under its own weight. Said *Fortune*:

"Using a set of assumptions drawn from general industry experience, and from the known details of the Ranger agreement, he estimated that if EFLIC sold off policies whose premiums came to $1 million in year one, the company would have to concoct $250 million of phony insurance by year five. In the tenth year alone, it would have to concoct over $3.7 BILLION of phony insurance—i.e., it would have to sell off that much to be able to pay all the renewal premiums due on phony business written earlier. By the tenth year the company would be claiming over $7 BILLION of phony insurance in force."

are alleged to have intentionally conducted incomplete and insufficient audits of EFCA, which resulted in the acceptance of certain fictitious items for auditing purposes and the issuance of unqualified certifications of EFCA's yearly financial statements.

EFCA became the darling of institutional investors —banks, insurance companies, and many pension funds. It was a financial services conglomerate with a fabulous growth record that apparently was immune from the economic ups and downs that affect the stock market and most other corporations.* In short, few bothered to really check what was happening, and Wall Street's high-priced talent bought EFCA's story lock, stock, and barrel.

So it was little wonder that Wall Street and some 10,000 EFCA investors were stunned by the news of massive fraud allegations. Hundreds, perhaps thousands, of individuals saw a good chunk of their life savings disappear overnight. Who can say how many personal hardships were caused by the EFCA disaster?

Some of the nation's largest banks, who had lent EFCA millions of dollars in a seemingly never-ending stream of credit so that the fairy tale of growth could go on forever, were also duped.

Equity Funding's roots went back to the late 1950's. Its forte was a unique product—a combination of mutual fund shares and life insurance sold as a package—the Equity Funding Program. Under this concept, customers would sign up to buy some fund shares every year, then borrow against them to pay the annual premiums on a life insurance policy. Each year for ten years the customer would continue buying mutual fund shares with Equity Funding lending up to 45 percent of the value of the mutual funds as payment on

*Indeed, the May, 1972, issue of *Fortune* rated Equity Funding as the most rapidly growing of all of the nation's financial conglomerates. In terms of assets among these same diversified financial companies, Equity Funding ranked forty-fifth.

life insurance premiums. The program allowed insurance premiums to be paid by the proceeeds of loans made to Equity Funding's customers who would sell their mutual funds shares at the end of a ten-year period. It was hoped by the individual who bought the package that not only would he use this technique to pay off his insurance premiums but that there also would be a neat nest egg of mutual fund shares left over.

The phenomenal growth of Equity Funding was suddenly braked during a downturn in economic conditions in 1970. But according to the indictment, Equity Funding's dynamic team of young executives led by Goldblum wasn't about to watch their company's stock, like so many other issues, nosedive in a bear market. That's when the indictment alleges that EFLIC began inventing the phony insurance.

Aside from attempting to piece together the mosaic presented in the indictments, investigators are still trying to learn whether funds were siphoned off for personal use by any of EFCA's officers. Attempting to trace funds which sloshed around EFCA's subsidiaries with little apparent discipline is a hard enough task. But when one overlays the domestic operations with EFCA's international sleight-of-hand, it becomes a worldwide scramble which may never be resolved and which made federal investigators theorize that the immediate scandal which on the surface appeared to center in the Equity Funding Life subsidiary was just a small part of a much more complex fraud involving the entire corporation.

Didn't anyone care? Could all this have happened under the noses of the regulators—the Securities and Exchange Commission, the insurance departments of Illinois and California, and the New York Stock Exchange, on which EFCA's stock was listed? The answer, of course, is a resounding "Yes!"

Essentially, Equity Funding Corporation of America was what's known as a holding company, with no real direct operations of its own, and was totally dependent for its revenue on its subsidiaries.

In addition to Equity Funding Life, acquired by Equity in 1967 and moved to California in 1968, there were three other insurance companies. One was Bankers National Life Insurance Company, located in Parsippany, New Jersey, acquired in 1971 for stock, and operating more or less autonomously. Bankers owned Equity Funding Life Insurance Company of New York, or EFNY, which was formerly the Palisades Insurance Company, a small company which operated only in New York State.

The other insurance company was Northern Life Insurance Company of Seattle, Washington, which was acquired in 1972 for approximately $40 million.

Outside of the disaster of Equity Funding Life, the other insurance operations survived unscathed.

The company's securities operations included three mutual funds: Equity Growth Fund, Equity Progress Fund, and Fund of America, the last-named a 1969 acquisition of the United States sales force of Bernard Cornfeld's Investors Overseas Services.

Two real estate subsidiaries were Equity Development Corporation and EFC Property Management Corporation. The former acquired and held land for development, particularly for the construction of apartment buildings in California and Arizona, which then sold as partnerships in which the public could purchase an interest. The latter managed the property, which included some 4,000 apartment units.

On an international level, Equity Funding was in the oil and gas exploration business under Equitex Resources Corporation. In 1969 the company marketed two limited partnerships for the purpose of exploration in oil. In addition, another subsidiary in this group was a member of consortiums which held interests in offshore concessions in Ecuador, Ethiopia, and Israel.

BEDEC International was its Rome-based subsidiary,

originally designed to enter into business deals with developing countries.

Equity Funding's international banking operations featured Equity Funding Capital Corporation, N.V., a Netherlands Antilles corporation which was the owner of the stock in Bishop's Bank & Trust Company, Ltd., a commercial bank based in Nassau, the Bahamas, engaged in international banking activities.

Its domestic banking subsidiary was the Liberty Savings and Loan Association of Beverly Hills.

The company's prize-winning cattle group, Ankony Corporation, was based in Grand Junction, Colorado, and was acquired in January, 1969. Ankony operated and managed partnerships distributed through the Equity Funding sales force. Over 190,000 acres of ranchland and over 27,000 head of cattle grazed on Ankony ranches in Iowa, South Dakota, Montana, Idaho, Colorado, and Texas.

The company's sales organization was its lifeblood and its incredible success in the face of seemingly adverse market and economic conditions was the envy of the insurance and mutual fund industries. Some 4,000 full-time sales representatives were scattered about the country. On the mutual fund side, the salesmen and agents sold not only Equity Funding's three mutual funds, but up to 300 other mutual funds with which the company had contracts as a dealer.

To finance all these activities, the company had negotiated over the years approximately sixty different lines of credit with some fifty different banks or lender groups.

The way this financial empire crashed is a bizarre adventure. Indeed, declared Robert M. Loeffler, a former executive of Investors Diversified Services, who became Equity Funding's reorganization trustee in April, 1973: "It seemed to me more fascinating than any other story that had come to my attention since *Alice in Wonderland,* which had always been a favorite of mine."

I
The Impossible Dream

GOD, it rained. Drops as big as a man's fist were drenching Los Angeles. The downpour hadn't stopped for a week. January, 1969, was one of the wettest months ever for the City of Angels.

Mike Riordan was dog tired. Not only had the likeable Irishman just finished an extra-long day of endless meetings, but a slight cold was making him feel miserable. Much more importantly, Mike wasn't getting as big a kick anymore out of running Equity Funding Corporation of America. Oh, the zest and spirit were still there. But the burden on the board chairman seemed to be getting heavier and heavier. Handsome Mike was even giving some thought to other ventures.

For the moment, Mike's main concern was maneuvering his Lincoln Continental through the flooded streets. As the unrelenting rain battered the street, Mike hunched forward with care to peer through the pitch-black streets as he drove from Equity's Wilshire Boulevard headquarters to his Mandeville Canyon home in the city's chic Brentwood section. As millions of Southern Californians were discovering that bone-soaking night, just getting home safely from work was an exhausting accomplishment.

Over the car radio, Mike half-listened to a report of the storm's devastation. The newscaster was saying that eleven-year-old Michael Hetrick of Hacienda Heights was presumed drowned after falling into a flood control channel. The youth was swept away by the fierce, rain-inspired current.

The announcer said that the Hetrick boy might have become the forty-eighth fatality from the storm that already had caused some $5 million in property damage.

Mike's attention picked up as the newscaster described mudslides oozing down the city's many canyons. The ground was drenched and couldn't hold much more water. Ten inches of rain in a week was creating havoc with city and county tractor crews struggling to clear the mud from the streets.

Mike thought about his $100,000 home flat up against the Mandeville Canyon hillside. He wondered, as he slowly drove his car through the rain-choked streets, how long the canyon road leading to his home, formerly owned by actress-swimming star Esther Williams, could be kept open. Handsome Mike's mind was also wandering to the thought of purchasing the then-floundering Miami Dolphins professional football team for $10 million.

He gave an involuntary sigh of relief as 2077 Mandeville Canyon Road finally came into view. Mike parked the car and entered the house. Jacqueline and the three children had already eaten dinner. It was late; Mike wasn't hungry but he was tired. He left Jackie to watch the late television news while he read in bed for a while before getting drowsy.

It hit with a loud *whop*. Jackie was startled and ran into the back of the house where Mike had been reading. She found her husband pinned under the bed, his leg broken. A mountain of mud had crashed through the rear of the Riordan house. Mike was conscious but in agony. Jackie dashed to call the fire department and then gathered up the children.

Battalion Chief Paul Augustine and Captain Charles Lechler of Engine Company 19 arrived about midnight. They found Mike alive but half buried in the oozing mud which had smashed through the bedroom's sliding glass doors. The big strong Irishman was pinned under a door and the bedframe, and the fire crew had difficulty just keeping his head out of the mud.

Mike had a great capacity for enduring pain and stayed calm as the fire crew worked to extricate him from the mud-cluttered debris. About half an hour later, Chief Augustine could see that his men were almost ready to pull Riordan free and went outside to check on a broken gas line.

The battalion chief had just returned from the pitch-black night and was in the living room which faced the bedroom when another thunderclap froze him in his tracks. A second mountain of mud had slammed into the house.

Augustine saw his firemen forced out of the Riordan bedroom like corks popping from a champagne bottle. Three firemen were wedged into the bedroom doorway. One fireman hit the bedroom ceiling so hard his helmet lodged in the boards. Then the mud receded almost as quickly as it had filled the room. The fire rescue team survived that second mud onslaught. Mike Riordan didn't.

January 25, 1969. The forty-one-year-old wonder boy of Wall Street was dead—drowned in a sea of mud.

Still the rain came. It had become the biggest storm in Los Angeles for any month in eighty years. By the end of the next day at least twelve families had been evacuated from Mandeville Canyon Road, where homes were now being washed out on a frightening scale. The road finally had to be sealed above the 2300 block. Almost sixteen inches of rain had fallen in nine days.

The street edition of the Los Angeles *Times* bannered: MUDSLIDES KILL NINE; RAIN DAMAGE GROWS. Eighty-two persons were dead. The rain had now caused some $15 million in property damage.

By a touch of irony, Michael Robert Riordan's obituary appeared on the same page with the weather report. The funeral would be Tuesday morning at the pretty Saint

Martin of Tours Catholic Church, a pink and beige, brick Italian Renaissance structure on Sunset Boulevard, in Brentwood, not far from the Riordan house.

For two days the Riordan family had stayed at Stanley Goldblum's elegant Beverly Hills home at 909 North Whittier Drive. Goldblum was the number-two man at Equity Funding. He and Riordan had put together a financial conglomerate that had Wall Street agog. Stan felt he should open his house to the Riordans.

The news of Mike's death quickly spread to his legion of personal and business friends in California, on Wall Street, and around the world.

Aside from Riordan and Goldblum, there were three other directors.

Nelson Loud, fifty-five, flew in from New York. Loud had been a director since 1964, when New York Securities Company, the investment banking firm he had helped found, managed the first public offering of Equity Funding's stock. Loud was a director of several other companies and had wide contacts among Manhattan's moneymen.

Theodore Goodman, another director, destined to die in October of that year of an incurable illness, was then barely forty. Goodman, an attorney, was the contact man between Equity and New York Securities.

Herbert Glaser, forty-one, a Harvard Law School graduate who had been associated with Equity since 1961, could reach the church in a few minutes from his Beverly Hills home. Glaser had been hand-picked by Mike and Stanley. He had become a director in 1962 and general counsel in 1968.

Yura Arkus-Duntov, while not a director, was the company's fifty-one-year-old mutual fund manager and a good friend of Mike's. He got the message while skiing in Gstaad, Switzerland. He journeyed to Lausanne, spent several hours making connections to Paris, and then flew on to Los Angeles to say good-bye to Mike. Russian-born Arkus-Duntov was soon to be named to the board as Riordan's replacement, bringing it up to its full complement of five.

The third storm in eleven days swept into Los Angeles that Tuesday and bolts of lightning struck three airliners as they neared the city's International Airport. No one was hurt; the planes landed safely. Arkus-Duntov was too tired to worry about the storm. Could Mike be replaced, he wondered.

"Mike Riordan dead?" Gordon W. McCormick muttered into the phone in the palatial living room of his hilltop estate in the San Fernando Valley community of Hidden Hills. A friend was telling McCormick of the mudslide. McCormick had made the Equity Funding concept click. "Go to the funeral? Of course not."

McCormick squinted and peered over his patio swimming pool into the black, rainy night of the valley far below. He was still bitter over the Goldblum-Riordan power play which had squeezed him out of his company in 1960. "I don't want to see any of that old Equity Funding crowd," McCormick thought.

At Jacqueline's request, a special requiem mass was held that broke away from the traditional mourning of the Catholic high mass. A traditional mass simply wouldn't be in keeping with her husband's freewheeling style. It took clout to make the changes in the church's sacred ceremonies. But the Riordans had wealth, influential friends, and the power that comes from such associations. James Francis Cardinal McIntyre, of the Los Angeles Archdiocese, and the Liturgical Commission allowed the changes. As a result, the vestments worn were white instead of black. Guitar music filled the church. The choir of schoolchildren from St. Martin's school was allowed to sing some of Mike's favorite songs.

Leading that choir was William A. Logan, just thirty years old but already acknowledged as one of the city's most popular church singers. Logan stood in St. Martin's choir loft, his black face accented against a white robe. He looked down upon the more than 500 mourners who were filling the modern six-sided church to capacity. Sprinkled throughout the audience were the familiar faces from Hollywood's entertainment industry. Dancer and entertainer Ray Bolger and singer Dennis Day were there. There was also Mike's pal, comedian Jonathan Winters. They were there to pay their last respects to the Irishman's insatiable appetite for enjoying life. They rubbed elbows with Wall Street hustlers and maîtres d'hôtels from some of Mike's favorite Los Angeles restaurants. Even the Riordan family's milkman took time off. Mike had that kind of human magnetism.

Logan opened with "I Believe." But it was the second number that created the sensation. Jackie felt the close business relationship with Goldblum should be symbolized by Logan singing "This Land Is Mine" from the film *Exodus*. Logan got more than a few dirty looks and derisive comments from some of the older women present—not members of the Riordan clan—for singing "that Jewish song" in a Catholic church.

But it was the third song that really captured the spirit of Mike Riordan. That's because Wall Street was Mike's world. He could hardly walk thirty feet down that Manhattan canyon before being stopped by someone who knew him. And Mike would invariably quip that Wall Street was The Impossible Dream. Every piano player in every Irish bar that Mike frequented in Manhattan—and there were plenty of those bars, some not so Irish—would immediately strike up "The Impossible Dream" when Mike strode through the tavern doors. So "The Impossible Dream" was a natural for Logan's third selection.

Comedian Winters, a good Riordan friend, may have thought back to that night in New York when he and Mike were putting a few down at their favorite watering hole. "Here's the bill, gentlemen," said the bartender. "What do you mean?" asked the incredulous Winters. "I don't pay bills. I'm a veteran." Or another time in a crowded Los Angeles elevator when the incomparable Winters turned to Mike and exclaimed very loudly, "Doctor, that's the last time I'm going to let you operate on me." Mike would double up laughing.

Perhaps Riordan even told Winters of his wild adventure the night of June 5, 1961.

A former radio-television sportscaster turned insurance salesman, a friend of Riordan's, lured Mike to Manhattan's Hotel Pierre on the pretense that Mike would meet some important Canadian financiers interested in mining securities. What Riordan didn't know was that his "friend" was working as a steerer and shill for a mob running a wild, rigged Cuban dice game called "Razzle." It seems that the friend was paying off a $900,000 debt to the ring.

Riordan found the $100-a-day suite lavishly supplied with champagne, caviar, and "businessmen" including the "financiers." He got within a hair of winning $40,000, as planned by the ring, when the dice (actually eight dice used in a progressive form of betting) went "bad." Suddenly Riordan found he owed the house $21,000.

With three blank checks supplied by the ring, Riordan paid the debt, but after reflecting on it overnight, stopped the checks.

A week later at his Wall Street office, Riordan began receiving threatening telephone calls. Later, he went for a forced ride with two of the gang, plus a 6-foot, 5-inch, 300-pound individual whom the ring used as their persuader. Riordan was informed that a contract was out for his murder unless he came up with the $21,000.

Badly scared, Riordan went to the New York district attorney with the story. There he learned that the gang already had shaken down a United Nations diplomat, theatrical and sports celebrities, and plenty of wealthy businessmen like Mike Riordan. The gang was immediately rounded up and arrested.

Mike would have gotten a big laugh when, at the end of the mass, it was announced by the priest that a reception would be held after the burial ceremony. The reception, read the priest from a piece of paper prepared by the Riordan family, would be held at the home of Stanley—and there was a pause that seemed like an eternity—Goldblum.

Certainly, it wasn't a traditional Irish name. It was a touch of levity appreciated by more than a few there that day. Mike's funeral, like his life-style, had a certain class.

The street was a mob scene. Fortunately it had temporarily stopped raining, but the mist was heavy. The crowd even spilled over across Sunset Boulevard, fronting the University Synagogue. Police helped herd the crowd, and the long funeral procession began winding its way to the San Diego Freeway, and then a few miles south to Holy Cross Cemetery. The Goldblums and the Riordans followed close behind the black hearse. The two families were so different and yet their lives had become closely intertwined. Mike, the Catholic kid from New Rochelle, the son of the president of Stern's department store, a Manhattan landmark. And Stanley, the Jewish kid from Pittsburgh, the son of a jeweler. Stanley, the stylish dresser, exuding the captain of industry image. Riordan, who bought his clothes off the rack and who used to take a ribbing when he wore that out-of-date overcoat his father had given him and which Mike wore when he made one of those frequent trips to Manhattan. Stanley, the loner, Equity Funding's "Mr. Inside." Mike, the ever-social "Mr. Outside." Goldblum, not a gourmet, not a big drinker. Mike, who knew his way around the best restaurants and bars. Stanley did not covet many friends and did most of his socializing with Mike's circle. But Mike's associates came from many worlds—Wall Street, politics, the entertainment industry, and even sports. Vince Lombardi, the famous coach of football's Green Bay Packers, was among those shaken by his sudden death.

But if Equity Funding's two top executives didn't have much in common socially, they were good for each other professionally. Since 1966 they had put together just the sort of financial services empire that Wall Street was looking for to satisfy the performance "cult."

Stanley was naturally distraught as the funeral cortege neared the cemetery.

"He [Riordan] was the greatest guy I ever met," said Goldblum as he looked back after the once mighty Equity Funding had become a shambles.

Goldblum first met Riordan in 1960 at what was then New York City's Idlewild Airport when Stan flew to the Big City from Los Angeles to help McCormick train and set up a national mutual fund-insurance sales force. Riordan and Jackie drove Goldblum to the New York Athletic Club. "The rooms were like cells," Goldblum recalled. "But it was cheap. That's why I stayed there."

Goldblum wistfully remembered that when his name was paged for telephone calls—a Jewish name was rarely heard in those hallowed halls—the ears of the Athletic Club's members would perk up.

Goldblum's thoughts may also have wandered back to the previous October when Stan and his wife, Marlene, and Mike and Jackie flew to Europe, rented a yacht complete with a crew in Nice, and spent a fortnight cruising the Mediterranean, including a visit to the island of Elba, where Napoleon was exiled.

"I'm glad we did it now," Goldblum said in recounting his friendship with Riordan and his associate's sudden death a few months after the trip.

But Stan also was a shrewd businessman. He began considering the economic impact on the shareholders of the death of Equity Funding's chairman. Mike's loss could shake the company to its roots and seriously impair the value of the stock. Stanley the businessman, Stanley the Equity Funding man, opted for action that very day to maintain investor confidence. Mike's name would have to be downplayed and a "business as usual" sign would, in effect, have to be hung out for all shareholders to see. There would have to be an informal board meeting that day at his house. It could be held unobtrusively in his den while turning over the rest of his home to a post-funeral reception.

Mike was buried on that misty day in grave 1, tier 192, in the grotto section of Holy Cross. As flowers were left on

Mike's grave, so it was remembered that one of his favorite sayings was, "Don't forget to smell the flowers." Mike liked to use that expression when business was getting him down or when he sensed that he was forgetting that there was more to life than Equity Funding. Well, Mike wouldn't be worrying about Equity Funding anymore. They left him on a pretty green hill with neatly manicured lawns and hedges.

It was Stanley's baby now. And the wheels already were turning to keep the empire growing into one of the nation's biggest financial conglomerates, a favorite of Wall Street.

It started to rain again as the long funeral procession wound its way out of the cemetery.

A freshly brewed coffee smell filled the comfortable Goldblum home on Whittier Drive. The crowd was again full of those familiar faces of Wall Street and Hollywood who, only a few hours earlier, had attended the church mass. And a few local political types showed up, too. Tom Bradley paid his respects. Bradley was also hustling votes against Sam Yorty, then the incumbent mayor of Los Angeles. Bradley would soon learn that he would have to wait four more years before savoring a victory over Yorty to become the city's first black mayor.

It was a large house that easily absorbed a big crowd in its mammoth-size rooms. It was a house built to appear comfortable, a home designed to look like it had always been there. From the inlaid wood paneling to the detailed woodwork around the moldings, it had a certain elegance.

Few bothered to mill outside around the pool or were curious about the meticulously equipped private gym facing it.

Jackie Riordan stayed mostly on coffee while others helped themselves to the smorgasbord attended to by Stan's live-in servant team. Mike Riordan's widow was more concerned about making arrangements to move herself and her children out of their mud-devastated house into temporary quarters until they could find a new home. They were to remain at the Goldblums' for a few weeks and then take up temporary residence next door in a house being vacated by film stars Paul Newman and Joanne Woodward.

Herb Glaser, Nelson Loud, and Ted Goodman had gotten the word that Stan wanted an informal directors' meeting in his library. Milton Kroll, Equity Funding's chief Washington counsel, also was there. And, of course, so was Arkus-Duntov, by this time just beginning to shed that numb feeling which comes with traveling halfway around the world in less than a day.

When the men sat down, Stan left little doubt why the informal meeting was being called. Shareholders would have to be assured that Mike's death would not adversely affect Equity Funding. As Dick Riordan, Mike's brother, would later agree, it made sense to downplay Mike to hold the company together. But concern also was expressed over the 400,000 shares of Equity Funding held by Mike, which were now part of the Riordan estate.

A question was raised by Kroll over whether the Riordan shares could be freely sold on the market without going through Securities and Exchange Commission registration procedures. Dick Riordan said the 10 percent of Equity Funding that Mike had was not a control block and wasn't subject to SEC approval if the family wanted to dispose of it right away. The issue was quickly settled. The Riordan family decided to sell off the stock over a calculated period of time so as not to depress Equity Funding's market position. The Kroll-Riordan exchange produced the only hint of tenseness at the meeting. Stanley was clearly ill at ease over the funeral of his partner. Mourners were still milling about in the rest of his house. Goldblum told Dick Riordan the company would have to issue some press releases which wouldn't have Mike's signature on them and outlined some other strategy to erase Mike's name. Dick quickly disarmed everyone by saying that was good corporate strategy and left the meeting. Dick Riordan had already decided he wasn't going to use his brother's stock to wedge his way onto the

Equity Funding board. A gut feeling told him that he couldn't happily associate with the Equity Funding crowd.

As the group emerged from the Goldblum inner sanctum, at least one of the meeting's participants felt it should have been delayed to another time. Mike had just been buried. It was hardly the time to carve up the spoils. Nevertheless, it was done. Stan was now ready to turn his full efforts to building Equity Funding into a financial colossus.

II
In the Beginning

"LIKE anything, it kind of grows."

Gordon C. McCormick reflected on the disaster that was Equity Funding. He gazed up at the ceiling of his expansive hilltop home in Hidden Hills, less than an hour from Equity Funding's Century City headquarters.

Born in Buffalo, New York, McCormick had studied business administration at Cornell University and moved to California in 1948. His first taste of what was to make him a wealthy man was a job with Investors Diversified Services, which was growing into the world's largest mutual fund organization. The portly McCormick, using literary license, reflected that by 1953 he was one of IDS's top representatives out of a nationwide staff of 5,000. Considering that his territory was San Bernardino County, which included the Mojave Desert, perhaps it was no idle boast. Gordon C. McCormick was indeed a persuasive, aggressive salesman.

In 1954 McCormick struck out on his own, hired and trained his own sales crew, and began selling both mutual funds and life insurance. By 1958 he had developed a system under which a customer could borrow on the cash value of the life insurance policy to pay the premium.

The year 1958 also was significant for another reason. That was the year McCormick hired young Stan Goldblum from a small Los Angeles insurance agency. Goldblum certainly was a bright guy, McCormick recalled. Yet, he added, for all his sales ability Goldblum appeared to have trouble closing and would tend to overstate his actual sales.

On June 1, 1959, McCormick formed the California- and Nevada-based Tongor Corporation, a contraction of Toni, his wife's first name, and his own first name. The company's objective was to act as a stockbroker with principal offices at 3761 Wilshire Boulevard in Los Angeles. McCormick then decided that his new company would do business as McCormick & Company and opened a second office at 315 Montgomery Street in San Francisco's financial district.

On March 31, 1960, McCormick changed the name to Equity Funding Corporation and soon afterward altered the company's legal purpose to an insurance agency, the forerunner of Equity Funding Life Insurance Company, which was to become the focal point of the scandal that was to rock the insurance and financial communities more than a decade later.*

To cover the mutual fund side of the business, McCormick formed a subsidiary on April 4, 1960, and called it Gordon C. McCormick, Inc., located at 1535 Wilshire Boulevard in Los Angeles.† The subsidiary was registered to sell mutual funds under the supervision of the National Association of Securities Dealers.

McCormick kept moving. He formed the parent company for the two subsidiaries on September 1, 1960, a Delaware corporation called Tongor Corporation of America, with headquarters at 37 Wall Street. Tongor's charter declared it was to be "engaged in the business of coordinating investments in securities and insurance." On January 12, 1961, Tongor was changed to Equity Funding Corporation of America, the name of the company at the time of its April, 1973, crisis.

---

*At the end of March, 1973, EFLIC was licensed to do business in forty-seven states.

†The name was changed in 1961 to Equity Securities Corporation, the forerunner of the Equity Funding Securities Corporation, which housed the mutual fund side of the business.

By 1960 McCormick's salesmen had two licenses—one to sell insurance and the other to push mutual funds.

The young company grew rapidly through the recruiting of salesmen who were enticed by the novelty of the insurance-mutual fund package, which they used as a "door opener" in their sales pitch. Part of the attractiveness was the fact that the stock market was performing well, which made it relatively easy to sell prospects on the value of mutual funds.*

The company was an agent for several insurance and mutual fund operations, among which was Keystone Custodian Funds, Inc., of Boston, where an aggressive young salesman named Michael Riordan was making a name for himself as a Keystone wholesaler who would contact agencies like McCormick's company to sell Keystone mutual funds to the public.

"I was selling more Keystone than anyone in the United States," said the unabashed McCormick. "Every month we sent Keystone one hundred fifty to two hundred thousand in mutual fund sales."

McCormick's aggressive sales force and its tactics were well known even then to the California Insurance Commission. His sales crew was constantly being criticized for what is known in the insurance industry as "twisting." However, McCormick was never charged with any wrongdoing. ("Twisting is insurance jargon for selling policies by persuading customers to cancel their current policies with competing insurance companies.) The prospect would then be expected to take the cash from the old policy and use it to

---

*On May 22, 1962, the Securities and Exchange Commission ruled that using mutual funds as collateral for a loan on life insurance premiums meant that the company had to come under SEC supervision and register under the Securities Act of 1933. Thus, on September 28, 1962, Equity Funding filed a registration statement with the SEC to register $10 million worth of securities to be used in its combination package and put out a company prospectus. But the statement didn't become effective until October, 1963, some thirteen months after it was filed. This had the effect of halting sales of the program during that time period and braked the company's growth.

purchase one of McCormick's products. Because this technique could tear down an individual's years of contributions into an insurance program, the practice is generally outlawed in most states. But Equity Funding, even in the later Riordan and Goldblum days of the 1960's, was accused by its competitors of maintaining twisting sales tactics.

"We were always getting heat from other insurance companies and insurance commissioners," a former sales executive said. "We were the suede shoes guys from Beverly Hills who twisted insurance."

Mike Riordan was a supersalesman, McCormick recalled. Riordan had surveyed McCormick's California operations in 1960 and was so impressed that he invited McCormick to New York. In the space of two weeks, Riordan and McCormick put together contracts with fifty-six New York brokerage houses to supply the securities for the mutual fund operation and signed up 1,037 agents to sell the combination program throughout the United States.

By this time McCormick had a potent organization. Eugene R. Cuthbertson, who owned Diversified Mutual Funds of Southern California, Ltd., based in Long Beach, put together a Long Beach sales force for McCormick. Raymond J. Platt, who had previously worked for the Equitable Life Insurance Company, was handling McCormick's San Francisco office.

McCormick appeared to be sitting pretty with a network of mutual fund and insurance agents and brokerage house tie-ins on every Wall Street corner—and all thanks to the contacts of Wall Street's most popular salesman—Michael Robert Riordan, Mr. Wall Street of the Keystone organization.

There was only one catch, moaned McCormick. He had overextended himself and didn't have the capital to properly finance the Riordan grand plan. The Irishman from New Rochelle moved too fast even for a sharpshooter like McCormick.

By mid-1960, Riordan, realizing McCormick's plight,

offered to buy into the Equity Funding operation. To discuss the prospect and how to expand his operations, McCormick, in October, 1960, called Goldblum, who was now training some of his salesmen (despite McCormick's early opinion of his sales ability!). Cuthbertson and Platt flew to New York for a meeting with Riordan at the Warwick Hotel. It turned into a confrontation between McCormick and his four key employees. They knew that their boss was financially strained and that they had him over a barrel. They also were well aware that they had a hot financial product on their hands and they wanted a piece of the action.

A subsequent meeting was held on October 24 at Glore Forgan & Company's Wall Street office. Goldblum, Riordan, Cuthbertson, and Platt offered McCormick a deal: They would split the company five ways. McCormick threw up his hands and declared that either he ran the company or he would pull out. Moreover, he shouted at the four, "All you've got is an idea that hasn't been put to a sustained test."

"I'll split it with you if you give me fifty-one percent," offered McCormick, growing more irritated with his colleagues.

Led by Riordan, the four turned down the offer, standing firm on their proposal to split McCormick's company five ways.

Then Riordan, in what was obviously a planned maneuver, reached into his pocket, took out his checkbook, and signed a check for what he had calculated to the penny was the value of McCormick's company—$55,392.14.

"You're a fool, Mike," McCormick said. "You're putting up all the money but still splitting equally with the other three."

But Riordan stuck to his guns and said take it or leave it.

McCormick took it.

Riordan just happened to have a contract with him and McCormick signed the fifteen-page document. It called for McCormick to turn over his shares to his four former employees. In exchange, the magnanimous agreement allowed McCormick to remove from his office a desk, three chairs, a table, an ottoman, an antique mahogany card table, a telephone stand, a fireproof safe (interestingly, accounting books and records relating to the company's early years are missing but there is no evidence that McCormick took them with him when he removed the safe), two family pictures, and his personal effects.

McCormick walked out to start his own insurance operation again. The Riordan-Goldblum era had begun.

III
The Early Years

RIORDAN finally severed his relationship with Keystone and came aboard full time as vice-president in June, 1961.* Riordan, Goldblum, Cuthbertson, and Platt each had received 23,750 shares of Equity Funding stock which had a par value of $2. Platt's role in the company diminished partly because he lost interest and partly through a health problem complicated by a drinking habit. Platt was bought out by the other three in May of 1963 for $51,074. Platt then sued his former colleagues for allegedly not living up to the deal, declaring they owed him some $600,000. In 1964 Platt died of a heart attack at Scandia, a posh Sunset Strip restaurant. His widow eventually lost the lawsuit.

The Riordan, Goldblum, Cuthbertson interests in the Platt litigation were represented by Jerome Glaser, whose brother, Herbert, was eventually to become a member of Equity Funding's board of directors. Herb Glaser, born in New Brunswick, New Jersey, in August, 1927, graduated from Harvard Law School in 1951. His legal association with the Equity Funding crew was to lead to his appointment to the company's board in 1962. He joined Equity Funding's management in 1968 as executive vice-president and general counsel.

*Riordan was appointed chairman of the board on September 1, 1964. Until that time no one had officially held the title although Goldblum, EFCA's president, had acted as chairman at board meetings.

Goldblum and Glaser got along well together and aside from their relationship at Equity Funding, they joined in at least two private deals—both real estate ventures—one in the San Fernando Valley and the other in Orange County, south of Los Angeles. Ironically, Glaser, after more than a decade of friendship with Goldblum, was to receive the shock of his life—that the chairman was involved in a massive securities fraud case. And, adding to the irony, it was Glaser who temporarily took over Equity Funding as it floundered helplessly in the first two weeks of April, 1973, until a federal judge could appoint a permanent trustee.

Equity Funding went public in December, 1964, through an offering of 100,000 shares at $6 each, underwritten by a new securities house, New York Securities Company. Nelson Loud, one of six general partners in that firm, was ultimately to become an outside director of Equity Funding.

In 1966 Riordan and Goldblum bought out Cuthbertson for approximately $870,000. That left Mike and Stan clearly in charge of Equity Funding.

From 1960 to 1967, EFCA remained a marketing organization exclusively selling life insurance, mutual funds, and the Equity Funding combination life insurance-mutual fund package. Virtually all EFCA's life insurance sales from 1964 to 1968 were made under an exclusive agreement with Pennsylvania Life Insurance Company. EFCA sold many mutual funds separately, but used only three Keystone funds in connection with the combination Equity Funding program.

The seeds of fraud appear to have been planted shortly after the 1964 public offering. Up to that time the company had been sailing along reflecting a four-year history of steady growth. Investors liked the idea of buying insurance as a protective hedge against mutual funds, and Equity Funding's vast sales force was happy because they received separate commissions on both the fund shares and the insurance policies.

Investigators believe it was in 1964, shortly after the company went public, that Riordan and Goldblum began experiencing trouble raising cash. That was when a system of phony loans was created which overstated the company's assets.

The first false financial statement detected by the Federal Grand Jury was documented on December 31, 1964, when, read the indictment, the company claimed as assets fake loans owed to it to finance the insurance premiums of its customers in the amount of $6,682,075.61.

According to the Federal Grand Jury indictment, the head of Equity Funding's own accounting firm, which had been auditing its books since it went public, knew about and covered up the inflated assets. Julian S. H. Weiner, the head of Wolfson, Weiner, Ratoff & Lapin, a then small firm with offices in Beverly Hills and New York, was indicted for conducting "insufficient audits and would accept and cause to be accepted substantial portions or all of the fictitious and inflated entries. . . ."

(The Weiner firm merged with the accounting firm of Seidman & Seidman on February 1, 1972.)

Weiner sometimes boasted that the Equity Funding concept of selling insurance and mutual funds as a package was both his idea and Riordan's. Equity Funding ultimately accounted for 60 percent of his firm's accounting business.

Also indicted was Sol Block, who was in day-to-day charge of Equity Funding's books in those years for the outside auditors. Block had an unusual claim to fame on the fabulous Equity account: He wasn't a certified public accountant. In fact, unearthed *The Wall Street Journal*, Block didn't become a CPA until April 27, 1973, well after the scandal broke. Not that Block didn't try. Block first took the CPA exam in 1961 and flunked all four parts—law, theory, practice, and audit, the *Journal* reported.

And finally there was Marvin Al Lichtig, Equity Funding's treasurer, formerly associated with Weiner and Block in the Wolfson, Weiner accounting firm, who also was indicted for allegedly participating in the same inflated assets game of the 1960's.

As stated in the indictment, these acts "fraudulently

overstate(d) the income and assets and misrepresented the growth and general business and financial condition of" the parent company.

The fraud temporarily surfaced in 1966. In that year, an Equity Funding prospectus showed the company sold $226.3 million worth of life insurance, most of it Pennsylvania Life policies. Yet, when Penn Life put out a prospectus the same year, it showed that Equity had sold only $58.6 million of Penn Life insurance.

Additionally, there were reports that Equity Funding fabricated some of its mutual fund sales reports, but these rumors were not substantiated.

At the same time, Equity Funding was having difficulties with regulatory authorities of various states.

A particular case in point occurred in 1967 when Harry M. Beyer pleaded guilty to two charges of bribery and one of conspiracy in connection with a 1964 incident in Minnesota. Beyer, a former Minneapolis businessman, was an officer of Penn Life (and the father of its board chairman), whose policies Equity Funding was selling as the insurance part of its insurance-mutual fund package. Beyer wanted to register the Equity package in Minnesota but, for some reason, sources close to the case believe, he was dissatisfied with the registration process, which normally takes only a few months.

At the same time, on June 4, 1964, Beyer made a personal loan of $1,500 to Joe Haveson, the late assistant commissioner of insurance in Minnesota. Haveson then went to David Kroman, a Minnesota Insurance Division attorney, and asked Kroman to write a memo which normally would have been written by an insurance supervisor giving the green light for Equity to sell its program there. Haveson and Kromer then split the $1,500 "loan."

In 1967 Minnesota uncovered a fraud-scandal within its Insurance Division and in the course of the ensuing state probe, the Beyer "loan" surfaced. On September 13, 1967, Beyer, who lived in Beverly Hills, paid $3,000 in fines and was placed on a year's probation. Beyer, then sixty-four and in poor health, could have been fined up to $10,000 or sentenced to ten years in jail. The limited sentence, however, was recorded as a gross misdemeanor and not a felony.

Equity Funding was suspended from doing business in Minnesota for 120 days in 1967 as a result of the Beyer case. The name of Equity was thus at least tarred in that state and that irked Goldblum no end. Moreover, Goldblum became more irritated over a statement by Minnesota authorities that Beyer had been reimbursed with Goldblum's knowledge by Equity Funding for his original $1,500 "loan" to the Minnesota officials.*

The Beyer incident came back to haunt Goldblum in later years. In 1971, Equity Funding acquired Banker's National Life of New Jersey. With Bankers, Equity inherited a Bankers subsidiary, Palisades Life. New York insurance authorities, upon learning of the Minnesota bribery incident, sent investigators to California to interview Goldblum. The New York officials felt the Minnesota affair did not augur well for Equity Funding in New York and the matter of Equity Funding acquiring a company in that state was still up in the air when the Equity Funding scandal surfaced.

Equity Funding also faced various complications in Pennsylvania, whose insurance officials weren't attracted to—and may have anticipated problems with—the mutual fund-insurance package. As a result, the company was prevented from selling the program in that state.

And so it went in the middle 1960's. Although mutual fund industry sales tailed off in 1966, Equity Funding reported a 47 percent increase in profits. Investigators now

---

*Minnesota's Department of Commerce declared that "Beyer paid said bribes with the implied approval of Stanley Goldblum . . . that Harry Beyer was subsequently reimbursed for said bribery payments by Stanley Goldblum with funds of Equity Funding . . . and that the reimbursements were made with the knowledge of the use to which said funds were put." (State of Minnesota, Department of Commerce, Securities Division, In the Matter of Equity Securities Corporation, Findings of Fact, Number 6, October 17, 1967.)

know this increase in the face of a poor market was caused by company officials artificially inflating assets. This sort of subterfuge, of course, supported the price of the company's stock and kept Wall Street hypnotized through 1969 into believing that at last there was a real corporate fantasyland immune to the roller coaster rides that the economy imposes on most of the financial community.*

More specifically, at the end of 1964, Equity Funding Corporation had $6.9 million outstanding in real and phony premium loans to purchasers of the combined insurance-mutual fund program.† This loan figure jumped sharply each year because of the mushrooming nonexistent loan scheme. At the end of 1965, the company listed the outstanding loans in the program at $10.4 million. By 1966 it was $16.5 million; 1967, $25.1 million; 1968, $36.3 million; 1969, $51.2 million; 1970, $66.3 million; 1971, $88.6 million; and 1972, the biggest jump, $117 million.

What was finally happening was simply that Equity Funding was purchasing phony life insurance for nonexistent mutual fundholders with the phony loans. Phony insurance sales generated phony profits. And the phony profits kept Equity Funding's stock flying high. So it wasn't

---

*EFCA stock hit a high of 80¾ in 1969, but dropped to 12¾ during the bear market of the early 1970's. Although the stock recovered somewhat to the mid-30's in 1972, it never again soared anywhere near its highs of the late 1960's.

†The trustee also believed that unlawful activities were going on as early as 1964. Here is that analysis:
"Fraudulent transactions involving the failure to record liabilities for borrowed cash may have occurred as early as 1964. Cash received from such borrowings was termed a 'free credit,' meaning it was regarded as available for the inflation of earnings, or for reduction of a fictitious or inflated asset account. The illegitimate uses of free credits were substantiated by fraudulent accounting entries and, in some cases, documentation was prepared involving fictitious companies and bogus transactions. By the end of 1972 it appears that the unrecorded borrowings had been repaid or somehow entered on the books. This had been done without impairing the reported performance of the company by inflating assets and earnings through other devices."
(Report of the Trustee of Equity Funding Corporation of America, February 22, 1974, p. 32.)

too difficult to raise real money from banks and through debenture issues so Equity Funding could, among other things, keep its investors happy.

As McCormick suggested, Equity Funding was like Topsy—it just kept growing.

Federal investigators believe Riordan and Goldblum had to know what was going on. If they were nothing else, they were the company's moneymen. This go-go financial conglomerate was their baby. Riordan, however, was never convicted or even accused of any wrongdoing during his lifetime.

But the greatest expansion was yet to come.

Riordan and Goldblum realized that although EFCA was showing substantial growth as a marketing organization, its prospects for becoming a major corporation were dim unless it actually owned and operated the companies whose products its sales organization sold. That was because EFCA received no future profits from the life insurance it sold and which was placed on the books of other companies; nor did it derive management-fee income from the growth in the assets of the mutual funds whose shares it also sold.

So between 1967 and 1972 a period of acquisitions took place which rapidly expanded EFCA into one of the country's major financial conglomerates.

Beginning in 1967, Equity decided to buy its own insurance company, and on December 12 it purchased Presidential Life Insurance Company of America, a small concern in the Chicago suburb of Elmhurst. With that deal, Equity Funding inherited Fred Levin, then thirty years old.*

Equity Funding moved Presidential Life to Los Angeles in

---

*Presidential was first incorporated in Illinois in June, 1959. EFCA paid $1,099,000 in cash for Presidential; a 5½% promissory note in the amount of $500,000 which was subsequently paid; 54,865 shares of EFCA common stock; and convertible notes which were later converted into another 66,600 shares of EFCA common. At the time of the acquisition, the three major shareholders of The Presidential Group, Incorporated, an insurance holding company, were John S. Pennish, its chief executive officer, American Express Company, and Lazard Freres & Company, an investment banking house.

1968 and in the next year Levin was named president of the subsidiary, which was later renamed Equity Funding Life Insurance Company. It was this company that was to find itself in the eye of the fraud storm a few years later. And it was Levin who was believed by investigators to have been Goldblum's chief lieutenant in creating and taking part in the phony insurance scheme, the counterfeiting of securities, and the other charges laid down by the grand jury.

Riordan had even bigger ideas. Mike dreamed of setting up an Equity Funding organization in Europe. He engaged the friendship of a Ralph Seligman, a lawyer and financier living in the Bahamas who attracted Riordan—if for no other reason—because he was a native of Ireland. The two stomped their way through Europe in 1967 from London to Paris to Amsterdam to Germany. Riordan obviously felt there was room for another American financial services group in Europe in addition to Bernie Cornfeld's Investors Overseas Services group. But the dream never materialized.

Seligman's wife, however, was to play a role in the late 1960's as one of three women who received Equity Funding directed commissions in the Bahamas. This practice became the subject of an investigation by the intelligence division of the Internal Revenue Service, which was interested in where the commission money was going. IRS never reached any conclusions in the case and ended up pointing the finger at no one.

In 1969 Equity Funding made its third major management acquisition in Samuel H. Lowell, then thirty years old, an accountant by training. Lowell came from Los Angeles-based Dart Industries. He joined Equity Funding as assistant treasurer and corporate controller in April, 1969, and his responsibilities included foreign investment. Lowell, along with Goldblum and Levin, was believed by investigators to be the third member of the EFCA "troika" which played a major role in the fraud.

Still riding a crest of optimistic stock reports by Wall Street analysts, the company kept expanding. Among other things, it purchased Liberty Savings in Beverly Hills; it ventured into the oil and gas business in foreign lands; it purchased a prize-winning cattle operation; and even picked up the United States assets of IOS, which Cornfeld had been forced to divest by the SEC.

But this period was not without its problems, too. Rumors had surfaced from time to time on Wall Street in the late 1960's that there was an Internal Revenue Service investigation being conducted into EFCA's accounting procedures.

There was.

The IRS probe actually started in 1967. (This was in connection with the IRS intelligence probe of EFCA's involvement in commission giveups.)

The IRS concluded that the giveups, or reciprocity to other brokers and individuals in the form of directed commissions, should have been counted as income. This, in addition to other accounting gimmickry, said the IRS, meant that EFCA owed the federal government $34 million in back taxes!

A long hassle ensued during which the IRS declared that depending on how the accounting was interpreted, the $34 million figure could be reduced to approximately $9 million.

On August 30, 1971, EFCA settled with the IRS for $165,000 for the year 1968, when Goldblum signed a deficiency agreement allowing the IRS to bill the company for the amount. A subsequent carryback tax loss recovered this amount plus $46,000.

The IRS wasn't the only federal agency probing EFCA's operations in the 1960's. Rumblings of troubles at Equity Funding were also heard by the SEC beginning in 1967. At first there were complaints of a back-office paperwork problem. But the SEC, after a look, generally attributed the paperwork snafus at EFCA to the back-office problems plaguing the entire securities industry.

Then, in early 1972, a strange case came to the SEC's attention. It involved William Mercado, the head of the company's data-processing organization, who had been making some attempts to streamline its computer hardware. Sometime during the third quarter of 1971, it appeared that Mercado had a falling out with Sam Lowell, EFCA's chief financial officer, to whom Mercado reported. Mercado was removed from his position by Lowell and let go by the end of the year.

At the time Mercado was fired, the SEC began hearing stories that EFCA's assets might be overstated. Mercado and two other employees were called in for questioning. Ray Garrett, Jr., who in 1973 became chairman of the SEC, recounted the investigation's conclusion to a United States Senate panel:

"The individuals [were] questioned [and] stated that there were no irregularities in the operations or accounting practices of Equity Funding and that earlier suggestions to the contrary resulted because the corporation had been founded by salesmen who were not qualified accountants. . . ."

Mercado specifically told the SEC he had no reason to believe there was any fraud going on and attributed any faults to sloppy bookkeeping. Assured that all this had changed and that the company had acquired good accountants and a tough compliance chief who would make sure the firm kept within the SEC's guidelines for selling securities, the agency shut down its investigation. Its basic reasoning was that Mercado—who, having been fired, would have had good reason to rat on the company if there was fraud going on—asserted he didn't see anything blatantly wrong. There was probably more smoke than fire, believed SEC officials.

A subsequent SEC probe looked into whether Mercado was actually trying to shake down Goldblum while he was being questioned by the SEC. Apparently Mercado and his attorney had 1970 figures which allegedly showed that EFCA's assets were $8 million under what was actually in the company's annual report. Mercado reportedly believed he could prove his claim on a computer run of the company's books. Lowell countered by declaring that Mercado's figures were incomplete. Eventually, Goldblum paid Mercado's attorney, Jim Jess, $2,900 in legal fees for representing his client before the SEC. Mercado reportedly wanted substantial termination pay but it wasn't clear if he got it.

Additionally, no hard evidence was made available that any extortion attempt was made by Mercado against Goldblum.

Another thorn in Equity Funding's side was the California Insurance Commission, which felt that in 1968 about half the company's insurance business was replacement business —that is, there was still wholesale "twisting" going on.

To ward off an investigation by the commission, Equity Funding promised that with each policy it sold it would solicit a letter of understanding from the insured policyholders which said, in effect, that they knew what they were doing. Or, as one insurance official said of the operation, the letter was tantamount to a canned statement which declared: "I know what you are doing to me and I know it hurts but I love it."

IV
Goldblum

Stanley Goldblum, the chairman of Equity Funding Corporation of America, is an extremely complex person. Gifted with a brilliant business mind, Goldblum, initially in tandem with Riordan, and then by himself, almost overnight pyramided a relatively modest mutual fund-insurance concept into a financial conglomerate that literally dazzled Wall Street. It was an outfit with big ambitions, both domestically and internationally. Goldblum and his talented Century City gang were well on their way to immense corporate power and wealth when their empire was shattered on April Fool's Day, 1973.

Away from the company, Goldblum was a reflective man who enjoyed contemplating life and humanity. When he wished, from memory, he injected passages into his conversation from philosophers he had read or from some of his favorite writers, including Shakespeare. He was an expansive man who could engage in endless conversation about a thousand subjects, easily cracking jokes, and then, just as suddenly, showing pique and outright anger when he felt misunderstood.

So it was on the afternoon of December 22, 1973, when Goldblum was interviewed for four hours in his sumptuous Beverly Hills home at 909 North Whittier Drive. Here was a giant of a man, both mentally and physically, whom one does not easily forget.

Two chapters are devoted to this man because, following Riordan's death, Goldblum was the driving power behind Equity Funding. It was Goldblum who plotted its financial path and it was Goldblum, the general, who successfully led his legions into *corporate war after corporate war until Equity Funding Life became his Achilles' heel.*

This book thus endeavors to capture some of the flavor and character of this corporate chieftain. It is not our intention to try Goldblum on these pages—that is the province of the courts. It is instead our objective to probe the kaleidoscopic personality of one who is charged with directing what many believe to be one of the most massive business fraud schemes ever concocted. Whether these charges are true or false, Goldblum indeed emerges as a fascinating product of our capitalistic system.

The first of two chapters on Goldblum deals among other things with his boyhood, his early business history, his personal interests, and his tastes and politics. In the second part of this interview, which is the last chapter of this book, Goldblum speaks out for the first time on the charges and looks back with 20-20 hindsight on how he might have avoided the biggest crisis of his life.

Rodney Loeb had no trouble recalling his first encounter with Stanley Goldblum. It was the third week of May, 1969.

Loeb had been recommended for the job by Herbert Glaser, EFCA's chief counsel, who wanted to start up an EFCA real estate operation. Upon graduation from Harvard Law School, and after service in the Air Force on the staff of the Judge Advocate General's office, Loeb was offered a job by former Supreme Court Justice Abe Fortas in the Washington law firm of Arnold & Porter. But Loeb decided instead to start his career at the Securities and Exchange Commission, ending up as a legal assistant to one of the SEC commissioners.

Loeb, by this time an experienced corporate attorney, a quiet, sophisticated gentleman, stood before Goldblum, the chairman of Equity Funding Corporation of America, in the company's fifth floor office at 9601 Wilshire Boulevard. Loeb, then forty-one, was interested in the job of general counsel for the fast-moving company. And there he was, in front of the imposing, impeccably dressed Goldblum. The chairman sized him up.

Goldblum looked over Loeb's conservative Ivy League

clothes (a holdover from his Harvard days), his somewhat smaller build, and his classic Semitic nose. Goldblum's eyes came to rest on the bottom portion of Loeb's rugged face. From ear to ear there was a full and well-manicured beard. Goldblum paused and then declared:

"If you're coming to work for this company you have to shave."

Loeb was thunderstruck.

"Is he testing me or is he serious?" thought Loeb. "How could he be serious? I'm not going to take a position with somebody so dominating he can tell me to shave off my beard."

And so Loeb replied in a quiet, slow cadence:

"You just lost yourself a general counsel."

Goldblum apparently thought that was a gutsy reply. And Equity Funding, thought the chairman, was a gutsy company which needed that kind of talent. Loeb was hired.

But the chairman never really got used to that beard. From time to time at meetings Goldblum would half joke to others with Loeb looking on : "You've met the house rabbi, of course."

Loeb came to learn that Goldblum wasn't really picking on his new company counsel. It was just that the chairman in many ways ran his company like an old-fashioned schoolmaster would run a one-room schoolhouse—even to expecting his "students" to show up on time for lunch in the twenty-eighth-floor boardroom or have a good excuse for being absent.

Parenthetically, Goldblum's organized lunches for his executives, begun in April, 1970, weren't entirely appreciated. At the outset, on April 13, 1970, Goldblum set the tone for the lunches by insisting that everyone be prompt because he did not intend to "be running a short-order kitchen." Some resented his requiring that his executive team be in the boardroom at precisely 12:30 P.M. To allow for outside business appointments, Goldblum permitted his team to schedule outside lunches on Tuesdays and Thursdays.

They ate seated at a massive twenty-seven-foot mahogany

table that was used for directors' meetings and executive conferences, while a pair of imitation-bronze eagles on fluted column pedestals at either end of the room gazed down upon the gathering. It was truly a modern-day version of King Arthur and his knights.*

Goldblum thoroughly enjoyed the sessions, during which he would guide the conversation on everything from politics to the fortunes of his company.

And, to his consternation, one executive even learned not to tamper with Gertrude the cook. The executive had asked Gertrude if she could come over to his house one night to help his wife prepare food for a party. Gertrude said fine.

But Goldblum was outraged when he heard about it. He immediately called the executive to his office and informed the startled individual that he couldn't have Gertrude.

The reason: Gertrude was Goldblum's personal cook at night and he wasn't about to let her begin moonlighting for other Equity Funding officers.

The kid from Pittsburgh had come a long way.

Goldblum's grandparents had lived near the Russian-Polish border before emigrating to the United States and settling in Pittsburgh.

One of Goldblum's grandfathers owned the American Trouser Company of Pittsburgh. Goldblum's father worked in the jewelry business there.

Goldblum was born on January 17, 1927, and spent his youth in Pittsburgh's Squirrel Hill area, a predominantly Jewish middle-class section of the city's east side. He had one brother, who has been known to use the name Ron Gordon, and with whom Goldblum says he has not been close.

In 1942 Eva and Victor Goldblum moved their family to Los Angeles, where Victor opened his own jewelry store and where young Stan spent a semester at North Hollywood High School.

The next year, Stan transferred to Los Angeles High

---

*At EFCA's bankruptcy auction, the conference table sold for $6,000; the eagles and pedestals went for a total of $1,600.

School (which, incidentally, has the motto: "Obedience to law; respect for others; mastery of self; joy in service; these constitute life"). Goldblum excelled in math and science, showing a fine grasp of figures and mathematical concepts. Although a good-sized lad, he didn't go out for any sports. To earn money on the side, Goldblum took a job at a Vic Tanny health studio, where he exhibited great interest in bodily exercise and physical fitness.

Goldblum's original ambition, he said, was to study medicine and become a doctor. That's why, he claimed, he enlisted in the Army at age seventeen under a military program which was to send him to Stanford University to take pre-med courses. This, he asserted, was his big chance to go to college and, since his family didn't have a great deal of money, provided an opportunity to begin his medical education at government expense.

Well, the Army program got caught up in red tape and Stan was sent instead to the University of Idaho. "That's when my career went awry," observed Goldblum.

After two years he was put on active duty and went through basic training at Camp Roberts in California. He was then assigned to Fort Benning, Georgia, where he was made a radio operator because, he believed, he had mentioned to his superiors that he had operated a ham radio as a youngster.

After his Fort Benning training, Goldblum was shipped overseas as a member of the Sixth Infantry Division and served in the Pusan area of South Korea (before hostilities broke out). "If I remember nothing else [about Korea], I remember the smell of the fertilizer in the fields," he reminisced.

Honorably discharged in San Francisco in 1948 as a private first class, Goldblum said he wanted to get back on the pre-med track. But in 1949 he married Leah Cherry, a girl he had known in high school and whom he had met through Louis Cherry, a classmate at Los Angeles High. For financial reasons he therefore switched his major to pre-pharmacy at the University of California at Los Angeles but quit after a year and a half to go to work.* His interest in medicine stayed with him through his adult years, however, and he still subscribed to the *Journal of the American Medical Association*.

Goldblum's first job after leaving UCLA was hauling scrap in Los Angeles for the now defunct Newman Scrap Metal business. "It was hard work," he recalled, "but I eventually ended up managing the operation."

He then joined the business owned by Leah's family, the Supreme Meat Packing Company of Los Angeles. Leah's father and two brothers ran the operation.

"I did everything," said a proud Goldblum. "I hauled meat, I ran the smokehouse, I made the sausage, I cut the meat, I rebuilt the plant." The latter was a reference to a problem the business was having conforming to Department of Agriculture rules. Goldblum said he straightened that out, too.

For five years, until 1955, Goldblum worked from 4 A.M. to 7 P.M., six days a week, at the meat-packing plant until "I just got tired" and resigned. "I was not using the ability I had."

(Goldblum resented the newspaper publicity he had received about this job since the case broke. It pictured him, he said, "as a cigar-chomping former sausagemaker and butcher.")

Deciding to try his luck with the insurance industry, Goldblum then held successive jobs with the Pacific Mutual and the Midland Mutual Life insurance companies in Los Angeles, and showed promise on the sales side at both firms. "I didn't know a life insurance policy or a mutual fund from an apple," Goldblum said of those years.

In 1958, Gordon W. McCormick, who was experimenting with a new insurance and mutual fund concept, put Goldblum on his sales staff. Ultimately, Goldblum was to take over the training of McCormick's sales force.

As Goldblum was advancing into a position of immense

---

* Curiously, when EFCA became listed on the New York Stock Exchange, Goldblum's biography said he was a UCLA graduate.

financial power, his relationship with Leah was becoming more strained. That was mostly because he was increasingly friendly with an attractive, blond woman, Marlene Cherry, a woman almost a decade younger than himself, and the wife of his brother-in-law, Joseph Cherry.

On July 16, 1964, Leah and Stan officially separated, with the divorce proceedings beginning on May 5, 1965. Even then, Goldblum was a wealthy man, as reflected by the divorce settlement.

Leah received $257,500 in cash; their Beverly Hills house at 9108 Alanda Place, valued at $68,000; $30,000 worth of house furnishings; the family's Jaguar sedan; a lump-sum final support and maintenance payment of $92,500; a $50,000 life insurance policy (written on Pennsylvania Life, for which Equity was the agent at the time) for Leah and their two children, Corinne and Gary; a $400 annual payment so that the children could go to summer camp every year; 1,667 shares of Equity Funding stock to be put into a trust for each child (which was subsequently sold off); and even $200 to take care of the maid's expenses for the rest of 1965.

Goldblum walked out of the settlement with 103,069 shares of Equity Funding and $142,500 in cash.

The final divorce decree was granted on May 12, 1966.

Two days later Goldblum married Marlene, who had divorced Joseph Cherry. The two girls from Marlene's first marriage, Jolene and Wendi, lived with the Goldblums. Stanley was described as a good, responsible father who, despite his wealth, did not overindulge his children.

Goldblum said he is not a very religious person. "I believe in God, but I don't want to get philosophical about it."

Both Stan and Marlene were intensely private individuals. Neither enjoyed the responsibility of entertaining that so oftens accrues to someone in Goldblum's position. This made for tremendous contrast with Mike Riordan, Goldblum's former close business associate, whose private life appeared to be a continuous series of soirees that took place in Los Angeles, New York and other international points, and which involved relationships ranging from iconoclastic Wall Street brokers to influential people in the entertainment and sports industries. In fact, noted one observer of those years, most of Stan's socializing was sparked by Riordan—when Stan chose to socialize.

Stan, on the other hand, was Equity Funding's bookkeeper, the moneyman, the guy who stayed in the background guiding every cent of the fortunes of the growing financial concern—which was his area of expertise—while Riordan performed the outside public relations function.

Stan and Marlene ("the kind of girl any decent guy would want to marry," noted a friend of the Goldblums) easily settled into their elegant Beverly Hills home near Sunset Boulevard.* The home's exterior didn't particularly stand out among the area's mansions, with their expansive, manicured lawns in a neighborhood noted for its antiseptic streets, where the only minorities are the domestics that work in the homes of the wealthy.

But the inside was lavishly decorated, incidentally, by the same two elderly female interior decorators who were one day to design the million-dollar interior of Equity Funding's lush twenty-eighth-floor executive offices.

The home has big rooms which, said one visitor, immediately left the impression that it was a captain of industry's house. As one walked into the house on the west side of Whittier Drive, there was a very large living room to the left of the entrance. The maid's quarters were to the right of the door and next to the dining room.

Straight ahead from the main entranceway and to the left was the den, where Stan liked to watch television. West of the living room was an even larger den Stan added to the house.

---

*Goldblum, true to his loner instincts, didn't make many friends among his neighbors. In fact, he said he never met his illustrious next-door neighbors, the husband and wife acting team of Paul Newman and Joanne Woodward, who had temporarily turned their house over to the Riordan family after the mudslide disaster.

It contained a magnificent baroque polished wood pool table, a large ornate chess set, an antique brass telescope,* and a recessed bar. The bedrooms were upstairs.

Antique prints, lithographs of some of the world's famous stock exchanges, and several large paintings lined the walls of the home. One, a large Spanish painting, hung in the den housing the pool table. Goldblum couldn't remember the name of the painter—"it's nobody you ever heard of"—but he commented that it had once hung in Madrid's famous Prado. "I liked it because it goes with the color of the room," remarked Goldblum.

Goldblum also had several Chagall lithographs on display. He even hung a Chagall in the downstairs powder room over the toilet and remarked to an acquaintance it was "a piece of whimsy."

But Goldblum was hardly a connoisseur of the arts. In many respects it appeared he bought simply to acquire, without the knowledge of what he was purchasing. The dominating painting in Goldblum's office at Equity Funding was a good case in point.

In October, 1972, he purchased a painting called "Checkmate." The painting, 3 by 4 feet, was hung over his office fireplace. It showed a group of elderly men, wearing somewhat Byzantine-looking clothes, watching a chess game.† Goldblum purchased the painting for $10,000. After the company went into reorganization, the trustee began selling off executive office furnishings on the twenty-eighth

---

*A minor feud developed over the antique "Monsieur Chevalier" telescope. It started when Goldblum took possession of the instrument shortly after he was ousted as EFCA board chairman. Goldblum claimed his wife gave him the telescope as a gift. The trustee, however, claimed it was company property purchased with EFCA money. Eventually, Goldblum relented and he allowed two attorneys from the O'Melveny & Myers law firm, handling the reorganization of the company, to pick it up at his house.

†Ironically, as far as the bearded Loeb was concerned, all the men in the picture—which hung on the wall opposite the chairman's desk—had beards!

floor in preparation to evacuate those quarters in a cost-cutting move. An art appraiser assessing some of the objects for sale happened to wander into Goldblum's office and studied the painting—so heavily varnished that one could hardly scrutinize it from any angle because of the reflected glare of the sun.

After a moment of contemplation, the appraiser said he wouldn't give $15 for it. (Nevertheless, it was sold for $5,250 at the February, 1974, bankruptcy auction.)

Other elements about Goldblum's office also seemed a bit excessive. That $1,700 telescope with the brass fittings certainly seemed out of place there.

A visitor once remarked that the telescope was a splendid-looking instrument. He then inquired if Goldblum ever actually used it.

"Certainly," replied Goldblum, glaring down at the Los Angeles Country Club, often accused of restricting Jewish membership. Goldblum declared he used the telescope to survey the club's spacious golf course, which dominated his northern view.

"Some day," he declared, "I'm going to buy that land and turn it into a housing development."

The large barometer near it on the west wall was acceptable as far as it went—but why have a smiling wooden face carved atop it?

Goldblum's oversized desk was always scrupulously neat, to the point of having his telephone tucked into his top left-hand drawer.

Matching leopard-skin sofas faced a coffee table in front of his desk, which was just a few feet from his private washroom.

But there was a strikingly human touch in that room, too. In the western corner of Goldblum's office, on a coffee table, Stan, until the day he was thrown out, always kept a picture of Mike Riordan. A picture of Riordan also sat on Goldblum's library shelf in his den.

To the distant west, Goldblum could look down upon the

lush environment of Beverly Hills, and to the south spread the downtown area of Los Angeles.

Like his home, the office had a lot of dark wood paneling. To many it was more akin to a king's throne room than to a place where the chairman of a financial conglomerate would choose to work. But it was in his spread on Whittier Drive where Goldblum was truly in his element.

Behind his house Goldblum had a pretty red-brick patio, his pool, and the grassy yard surrounded by a brick wall.

His gym, once the pool house, was carpeted and contained $100,000 worth of stainless steel muscle-developing equipment. Adjacent to the gym was a sauna and a dressing room. The gym's walls were hung with charts displaying Goldblum's physical progress with weights and stress machinery.

Two wall-to-ceiling mirrors at either end of the gym allowed Goldblum to watch himself train. He was very proud of his prowess in the gym, where he worked out three times a week (which included 4 P.M. workouts even while he was EFCA's chairman. During that time he would not break his rhythm to take company calls.)

Stan boasted he was in Olympic weight-lifting condition, and even invited one of the authors to feel a muscle in his arm. It was indeed hard as a rock.

The authors were urged to try out some of the weight-lifting devices, which looked like Rube Goldberg machines linked together with springs and pulleys. It was all these puny journalists could do to lift the weights once or twice. Stan then proceeded to play with them like Ping-Pong balls and said he could have the authors in the same shape in six months.

"I always wanted to have a gym like this and when I finally got the money I did it," he declared.

"Stan's physical size grew before my eyes," recalled an associate. "You could see Stan's neck getting bigger—sixteen, seventeen, eighteen and one-half—and his biceps would bulge and his clothes would get tighter."

"Your body is your home," Goldblum would tell his

colleagues at work. "You live inside your body. You should take care of your home."

In conjunction with his dedication to physical fitness, Goldblum also taught himself to control his breathing to a point where he could breathe with his chest instead of his stomach. "Most men breathe with their stomachs and their muscles get flabby," Goldblum would say, all the while his chest moving up and down as he inhaled and exhaled. It was almost akin to the practice of Yoga. In fact, one time Goldblum studied an article in *Scientific American* which described doctors experimenting with humans controlling their own blood pressure through conscious control of breathing and the use of some of the Indian mystical arts.

As in everything else, Goldblum had expensive taste in automobiles. He owned a Ferrari and leased two Rolls-Royces. After the executive coup of April 2, 1973, however, the Rolls-Royces were disposed of and the family drove two 1973 automobiles—a Dodge Dart and an Oldsmobile.

Goldblum had recently purchased—but then sold when the scandal broke—a second house south of Los Angeles, in Newport Beach, fronting the Pacific. Until that time, the only sports activity the muscular chairman had taken part in was working out in his gym and riding his Honda motorcycle over dirt tracks.

But the Newport Beach home afforded Stan the opportunity to learn how to sail, so he bought a yacht. It also gave him a chance to tell his friends that he would soon be a competitive sailor. One day, to exhibit his competitiveness Goldblum "blew" his sails in a strong wind—that is, he used too much sail for the purpose of gaining speed. The wind tore the sail into shreds and that particular yachting lesson cost Captain Goldblum $1,500.

Goldblum did nurture a few lasting personal friendships such as that with the late Eugene Wyman, the nationally known Democratic Party organizer and fund raiser who lived not far from the Goldblums. Some of his acquaintances included comedian Buddy Hackett, whom Goldblum met on a vacation in Acapulco, and singer Glen Campbell who, as Goldblum's guest, sang at the 1971 St. Patrick's Day party the chairman gave for some of his personal and business friends at the posh Le Bistro in Beverly Hills.

Goldblum claimed he "had a lot of social acquaintances and few good close personal friends. Life is too short to cultivate more than just a very few friends." (He quipped that his definition of a good friend is "a person who will sign a note for you without asking why.")

Since the Equity Funding scandal was splashed across the nation's news media, Goldblum has had to restructure his life-style. "The few friends that I had are still my friends," said Goldblum. "But the social relationships have ended. The acquaintances are all gone."

Goldblum is a man of contrasts, who would pull out a few hundred dollars for a down-at-the-heels salesman while coldly firing dozens of senior management executives shortly after acquiring Bankers Life of New Jersey.

He could, in front of others in his office, reach into his pocket to give money to his brother, with whom he did not get along, or admonish a regional sales manager for putting too much postage on a sales report mailed to the home office. Meanwhile, unknown to most of his executives, he raised his annual salary from $100,000 to $125,000; his monthly expense allowance from $1,000 to $3,000 at the start of 1973 while putting out memos to his lieutenants that the company was embarking on an austerity program.

One of the hundreds of ironies in Goldblum's business conduct can be observed in the tough way he kept law and order within the company on the one hand and the sloppy—bordering on chaotic—bookkeeping and financing he allowed on the other.

The insurance subsidiary had a salesman who sold one of the company's ten-year mutual fund-insurance programs to an eighty-nine-year-old woman. Larry Williams, a former SEC investigator who was hired to make sure the company was conforming to SEC regulations, found out, however, that the agent had in fact picked up the elderly woman at a home for the aged during one of her more lucid periods, had spirited her away to her bank, and practically held her hand as she signed a check to purchase the program.

Williams was outraged and demanded that the salesman be suspended for sixty days. But Goldblum, more Roman than the Romans, fired the salesman on the spot. The chairman simply would not tolerate dishonesty among his sales crew.

This was the same Goldblum whose company, unlike other corporations, had no internal audit, and who allowed millions of dollars to slosh around from subsidiary to subsidiary virtually without restriction in an atmosphere practically devoid of financial discipline.

This was also the same Goldblum who served on the Southern California District Business Committee of the National Association of Securities Dealers, which handled all ethical and compliance problems for the region. Furthermore, it is believed that Goldblum had an excellent shot at becoming a member of the NASD's national board of governors in 1973.

Whether Goldblum read extensively is a matter of debate. One fellow executive believes his chairman became bored after two pages of almost any book. A neighbor says, however, he would read voraciously, particularly books on current events. "If I read a book on Kissinger, Stan had read three books on Kissinger," said the acquaintance.

In any case, his smaller den, where he watches television, has several book-packed shelves. Among the books were *The Godfather*, by Mario Puzo; *The Grandees, America's Sephardic Elite*, by Stephen Birmingham; *The Rich and the Super-Rich*, by Ferdinand Lundberg; and *Honor Thy Father*, by Gay Talese. An expensive Picasso artbook was on the coffee table.

There can be little debate about Goldbum's memory for Shakespeare, however, from whom he liberally quoted. Once, Goldblum had a friend over and the two, after a few drinks (Goldblum usually drank sparingly, but apparently not on that night) challenged each other to a duel to see who could quote the most Shakespeare. The friend had studied Shakespeare in college and was astonished that Goldblum could easily recall more lines from more plays.

Goldblum liked to remember that when he was young he also read Nietzsche and Schopenhauer, but those with whom he would try to philosophize did not believe he was a very ponderous thinker. In fact, there were times when he exhibited a marked degree of insensitivity to those who were better educated and better bred and who thought Goldblum a bit coarse for their taste.

"I appreciate the fact that you're trying to make me more sophisticated and more intelligent, but would you please let me alone—I'm tired of receiving your goddamn material," Goldblum once wrote in a memo to a colleague who thought he was doing his boss a favor by consistently sending him "enlightening" business and nonbusiness articles in the interoffice mail.

A man of many moods, Goldblum could be relaxed and friendly with Fred Levin, the head of his insurance operations, cracking jokes and trading stories.

But to an executive he tolerated only for business purposes he would clam up as he did on one occasion in New York. The executive was riding with Goldblum in midtown Manhattan to a board meeting. In an effort to make small talk, the man asked Goldblum if he had seen a movie on the plane ride from Los Angeles. "Yes," replied Goldblum. The answer told the executive that Goldblum didn't wish to pursue the conversation and the ride continued in an awkward silence.

It was difficult to judge just how politically aware Goldblum was. "Politics to him was the business of getting the right people into government," said a knowledgeable Los Angeles political hand who knew him. "He wasn't sophisticated in the sense of understanding organized politics."

An EFCA director who had been a dinner guest at Goldblum's house felt he was almost "totally uneducated" in modern-day politics.

Goldblum considered himself a political pragmatist who voted for Democratic Senator Hubert Humphrey of Minnesota for President in 1968, but, as a registered Republican, cast his vote for Richard M. Nixon's reelection in 1972. Goldblum often spoke out among friends against what he considered the socialistic views of Senator George McGovern of South Dakota, Nixon's opponent in 1972. Goldblum claimed McGovern's programs would soon bankrupt the country.

"I couldn't in good conscience support McGovern," said Goldblum. "He had a lack of control of the people around him."

Actually, Goldblum was simply reflecting the conservative Democratic political calculus of Beverly Hills, which has a big contingent of wealthy Jewish businessmen who would normally vote Democratic but who couldn't buy McGovern's platform, particularly the South Dakotan's ultraliberal social welfare programs.

Then, reflecting on the Watergate affair, Goldblum said that "maybe a vote for Nixon was wrong after all. We're only a few steps away from a police state."

Goldblum also gave $500 to Roger Hilsman, who served as Assistant Secretary of State for Far Eastern Affairs under President John F. Kennedy, and who later taught at Columbia, when he ran for Congress from Connecticut. He also loaned him $5,000 in August, 1972, but that was repaid.

Hilsman, who was on the board of directors of the three Equity Funding mutual funds, recalled that Goldblum said he would have liked to give him more money toward his unsuccessful campaign, but said he had spent so much trying to stop McGovern that he had no more to donate so he would make the loan.

Some of Goldblum's political views were even considered to be a throwback to the 1950's, allowing for practically unlimited defense spending to keep "the Russians or somebody" from threatening America's security.

The Equity Funding chairman clearly enjoyed the exhilarating feeling one gets in rubbing elbows with the powerful and in believing that through political contributions he had some sort of say about the internal machinery of that power structure.

So it was no surprise that when Humphrey became the Democratic candidate against Nixon in 1968, Goldblum contributed upwards of $100,000 to Humphrey's campaign. As a result, naturally, Goldblum was able to visit with Humphrey at Eugene Wyman's Beverly Hills home while the Minnesotan was on a campaign swing through the West.

Goldblum had been easily attracted to Humphrey's middle-of-the-road politics which were, in many ways, a throwback to the New Deal. "I was very impressed," Goldblum remembered of the meeting.*

In 1970 Goldblum was introduced to John Tunney, and again took an immediate liking to the attractive young California Democratic candidate seeking a U.S. Senate seat.

Goldblum ultimately contributed $25,246 to the successful Tunney Senate campaign. And Goldblum is believed to have helped Tunney with some travel details on a trip Tunney made to Israel in 1970. Goldblum had met Israeli Premier Golda Meir and Defense Minister Moshe Dayan, had traveled to Israel, and had been a substantial contributor to Israeli causes. (Interestingly, a 1972 Goldblum pledge of $350,000 to the United Jewish Appeal went unfulfilled, but sources said there were legitimate tax reasons involved.)

Goldblum was later invited to a Golda Meir dinner at the White House and said he shook hands with Nixon. (But, he added, "Nixon wouldn't know me if he saw me.")

Among Goldblum's bookshelf prizes was an urn from the Bronze Age encased in glass with the inscription: "Presented in grateful recognition of your support and commitment to the State of Israel." It was signed by Golda Meir. (The

---

*Goldblum, however, turned down an opportunity to be Humphrey's Southern California campaign treasurer. With the exception of Levin, the inside EFCA directors had advised Goldblum to reject the offer and keep the company out of politics.

bookcase also has a picture of Goldblum with Dayan, taken while the latter was visiting Los Angeles.)

Senator Birch Bayh of Indiana, another Democrat, also attracted Goldblum. Bayh had breakfast at Goldblum's home but never received any money from him. "I couldn't support everybody but I was very impressed with Bayh," Goldblum said.

Goldblum did make substantial contributions to Nixon. As late as November and December, 1972, Goldblum contributed stock worth approximately $31,822.43, despite a Republican campaign surplus amounting to about $4 million.

Because of his Nixon contributions, Goldblum also became acquainted with Maurice Stans, the former Commerce Secretary and then director of Nixon's campaign finances. As a result, Stan and Marlene were invited to, but didn't attend, a White House dinner after Nixon's reelection, a normal reward a President bestows upon his bigger contributors. Goldblum received a memento of the dinner, a pair of White House cufflinks which he enjoyed showing to his friends.

In October, 1972, Marlene and Stan attended a star-studded Democratic dinner at the Wyman home to raise money for candidates for Congress. By all accounts it was a magnificent affair, under the stars, with dinner served in tents. The dinner, one of two held by the Democratic Congressional candidates that year, brought out the likes of Senate Democratic Leader Mike Mansfield, House Speaker Carl Albert, and almost every big-name Democrat in the House and Senate. Janet Leigh, Jackie Cooper, and others from Hollywood's film industry also were present.

Marlene and Stan dined on steak and wine and danced to a full orchestra. As the music of violins was heard in the chill of the air that night, it must have been a heady feeling for the chairman, a moment of high spirits and elation. For this privilege he paid $46,423, consisting of a contribution of 1,400 shares of EFCA to the National Committee for the

Reelection of a Democratic Congress. The contribution was recorded by the Democratic committee on October 10, 1972.

Some say that Goldblum even aspired to political office some day, but that he probably would have happily settled for an appointment as ambassador almost anywhere.

In 1971 Goldblum was delighted to receive the honorary title of Consul General to Senegal at a time when Equity Funding was negotiating to build an elegant hotel there in partnership with the Hyatt Corporation. But the Senegal honorarium bestowed upon him would be as close as Goldblum would get to political power. (Goldblum said he never aspired to be a full-fledged ambassador, anyway.) He said he enjoyed the honorarium, which basically involved taking care of any problems of Senegalese students in Los Angeles.

And so we must face the same burning question that the prosecution must have pondered as it put together the 105 counts of the massive federal criminal indictment.

Even if a man as bright as Goldblum was in on originating the fraud—as the indictment alleges—why, with all his amassed wealth, didn't he pull out after he had become a millionaire a few years earlier?

Perhaps the answer lies with the statement of one Goldblum associate, who declared that at one time Stan, and Mike Riordan, in the mid-1960's, finally sensed they were shaping a company of immense wealth and power. "They felt they were on the threshold of this giant thing—they were going to shape the destiny of the universe," said the observer.

After the indictment, Goldblum gave no thoughts to leaving the country, intimates said, because he had no sense of guilt or that anything was really wrong. (In July, 1973, to make sure, the United States Attorney's office requested that he voluntarily turn in his passport, which he did through Thomas Sheridan, his attorney).

Following his April 1 ouster, Goldblum went into seclusion in his Beverly Hills home. How he spent his time and paid his bills while awaiting trial wasn't clear. With half a million dollars of his money frozen in litigation amid the scandal, Goldblum had to sell a real-estate asset in the San Fernando Valley that gave him an additional $750,000 on which to live.* At this writing, he was last seen in public in Los Angeles in December, 1973, to face arraignment on the federal charges. His bond was set at an extremely high $250,000.

The extent of Goldblum's involvement in the fraud and his motivations may never be properly understood. Declared a close friend:

"I don't know whether he thinks he's guilty or not guilty, whether he thinks he can put up a successful defense or whether he's willing to go to jail. I don't understand [Goldblum's involvement] and I don't think anybody else understands it. Maybe Stan doesn't understand it."

---

*Goldblum said that after he was ousted, his wife went to work in a white collar job for the first time in her life.

V
Sam and Fred

SAMUEL B. Lowell and Fred Levin were the top two officers under Goldblum. They had very little else in common, although when the Equity Funding scandal broke on April 2, 1973, they were both heading toward divorces brought about by events at the company.

For openers, they were of far different temperaments.

Levin could be endearing or he could intimidate an employee, becoming downright rude even in front of fellow workers. He exhibited humility and outrageous conceit. But for all his faults, Levin was extremely bright and combined intelligence with a hustler's instinct. He was just smart and ruthless enough to attract Goldblum, who had selected Levin to succeed him as president when Goldblum would retire from the company by 1976.

Lowell, too, was very bright.* But Sam lacked Fred's ruthless drive. He was more indifferent toward his EFCA colleagues. And, when it became clear about a year before the scandal broke that Goldblum had tapped Levin for the top job, Lowell lost interest. Lowell's colleagues noticed that he spent increasingly less time at the company. Sam had other pursuits. He was a tournament bridge player and owned an interest in the Wild Whist Bridge Club in the Westwood section of Los Angeles. After the indictment,

*Lowell even won some writing awards for his publishing efforts in professional accounting journals.

Lowell claimed he was spending all his time playing competitive bridge and giving bridge instruction.

In a sense, Sam and Fred were physically somwhat alike during their days at EFCA—almost akin to Tweedledum and Tweedledee. Both were rather short men, portly, wore glasses, and loved to indulge themselves in the good life that their comfortable five-figure salaries plus stock bonuses (all told over a quarter million dollars annually) afforded them.

Lowell was born in New York City on October 1, 1939. He received a Bachelor of Science degree from the University of Florida in 1961 and a Master of Business Administration from New York University in 1964.

From February, 1964, to March, 1968, Lowell was an auditor with the accounting firm of Haskins & Sells, which once audited EFLIC's books. Then, between March, 1968, and April, 1969, he served as treasurer of Bonus Gifts, a subsidiary of Dart Industries.

There were lots of ironies in the EFCA case. One of Sam's jobs while he was an auditor at Haskins & Sells was to help companies find embezzlers and clean up their internal operations.

Lowell joined EFCA as assistant treasurer and corporate comptroller in April, 1969. He was appointed executive vice-president of EFCA less than a year later. On May 24, 1971, Lowell was elected to EFCA's board of directors. Sam had responsibility for EFCA's finances, both domestically and internationally. Specifically, he supervised the operations of Bishop's Bank, Equity Funding's subsidiary in the Bahamas. He was also in charge of the finances of EFCA's funded loan programs. In his position, Lowell had to be considered the financial architect of the corporation.

Lowell and his second wife (he was divorced), Barbara (or Babs), had two daughters and lived in Pacific Palisades, a pretty, upper-class community overlooking the Pacific. Barbara Lowell knew little about her husband's work and accompanied him on just one overseas business trip to Rome in 1969.

Those who knew Sam said that he was an elder in the Presbyterian Church.

An acquaintance of Lowell's said that Sam once bragged he was a descendant of the famous Lowells of Massachusetts. A knowledgeable member of that prestigious clan, an investment banker who once attended a luncheon in Boston with Sam, said the subject never came up. He added that if Sam was a descendant, "it's news to me."

(All efforts to personally interview Sam were rebuffed, although one of the authors did make phone contact with him through the Wild Whist Bridge Club.)

Fred was born on Chicago's North Side on June 27, 1937. He received a Bachelor of Science degree from Roosevelt University in Chicago and his law degree from Chicago's De Paul University.

Levin was brought up by parents who strictly followed Jewish orthodox laws. His father was a kosher butcher. Moreover, there was a rumor at EFCA that Fred was a descendant of the Vilna Gaon, a great Talmudic scholar of the 18th century, who lived in Poland. But Levin said that wasn't so.

With this sort of upbringing it is no surprise that Fred gave some thought to becoming a rabbi. Therefore, during his high school years Fred also studied at Hebrew Theological College in Chicago. One of the rabbis there remembered Fred as being "a very good student, very bright." At that time the college didn't have a sister high school; it took only advanced students in Hebraic studies into what it called Chicago Jewish Academy, from which Fred graduated in 1955. "He was [already] on the college level in his Talmudic studies," recalled the rabbi.

From 1961 to 1964, Levin was a lawyer with the Illinois Department of Insurance.

One of Fred's closer colleagues in the legal section of the Illinois department recalled that part of Levin's duties involved checking to determine whether an insurance company was inflating its assets—one of the charges ultimately leveled at EFCA.

Levin was "a typical young brash attorney," said the older colleague. "By brash I only mean a nice person. A charming person you could almost say."

One thing that attracted him to Levin, said the acquaintance, was that Fred was a practicing orthodox Jew. "You don't find many like that," he said.

"He kept his religion fairly well. . . . I thought, 'Well, this is really a nice fellow.' My son at that time wanted to be an attorney and I used to think, 'I hope he's like Fred when he grows up.'"

Levin also had a degree of compassion. When his older friend incurred a long illness, Levin called frequently to inquire into the state of his health—even after he left the Illinois agency.

In 1964 Levin joined Presidential Life Insurance Company in Chicago as the firm's secretary and counsel.

In 1967 Presidential was acquired by EFCA and in 1968 it was moved to Los Angeles.* Fred came with the deal and in 1968 was named president of the insurance subsidiary. In July, 1970, Presidential was renamed Equity Funding Life Insurance Company. EFLIC was still chartered in Illinois when the scandal broke.

Fred was elected an executive vice-president of EFCA in April, 1969, with responsibility for the company's life insurance subsidiary, its 4,000-man sales force, and the marketing programs of the insurance division's over 100 offices across the country.

Levin was elected an EFCA director on May 24, 1971.

*EFCA made four applications to the Illinois Insurance Department to keep Presidential's legal residence in Chicago, but physically move its offices to Los Angeles. This was considered unusual by the Illinois authorities. They finally consented on the fourth application. Reports later circulated that Levin attempted to bring pressure on his former colleagues at the department to okay the move—but the reports were never substantiated.

Levin and his wife, Carol, lived in an upper-class section of Santa Monica, also near the ocean. They had two children.

Levin granted only a brief interview when confronted by one of the authors, who had traced him through the U.S. Postal Service to an apartment he was sharing with his brother in the Marina Del Rey area of Los Angeles, considered the city's swinging singles section of posh apartment complexes nestled behind yacht harbors, beaches, and high-priced restaurants and nightclubs.

Levin said he had told all he knew to United States Attorney John Marshall Newman, the young Harvard Law School attorney supervising the drawing up of the indictment, and therefore had nothing further to say. He claimed he had never felt better physically, having lost over 100 pounds in the past year. Levin had grown a mustache, wore tinted glasses, and hardly resembled the Fred Levin of Equity Funding.

At a second chance encounter at Los Angeles International Airport, Levin suggested there was a lot yet to be made public about the case.

During the heyday of Equity Funding, Sam and Fred lived well. When they were in New York they frequently rented limousines rather than take cabs. This practice applied whether they were there on company business or taking in a Broadway show. They stayed at the finest hotels and dined in restaurants in the style of the *Michelin Guide*—paid for by Equity Funding atop of their $1,000-a-month home entertainment accounts.

When Levin visited Bankers Life, for example, he stayed near Central Park and would rent a limousine for the two-hour ride out to Bankers' offices in Parsippany, New Jersey. The cost was about $38 an hour for the chauffeured Lincoln and the driver would wait for Levin—all day if necessary—and drive him back to Manhattan. One round trip for Levin cost EFCA as much as $300.

Sam and Fred were also quick to take advantage of EFCA's

business relationship with Los Angeles-based United California Bank. On January 14, 1972, Barbara Lowell signed for a $250,000 line of credit at UCB using EFCA stock as collateral. On February 23, 1973, her husband drew down $50,000 and, according to bank litigation, still owed $38,717.88 to UCB when EFCA went into Chapter 10.

Sam apparently had other loans outstanding with UCB as well, because on April 2, 1973, when the fraud story broke in *The Wall Street Journal,* the bank seized $106,282.12 the Lowells had in the bank to partially offset what UCB claimed was $169,000 in loans the Lowells had outstanding.

Coincidentally, on January 28, 1972, just a few days after Babs established her $250,000 line of credit, Carol Ann Levin did precisely the same thing at the same bank for the same amount using the same collateral.

Fred drew down $76,469 of the Levins' line of credit on June 7, 1972, which still appeared to be outstanding on April 2, 1973. He borrowed another $55,000 on January 26, 1973, and, according to UCB records, paid back only $15,000 before the fraud charges surfaced.

Babs said she didn't know why Sam wanted her to open up such a big line of credit. She said she just did what Sam told her. Carol Levin couldn't be reached for comment and, according to one source, had become highly upset over the scandal and left the state.

An attorney representing UCB in the lawsuits against Lowell and Levin to recover the loan said it wasn't particularly unusual for corporate executives to open personal lines of credit of that size.

Unlike Sam, one either immediately liked or detested Freddie (as many called him)—there were few indifferent opinions among his colleagues.

One underling said Levin was very difficult to approach or talk to. But another who worked directly under Fred liked him very much. "I enjoyed working for him. He was able to challenge me. I like him to this day. But I have no respect for his morality and I feel that what he did was wrong. Whatever happens to him, he was fully aware of the circumstances of the fraud when he did it.

"If he [Levin] walked up to me today and wanted to talk I'd do it very happily. But I don't know whether I'd buy a Mazda from him. I'd always wonder if there was something wrong with the car."

The latter was a reference to Fred's job as a Mazda salesman for Westwood Mazda, where newspaper accounts said he became the number-one Mazda salesman on the West Coast. Fred was certainly an excellent salesman, said one of the auto company's officials, but he wasn't the top salesman. Fred was with Mazda about seven months, almost up to the time of the indictment, before resigning and deciding to remain in seclusion. He complained that he was constantly being harassed by newsmen walking up to him on the car lot and asking for interviews. That, he said, was part of the reason that he decided to alter his physical appearance.

Fred could be generous—if the following piece of nepotism could be considered in that spirit.

Marshall Abraham, Fred's forty-year-old brother-in-law, was a Chicago real estate developer. A few years ago, Abraham recounted, Fred called out of the blue and asked if he would serve on the board of directors.

"I said, 'Impossible, I'm just a little schmuck. Who ever heard of me? Who wants me?'" Abraham recalled telling Fred.

Fred reassured Abraham that it would be a nice tribute to him, an honorarium.

"But I can't go to any meetings, I don't know anything about the life insurance business," Abraham protested.

Fred again assured his wife's brother that that, too, was all right.

"I reasoned he [Levin] was doing something for the family," Abraham recalled. Abraham said he had no idea how long he served on the board. In fact, he said, he didn't really know what board he was on because he originally thought Fred was offering him a position on EFCA's board of directors when it actually turned out that it was the board of Equity Funding Life.

"I thought I was going to be a big shot on the board of directors of a New York Stock Exchange company," blurted Abraham. "I wouldn't have taken it if I had thought it would be on the small board."

Abraham finally agreed to serve, but he was never called on to vote. In fact, by his own admission, he never did anything, with one exception. He bought a considerable amount of EFCA stock before the collapse. He wouldn't say how much except that it came to "five figures."

"Like a dummy, a month or two before this thing happened I bought an awful lot. I'm ashamed to talk about it." But he added that the stock purchase was his own decision, for which he couldn't blame Fred.

When the stock took a battering, Abraham asked Fred what was happening. He said that Fred told him, "Everything's fine. Our earnings weren't too strong."

After the scandal broke, Abraham was called in by investigators and, "They all laughed at me. I'm a schmuck with ears—that's what it comes to."

Signs of big trouble were everywhere that last week in March. Abraham called his sister in Santa Monica. He said Carol was "like a basket case over the telephone." She couldn't understand what was happening.

On March 27, the day the New York Stock Exchange stopped trading in EFCA stock, Abraham flew to Los Angeles and, for the first time, visited the Century City headquarters. His attorney, who happened to be in Sacramento on separate business, joined him.

After a four-hour wait outside Fred's office, Levin finally showed up, remembered Abraham, "looking distraught."

"What's this all about? asked Abraham.

"Big trouble here," Levin replied.

Abraham said he advised Levin to get hold of himself and remain calm.

By that time, said Abraham, "my sister was crushed."

Looking back, Abraham said: "Freddy's not a bad guy, but what he supposedly did to people is terrible. It's hard to believe. I don't understand it. When it came out . . . I yelled and screamed at my brother-in-law and to this day I still don't understand it. I swear I don't. I don't think anybody does."

There are those who feel that Fred went too far too fast and was in the end simply consumed by his own ambition. They say this might account for streaks of ruthlessness in his personality. A manifestation of this tendency to intimidate occurred, for example, when Fred took on the responsibility of firing the top management of Bankers National a few days after EFCA acquired the New Jersey insurance company in October, 1971.

A few days after the announcement of the Bankers acquisition, Levin attended a board meeting at the Parsippany headquarters. Here Equity Funding's brash young executive sat down with the eighteen board members of Bankers, a conservative insurance company. The meeting lasted about four hours, throughout which Levin kept up a constant round of chatter, asking rapid-fire questions about the company and, every once in a while, cracking a joke or two.

"I was great. Wasn't I terrific? Didn't I wow them?" repeated Levin as he rode to the New York airport in a limousine full of other EFCA executives after the meeting. "Boy, did you hear the way they laughed at my jokes? They were eating out of my hand."

One of the EFCA executives later questioned Fred's behavior in the limousine and was assured that the then thirty-three-year-old Levin indeed had the intellectual capability to run EFCA's insurance operations. It was just that he had an insecurity flaw in his character, possibly attributable to his meteoric rise within the company. Part of this insecurity also may have been evidenced by Fred's habit of biting his fingernails in public.

Fred's immaturity also manifested itself in his habit of criticizing employees in front of their colleagues. Again, this was passed off as a need to build himself up in the eyes of others. Fred Levin, like Stan Goldblum, his boss, very much wanted to be a success in every way and to make absolutely sure others knew he was successful—both professionally through his influence on the corporate course EFCA was pursuing and through his ostentatious tastes.

Fred's orthodox Jewish upbringing carried over into his home life, where his wife, Carol, kept separate dishes for meat and dairy products, as mandated by kosher dietary laws.

Unlike Goldblum, Levin took more of an active part in his community. He belonged to the Jewish Congregation of Pacific Palisades, where he served on the board of directors and was a member of the temple's finance committee. (The congregation, through its investment fund, held some EFCA stock, but unloaded all of it in 1972 when it decided to get out of the stock market altogether.)

One member of the congregation observed that both Levin and his wife appeared to be rather high-strung and nervous. He doubted whether Fred was immoral in his corporate relationship with other people. Rather, he observed, "Fred is amoral. It never entered his mind that what he was doing might be immoral and he would do it again."

Levin left the congregation about a year before the scandal surfaced.

Apparently the ethical and moral doctrines so deeply imbedded in an orthodox Jewish upbringing didn't quite make a complete imprint on Fred, particularly in his dealings with underlings. A good case in point is the method he used to fire Douglas Schoenfeld, the marketing vice-president of Bankers National, and one of the top positions at Bankers, directly under Fred.

William F. Good remembers the incident well because he took Schoenfeld's place.

Bill Good was with Bankers between 1954 and 1969, when he left to become president of a life insurance company in Michigan. But a merger involving the Michigan company had Good looking for another job about two years after he had left Bankers. Sales of Bankers National had plummeted and Levin contacted Good shortly after EFCA acquired the New Jersey insurance company. He urged Good to rejoin his old firm and Good accepted.

Levin told Good he would start on November 1, 1971, and that he, Levin, would introduce Good to Schoenfeld, the man he was to replace. "Christ, that's callous, Fred," Good remarked.

But that's the way Fred did it. On the morning of November 1, Levin asked Good to wait in a small office adjacent to the president's office. He summoned Schoenfeld and then asked Good to step into the room. Schoenfeld had heard of Good but hadn't met him. If Schoenfeld felt uneasy it may have been because it was barely two weeks after EFCA had taken over Bankers and there had already been a ruthless massacre of senior officials who EFCA executives, particularly Levin, felt would not fit into the Equity Funding mold. But Schoenfeld had been led to believe he was to be spared.

Levin told Schoenfeld that Good was returning to Bankers.

"In what capacity?" asked Schoenfeld.

"He's going to take your place," declared Levin. "Here's your resignation letter. Sign it. You're resigning." (All the other Bankers officials who were forced out were also given letters of resignation to sign.)

Schoenfeld was shattered. He was the last holdover officer to be fired. Good recalled that he was so shaken by the incident that when he went into Schoenfeld's office afterward, he could hardly hold a cup of coffee.

Some of Levin's associates believe that Fred took some degree of ghoulish glee in getting rid of the fourteen older Bankers Life executives. Levin liked to tell the story of how he had considered the routine of "the lady or the tiger" but

SAM AND FRED

never went through with it. The idea was to station Jim Smith, one of Fred's vice-presidents, in one office and Levin in an adjacent office connected to Smith's office. Levin was to do the firing and Smith was to give orientation talks to those employees being retained. Levin's plan was to secretly switch offices with Smith so the employees wouldn't know if they were going to be fired or kept on.

Perhaps religion eventually got to Levin.

On March 28, 1973, Levin, accompanied by Jim Smith, who was also the administrative head of EFLIC, went to the Century City branch of Wells Fargo Bank, where they withdrew $5.5 million in EFCA funds, negotiable bearer certificates of deposit. This was just a few days before EFCA's collapse.

Investigators got word that Levin was planning to leave the country after cashing in the CD's, and this ultimately proved to be the catalyst for the California Insurance Commission's decision to seize the company. There were reports that Levin was talked out of running off with the cash by some members of his family. In any case, on March 30, the $5.5 million in CD's was returned to Wells Fargo by Levin, where it was kept in a special EFLIC discretionary account.

In the end, Levin decided to cooperate with the United States Attorney after retaining Joseph Ball, a nationally known criminal trial lawyer, as his counsel.

No one has said however, that Fred was contrite. In fact, one of the members at the Pacific Palisades Jewish Congregation observed: "Fred enjoyed the game."

As the scandal began to surface, it was Sam Lowell who was the most shaken of the three by the swiftly moving chain of events.

The disenchanted Lowell, realizing that Levin was going to succeed Goldblum as EFCA chairman, began thinking about planning his financial future so that he could retire in a few years to a life of tournament bridge. Then, after he was kicked out by his fellow directors, Sam turned full-time to his passion for bridge in an effort to blot out his disastrous fall.

Lowell's lack of interest in EFCA may have been responsible for a snag that almost developed when EFCA was negotiating a $75-million-dollar revolving credit agreement with a four-bank consortium headed by First National City Bank of New York. EFCA was going to use $32 million of the agreement to purchase the Northern Life Insurance Company of Seattle and had to have the deal signed by June 29, 1972, the deadline set by the banks. But a few days before the deadline no one could find the loan documents. It seems they had been sitting on Lowell's desk for three weeks in a pile of mail.

The agreement had to be hammered out at Citibank's New York headquarters. A search commenced for Lowell, who was found in New York (no one knew exactly what he was doing there, but he had almost carte blanche authority as head of corporate finance to travel when and where he wanted). Apparently Lowell wasn't in Manhattan on the Citibank deal, but when notified of the pressing need to have the loan agreement concluded, he agreed to be in Citibank's headquarters for the final meeting which took place in the first week of June, 1972.

One of Sam's acquaintances lived on lower Seventh Avenue in Manhattan. Because she has a responsible position as a college professor and probably had nothing to do with the fraud allegations, we shall give her the name of "Mary X."

Sam was directly or indirectly responsible for siphoning off $2,005.18 to furnish Mary X's apartment.

The invoice for the furniture was issued on October 10, 1972, and has the handwritten name "M. Sultan" on it (Michael Sultan, EFCA's comptroller, reported to Lowell) and the additional handwritten notation, "OK to pay." The notation "charge to sales promotion" is crossed out. The invoice lists the furniture as sold to EFCA's New York office at 60 East 42nd Street.

The actual check—EFCA check #17447 drawn on the Wells Fargo branch at Century City—was dated October 20,

1972, and made payable to S. Gibson & Sons, Inc., a New York City furniture dealer. The furniture included a double-sized convertible sofa—the most expensive item, with a $450 price tag—in addition to chairs, tables, and various other furnishings.

The name of Miss X appears on the inventory list. The twenty-five-year-old Miss X acknowledged that she considered herself a close friend and confidante of Sam's.

Miss X declared she knew who Sam worked for and was "absolutely floored" when she read about the Equity Funding case in the newspapers. Nevertheless, she added, it was about two years since she last saw him and therefore had no intention of returning the furniture to Equity Funding.

The name of Miss X has surfaced in connection with Sam Lowell in another area, possibly of more interest to investigators.

In May, 1972, Sam took a two-week trip to South America. The ostensible reason for the trip was to look into further financial deals for either EFCA or Bishop's Bank.

The official story Lowell gave the company for going to Brazil, one of the countries on his itinerary, was that he was going to arrange some financing.

"The rumor around the company was that he was taking a large sum with him and that he was going to leave it down there someplace," said former EFCA executive Ronald Secrist, who was instrumental in blowing the lid off the case.

"[But] I don't think you will ever get proof in court," Secrist said.

Miss X said she accompanied Lowell on the trip. Also along, but staying at a separate hotel, was Roger Coe, the president of Bishop's Bank, who like Miss X speaks fluent Spanish.

Bishop's did extensive commercial-paper business in South America, and Coe, no doubt, was traveling on legitimate business.

What Lowell's business itinerary included, and whom he saw, were under investigation at the time this book went to press. Lowell, whose job it was to represent EFCA in its dealings with banks, journeyed from Rio de Janeiro to Chile and Argentina. It is reported that he met with influential powers in some of these countries.

Miss X refused to comment on what cities she and Sam visited or whom they met. Furthermore, she declared she didn't know what Sam's business schedule was in South America or whether—as Secrist alleged—he opened accounts in any banks. "I wouldn't have any idea if Sam was involved in depositing money in South America," she said.

Is Sam innocent, a victim of circumstances? Miss X couldn't directly comment. "Sam is really, really bright," she said. "I've met few people who have equaled his intelligence. If Sam wanted to cheat at something, he could plan very sophisticated techniques. But Sam, it seems to me, was too bright to do something that would eventually backfire, that obviously had to hit him in the face at some point.

"I don't see him doing something like that because above all he was so bright that he knew what he could get by with and he knew what he couldn't get by with. . . ."

In the end, Lowell saw he was headed for financial disaster. A last-minute attempt to transfer some of his funds to Bishop's Bank failed. During that last week of March, 1973, as the investigative net was closing around EFCA, Lowell was an emotionally distraught man who felt desperately alone. Moreover, Sam was in a financial bind caused by the sharp drop of his EFCA stock and his high bank borrowings against this stock.

It was during that week that Sam contemplated suicide. His immediate rationalization was that he would take his life to shield his wife from the scandal, Sam told a friend.

Fortunately for Sam the friend talked him out of killing himself. Sam later confided to this individual (who preferred to remain anonymous) that he had more than just financial problems and that the rumors concerning EFLIC were not only true, but it was far worse than the investigators yet knew.

Lowell's comments were contained in a four-page "confession"—a memo made by the friend on March 30, 1973, after listening to Sam describe his involvement in the case.* Copies of the memo were given to the Federal Bureau of Investigation and the United States Attorney's office.

According to the memo, Lowell implicated Fred Levin for maintaining a separate company office in Los Angeles which prepared "phony insurance policies. . . ."

Sam also pointed the finger, according to the memo, at Jim Banks, Art Lewis, and Lloyd Edens—members of EFLIC's middle-management team—as being involved in the fraud.

The memo continued:

"Sam indicated that he was an officer and a director of one or more of the insurance companies and that while he had no knowledge of the scheme, he should have had knowledge of it and that he himself had done other things for the company which were *very* questionable and in view of the other things no one would believe that he did not know about the insurance fraud."

Sam, according to the memo, also declared that when he first joined the company in 1969, he learned of a loan (counted as an asset on the company's books) which would never be repaid to EFCA. Sam went to Goldblum with the information.

The memo then asserts:

"Stanley Goldblum allegedly told him [Lowell] that if he did not leave that he would expect him [Lowell] to help cover up the loan.

"Sam indicated that he created a phony company which was receiving phony commissions from Equity which were being amortized over a period of seven or eight years and that eventually over that period of time the phony loan would be amortized off the books. . . ."

The memo continued:

"He [Lowell] doubted that either Herb [Glaser] or Rodney

---

*The "confession" was recorded by the friend from memory onto tape shortly after listening to Lowell.

[Loeb] know anything as both were too honest to allow anything to go on.

"Sam further indicated that Stanley [Goldblum] should have been aware of what was going on but that he was so happy with the 'earnings' that he never sought to question any more than he absolutely had to."

In a subsequent conversation with the same acquaintance, Lowell denied he had made any personal profit out of the fraud, adding that the entire scheme was to manufacture earnings and not to pocket money.

Moreover, Sam told the person, he [Lowell] knew for some time about the fraud as it pertained to manufactured earnings. (This seemed to conflict with his earlier statement that he had no knowledge of the scheme.)

In the end, Fred and Sam saw their personal lives decimated by the EFCA case.

And so it was a seemingly contrite Levin who, on Friday, January 18, 1974, stood stiffly at attention before Federal Judge Curtis and replied only, "Yes, your Honor" when asked if it was true that he had entered into a conspiracy involving mail and securities fraud, falsified documents, and bogus insurance policies.

At this writing, Lowell was maintaining his plea of innocence.

The International Operations

Piecing together the mosaic that was Equity Funding's international operations is somewhat akin to putting together a complicated abstract jigsaw puzzle blindfolded. The investigator feels like the frustrated mouse traveling through the maze, attempting to penetrate patterns of money movements only to find dead ends and having to begin again.

Like Equity Funding's domestic operations, it was almost as if it was purposely planned that way: That is, the more red tape and corporate bureaucracy, the less chance of any questionable deals surfacing. From the Caribbean to Europe, money sloshed back and forth and where it stopped nobody may ever know.

There was a phony Yugoslavian commercial-paper transaction signed by a mysterious Dr. Wangerhof and tied to a fictitious business deal designed to inflate assets involving a Panamanian "shell" company.

There was a probe by Internal Revenue Service intelligence investigators into hundreds of thousands of dollars which may have been siphoned out of the United States through the Bahamas. There was the comic-opera pasta-factory caper in Rome. There were the unsuccessful endeavors of Joseph Golan to make Equity Funding a sort of corporate godfather to the world's poorer nations.

To be sure, there were honest efforts to succeed on the international front—such as those mounted by Dov Amir, the ex-Israeli who headed the company's offshore operations, particularly in the area of oil and gas exploration. But these, too, were snakebitten, and millions were lost in investments that never paid off.

At one time, Mike Riordan had dreams of building an international financial empire for Equity Funding that would have dwarfed Bernard Cornfeld's Investors Overseas Services. In the end, with the exception of a bank in the Bahamas, the company had little to show for its efforts. More importantly, international negotiations have begun in an effort to discover if money was "dropped" in various foreign banks and whether the fraud uncovered in Equity Funding's domestic operations involving EFLIC was only the tip of the iceberg.

Let us first begin on a light note. Part I deals with the purchase of the pasta factory in the heart of Rome and ends up with the Vatican outsmarting the Century City Slickers.

VI
International Operations—
Too Much Spaghetti

THE *Liberté* was no longer France's most modern luxury liner. But in 1961 she still had that certain pride and elegance that her more recently built sisters hadn't had time to acquire. Of course, by then the jet also competed for the transatlantic travel dollar. But for those who loved to indulge themselves, the luxury offered by the *Liberté* simply wasn't available in the jet age.

Yura Arkus-Duntov loved the good life. To this tall, handsome Russian aristocrat, the *Liberté* was *the* way to cross the Atlantic from France to New York, a fitting end to a business trip. He could dawdle as waiters and cabin stewards catered to his whims. And, just as importantly, he could easily imagine he was still in the France he loved for a few extra days. Indeed, the *Liberté was* the France where he had lived for a dozen years. To Arkus-Duntov, the *Liberté* was the Hotel George V, Maxim's and the Louvre all wrapped into one glorious floating palace.

The *Liberté* had been at sea only a few hours when Arkus-Duntov found himself strolling along one of its decks after a glorious feast that needed walking off. A chance shipboard meeting brought him face to face with Joseph Golan, a taller, dark-complected Israeli, the son of a prominent pioneering family in the Jewish Holy Land.

The shipboard encounter turned into a friendship that was to last for several years—culminating with a disastrous business relationship. But, of course, on that cool, calm night at sea in 1961, neither Arkus-Duntov nor Golan had ever heard of an emerging outfit ten worlds away in Beverly Hills, California, called Equity Funding Corporation of America.

Arkus-Duntov recalls he initially was attracted to Golan because the Israeli said he was very friendly with the French philosopher Jacques Maritain, whom Arkus-Duntov wanted to meet. Golan provided the introduction.

He also was impressed with the kings, presidents, ambassadors, and statesmen Golan said he knew (Golan mentioned that his own father was an Israeli diplomat).

Arkus-Duntov was born in Russia in 1917, but was educated in Western Europe. In 1938 he received the License en Sciences of Paris University, specializing in fluid mechanics and technical aeronautics. He went on to do graduate work toward a PhD at the Institut Aérotechnique de St. Cyr and then served in the French Air Force in 1939 and 1940. Until 1949, Arkus-Duntov and his brother worked in experimental machine shops, mostly on auto racing engines—a field in which his brother was to make a name for himself.

From 1950, Arkus-Duntov spent a decade with the Curtiss-Wright Corporation of New Jersey as a project engineer, where he could put to use his experience in engine and helicopter design. In 1959, he joined the fledgling Dreyfus Corporation as a technical adviser and investment officer.

It wasn't until 1966 that Equity Funding attracted Arkus-Duntov. Goldblum hired him as president and a director of EFC Management Corporation, an Equity Funding subsidiary that was to be responsible for three domestic mutual funds: Equity Growth Fund, Equity Progress Fund, and Fund of America. In 1969, the debonair Russian was to be named one of EFCA's directors.

Golan was born and educated in what is now Israel. After Israel became a state in 1948, he became an activist in the

Zionist movement. Golan still has a large family in Israel, some of whom are prominent in its politics. Golan himself was a member of the Haganah, the Jewish underground army formed before Israel achieved statehood. Afterward, Golan went to Paris where, in the 1950's, he was involved in the left-wing student movements of that era. It was an important time for Golan because he was able to make friends with many of the young black African student activists. These were the same black activists who were to become rulers of emerging African nations a decade later. Golan's association with men such as Léopold-Sédar Senghor, later to become president of the Republic of Senegal, was to lead him to form his own economic development corporation in Rome, called BEDEC International, and was, in turn, to have a profound impact one day on Equity Funding.

Golan was thought to be one of those products of European and Asian intrigue—a soldier of fortune, a man of cloak-and-dagger abilities. "That's nonsense," said one acquaintance. "He is an international businessman and nothing else." What was known was that Golan spoke several languages fluently and did indeed have extremely high-level contacts with many of the world's governments, particularly among the emerging nations of Africa.

During the stock market euphoria of 1967–1968, Arkus-Duntov urged that EFCA reinvest the profits being generated by its three mutual funds. "We wanted to put some of the profits of the mutual funds into the development of natural resources in underdeveloped countries, particularly in Africa," Arkus-Duntov said. And who would be the perfect liaison for this sort of job? Why, his old friend from the *Liberté*, Joseph Golan, of course.

In 1969 Arkus-Duntov introduced Golan to Goldblum as the right man at the right time to do the right job. Goldblum gave the green light for Golan to represent EFCA abroad. In the process he acquired Golan's small company, BEDEC

International, and put Golan on salary with some stock options.

At the time, Golan and his company were in Rome. This, in turn, became Equity Funding's office on the Continent. It was small and unassuming, located across from a large park and not too far from the old walled section of the city which also was the home of one of Rome's largest industrial complexes—the Pantenella pasta factory.

The Pantenella complex sits on a number of acres in the middle of Rome. Founded in the 18th century by a wealthy Roman family, it consisted of the main pasta production plant, grain silos, and an administration building.

Golan, who had been attempting to promote several deals for Equity Funding around the world, had been with the Century City financial conglomerate for about a year when he recommended the purchase of the pasta complex.

Goldblum, Lowell, his top corporate moneyman, and Glaser, head of real estate operations, all favored the purchase on the simple assumption that EFCA was practically stealing the property and, given its location in the center of Rome, the real estate could only skyrocket in value.

The primary owner of the factory was the big Trieste-based Assicurazione Generali Insurance Company. The other owner also was well known: The Vatican.

Indeed, the purchase was a steal! The price tag was $16,000 with the caveat that the American company would refurbish the factory and ultimately move it out of Rome to a modern industrial park, while Equity Funding would retain the valuable property. With that stipulation Equity Funding got an unusual sweetener in the deal—a $5-million loan from Rome's Efi Banca, earmarked to rehabilitate the factory. It was reported at the time that the Vatican played no small part in getting the bank loan for EFCA.

The deal was finally consummated by Golan, who acted as EFCA's agent in receiving 93 percent of Pantenella's stock (the rest was publicly held). Even the 6-percent loan rate during the money crunch of 1970 was considered a bargain.

Equity Funding now had international status. That fast-dealing, fast-talking Western bunch from Century City gulch had themselves a real Italian spaghetti factory. Goldblum was elated. But spaghetti was the farthest thing from his mind.

"We weren't interested in the spaghetti," Goldblum recalled. "We wanted a quick turn-around profit on the real estate. It was a real estate play, that's how I would describe it. We bought the factory and planned to fire the people—the Vatican couldn't fire people.

"We were going to tear it down and build an apartment house. Equity Funding was not in the spaghetti business. We paid nothing for it because it wasn't worth anything."

In any case, Stan and his wife, Marlene, and Sam and Barbara Lowell went to Rome in the spring of 1970 to close the deal. It would be an interesting scene: delegates from a young financial empire just beginning to flex its international muscles meeting with delegates from a somewhat older and much richer empire—the Vatican.

The night before the closing, the Goldblums and the Lowells hit the town and didn't get back to their Rome hotel until the wee hours. The next morning, Lowell was the first to rise and exclaimed, "Oh my God, Babs, we're going to be late. We're due at the Vatican at ten A.M."

Lowell immediately dashed into the Goldblums' adjoining room and began shaking his boss.

"C'mon, Stan, we're due at the Vatican at ten A.M." shouted Lowell.

Goldblum turned slightly in bed, and with one eye half open asked Lowell: "Will the Pope be there?"

"Of course not," replied Lowell, watching the clock pass 9:30. "We're to meet the monsignors in charge of investments."

"Then," replied Goldblum with a yawn, "if they're not sending their top guy, we're not sending our top guy, either."

Goldblum rolled over and went back to sleep.

Goldblum later called this story "bullshit" but said Lowell enjoyed telling it.

There were few other laughs that Equity Funding got out of the deal. In the first place, the Italian unions wouldn't allow any of the employees to be fired or the plant to be moved. Secondly, labor strife became so rampant that the workers even took over the plant for awhile and mounted a sign in front depicting Equity Funding as the Ugly American—an Uncle Sam with horns. Violent labor strife is nothing new to Italy, but in this case the workers went so far as to storm Golan's office and attempt to burn it down. Thanks to Rome's finest, they didn't succeed.

So Equity Funding found it was in the same fix as Generali and the Vatican. It had a factory with 600 employees which operated at a loss. The previous employers, for obvious public relations reasons, couldn't shut the factory down or move it, and now neither could Equity Funding.

Toward the end of 1970, things went from bad to worse. Golan wired his old friend Arkus-Duntov that unless EFCA sent $400,000 immediately to meet the payroll, the spaghetti factory would go bankrupt.

In November, 1970, Golan got the $400,000.

Hardly more than a month later, just before Christmas, Golan said that more money was needed to save the factory from going belly up.

Goldblum ordered Arkus-Duntov to fly to Rome to find out what was going on. To his astonishment, Arkus-Duntov found that Pantenella was in a virtual state of bankruptcy. "Every penny we would have put in would disappear," Arkus-Duntov analyzed. "One hundred thousand wouldn't solve it and one million dollars wouldn't solve it." The $400,000, he found, had already disappeared into the financial morass of Pantenella.

Arkus-Duntov consulted with some friends he had in Rome who told him that in view of the state of Italian politics and the state of affairs at Pantenella, EFCA was insane to have ever become involved with the venture.

By this time, Arkus-Duntov's friendship with Golan was rapidly cooling. It was clear that there was no way the workers could be displaced, the factory closed, and a quick real estate profit made. There were other problems for Arkus-Duntov as well. He was desperately trying to avoid the adverse publicity which would result over a subsidiary of EFCA about to go bankrupt. And the original owners refused to take the factory back because the pasta operation had incurred heavy debt before EFCA bought it.

EFCA had originally been told the land on which the pasta complex sat might be worth $8 or $10 million. Now, with the present situation it was hardly worth the price of a used Fiat.

Arkus-Duntov finally concluded that Golan, who had been named Pantenella's general manager, would have been better off running a blintz factory than a pasta operation. For six months Arkus-Duntov glumly commuted between New York and Rome in an effort to spin off the spaghetti works. In the meantime, a harried Goldblum was getting conflicting reports from Arkus-Duntov and Golan on the status of the factory—in one case a story that nothing could save it; on the other hand, requests for more cash to turn the operation around.

Assessing the man he hired, Arkus-Duntov said that Golan "didn't know anything about the accounting of Pantenella, didn't know how to run it, and never appraised us of the true political problems." Whether this was true, or just disappointment or sour grapes on the part of Arkus-Duntov, is an open question and may never be known. In any case, it is hotly disputed by Golan.

There was another problem that Arkus-Duntov didn't consider. It was explained to Arkus-Duntov by Allessandro D'Urso, the new legal counsel he had hired in Rome to pull EFCA out of the deal.

It seemed that while all of this was going on, a couple of top executives at EFCA decided they could make better use of the original $5-million loan that had been part of the purchase package and which had been targeted to modernize the factory. Instead of using the money for this purpose, it was transferred out of Rome's Efi Banca to the Unione Bank of Milan. Then, Golan, under instructions from the EFCA home office, was instructed to use the Milan bank's passbook as collateral to borrow $5 million from the Amicor Bank of Switzerland, this time denominated in Swiss francs.

The $5 million was then brought back to the United States to be used for new EFCA adventures. But what the intrepid EFCA executives forgot—or chose to forget—was that the $5 million had been strictly earmarked to be used to overhaul the drab factory. Since it was indirectly siphoned out of the country, a currency violation had been committed under the Italian currency control laws.

"Have you heard about the currency violation?" D'Urso asked Arkus-Duntov one fine day in Rome while the two were still in the throes of trying to unload Pantenella.

"Not another headache," declared Arkus-Duntov who no doubt was thinking that no real estate, no matter how valuable, was worth that kind of aggravation.

Arkus-Duntov said the money must be returned at once and called Loeb.

"You have got to find us five million at once," chief counsel Loeb relayed to EFCA comptroller Mike Sultan. And Sultan didn't waste a minute in consulting Goldblum who, although annoyed with what he considered meddling by Arkus-Duntov and Loeb, okayed a deal with friendly Citibank, which loaned Equity Funding $5 million through the American bank's Rome office. That $5 million was later paid off.

Thus, the cycle was reversed. The Swiss bank was quickly repaid; the Milan bank passbook was returned; the money was pulled out of Unione Bank of Milan; and Efi Banca in Rome received its original loan back in early 1971. Although the loan was, in effect, paid off three years in advance, Efi Banca still charged Equity Funding $67,000 in interest that would have been levied if the loan had stayed on its books for the full period. To try to placate the Italian authorities, Equity Funding executives decided to pay that off, too, despite Goldblum's vigorous opposition.

But the Italians weren't placated. Equity Funding was suddenly a defendant in an Italian currency violation case because the Efi Banca loan was used as collateral to get money out of Europe through Switzerland and back to the United States—manipulation that the Italian authorities said ran directly counter to their country's currency laws. The Vatican was having the last laugh.

(It was not unnoticed by some of Equity Funding's management that the $5-million loan could have been assimilated into EFCA's books without reporting it to shareholders—and one federal investigator theorized that was the real purpose behind the purchase of the pasta factory, to get the $5 million for new ventures during a period of tight money.)

Certain Italian officials would love to have Stan Goldblum return to their colorful country again, but it's probably safe to say that if American authorities allow the former Equity Funding chairman to once more travel outside the United States, he'll probably opt to pass up the sybaritic pleasures of the Roman countryside.

A second violation—this time involving Pantenella stock —also cropped up just as D'Urso had finally found a buyer for the factory in 1971.

Moreover, the stock violation appeared to be an even bigger can of worms, which somehow didn't point the finger directly at Equity Funding, but certainly stemmed from its love affair with pasta.

As previously mentioned, Golan, in managing the factory complex, had become the transfer agent for 93 percent of the factory's stock. And, once again true to Equity Funding's tradition of trying to make a buck with other people's money, Goldblum asked Golan to use some of the Pantenella collateral to raise additional cash.

"Can you borrow any money using that stock?" asked the inquisitive Goldblum even after the company had already decided to sell the factory.

"I'll try," replied the always enterprising Golan.

And Golan went to an Italian moneyman named Gian-Franco Pilella, who was on Pantenella's board of directors and was also one of the largest stockbrokers in Italy.

What Golan, Goldblum, and the Equity Funding crowd didn't know, however, was that Pilella himself was on the brink of bankruptcy. Golan gave Pilella 28 percent of the 93 percent of the Pantenella stock and Pilella was ostensibly to use it as collateral to raise money for Equity Funding.

Pilella, however, used the 28 percent for collateral to get a loan for himself designed to resolve his own financial difficulties. It didn't work and Pilella went bust. And the 28 percent went down the drain.

Pilella's plight also was unknown to attorney D'Urso, who was locking up a deal to unload the pasta complex to a Neapolitan businessman, Roberto Memmo, who, on behalf of his business group, had plunked down the Italian equivalent of $16,000 for the Equity Funding interest in the Pantenella complex. Golan tried to retrieve the 28 percent from the Banco di Santo Spirito in Rome, which had taken it from Pilella as collateral on Pilella's loan. The Banco di Santo Spirito said no soap to Golan's request.

Memmo was left holding the bag. Memmo's backers asked "Where's the 93 percent?" An investigating Italian magistrate pointed a finger at Memmo and said if there was any fraud, Memmo was somehow involved. And beleaguered Memmo turned around and threatened a multimillion lawsuit against Equity Funding for failure to deliver on the deal.

Memmo and his backers still owned 65 percent of the spaghetti factory at the writing of this book. Like the whiz kids at Equity Funding, Memmo couldn't help but ask himself if a $16,000 piece of real estate in an historic section of Rome was worth all that aggravation.

Arkus-Duntov finally fired Golan after disposing of Pantenella. "I brought him in as a public relations [contact] to the African countries, I didn't bring him in to run a spaghetti factory," summed up Arkus-Duntov.

Golan maintained the pasta fiasco was none of his doing. Reached in Paris, he commented:

"It was a very sad part of my life. I think now that they [Equity Funding] are a bunch of crooks."

Golan said that when he saw the way EFCA was handling the venture he decided to pull out—he wasn't fired.

In any case, Goldblum returned BEDEC to Golan upon Golan's exodus. That hardly soothed Golan's ruffled feathers, however.

In retrospect, Golan said EFCA didn't know how to manage the spaghetti operation. "They didn't take it as a serious venture—it was one of those things you buy and sell . . . they could have had a very healthy factory in Italy." (Indeed, a silver cup for outstanding pasta was awarded the company by the Italian food industry while EFCA owned it, and the cup sat prominently in EFCA's boardroom in Los Angeles).

Golan claimed that EFCA didn't realize pasta is a basic Italian food and therefore big business in Italy. It could have been a profitable venture, he said. EFCA's big mistake, charged Golan, was attempting to run the factory like playing the stock market. "A factory is not like the banker in the market where you buy in the morning and sell in the afternoon," he said.

To underscore his point, Golan declared that Pantenella "is operating today and it is not losing money."

Whomever one believes—Arkus-Duntov or Golan—there is one fact, as emphasized by Golan, that cannot be refuted. Today the shares of Pantenella are worth more than the common stock of Equity Funding.

VII
International Operations— *The Maze*

MIKE Riordan had a private ambition to substantially expand Equity Funding's international business, particularly into Europe.* Riordan had been impressed with the success of Bernie Cornfeld's IOS operations and believed there was certainly room there for two financial wizards from the United States.

In 1967 Riordan capitalized on his recent friendship with Ralph Seligman, the lawyer who lived in the Bahamas.

On a trip to Europe, the two visited financial institutions in Brussels, Paris, Amsterdam, and in various cities in Switzerland and Germany, exploring possible lines of credit for Equity Funding and other business opportunities.

Seligman also traveled on behalf of Equity Funding to Hong Kong and other Far East cities, as well as to the Union of South Africa, in hopes of setting up EFCA distribution networks in these areas.

---

*Levin later also had his eyes on Europe. That's why, he told a board of directors meeting on March 8, 1973, Equity Funding should acquire First Executive Corporation, a Beverly Hills-based life insurance holding company with a subsidiary insurance company in Germany. Levin told the board the German company could be used as a base for insurance expansion into France and Italy as well.

Levin also said he might consider selling a piece of EFCA's proposed European plan and combining operations with IFI, an Italian insurance group, and that he had already opened discussions with the big Italian combine while in Italy on his way back from visiting the German firm.

But because of a lack of financing, Riordan's dream of an international sales organization never materialized.

Seligman's close association with Riordan was nevertheless fruitful. His wife and two other women were to subsequently take part in a commission arrangement involving EFCA and its brokerage house, the Wall Street firm of Dishy, Easton & Company, which was to become the subject of an investigation by the Securities and Exchange Commission. The SEC then asked the intelligence division of the Internal Revenue Service to take a look.

The SEC probe of Dishy, Easton was part of the agency's extensive study in 1968 of the so-called give-up system of commissions that had become so popular on United States stock exchanges. Under the informal rules of the give-up structure, brokerage firms allowed companies with whom they did business to direct where part of their brokerage commission should go. This was a way of saying, in effect, "thank you" to another broker for services rendered. The original broker didn't mind because the securities business was booming in 1968 and the whole system of reciprocity within the confines of clubby Wall Street seemed to be working out well. Reported misuse of give-ups by some brokers and mutual funds led the SEC to recommend their abolition, which was accepted by the New York Stock Exchange in December, 1968.

In the case of Cornfeld's IOS, commissions were directed to the research house of Jesup & Lamont which then split with Gloria Martica Clapp, a Cuban, who along with her Boston lawyer husband, an IOS tax adviser, built themselves a million-dollar home on Paradise Island in the Bahamas.

In the case of Equity Funding and Dishy, Easton, of the three women involved, two lived in the Bahamas and one, an attractive redhead, worked out of her apartment in Monte Carlo.

One of the most common give-up arrangements Equity Funding had was with Keystone Custodian Funds, Inc., the Boston-based financial management firm which was selling big chunks of its mutual funds through the EFCA sales force. EFCA would direct where it wanted Keystone to send part of the commissions earned on business. Keystone had no objection, since Equity Funding was the largest sales organization for Keystone funds. One investigator looking into the arrangement said Keystone had hundreds of letters on file from EFCA directing how the give-ups should be split.

The IRS believed that Mike Riordan and Stan Goldblum were personally directing many of the give-ups. The main benefactors were Dishy, Easton,* which did business with EFCA and the three women: Ralph Seligman's wife, Lorna;† Edith McLeod, the wife of an official of Bishop's Bank in Nassau; and Marlene Freedman, the attractive young woman who knew Riordan and who was of particular interest to IRS investigators.

At the time of the SEC and IRS probes into the commission fee deals and EFCA's operations, Bishop's was owned by a shareholders group which included Stanley Easton, Bernard Dishy, Riordan, and Goldblum. In 1969, EFCA began purchasing Bishop's in a two-stage transaction for almost $600,000.

As the Dishy, Easton officials testified before the SEC on July 18, 1968, Marlene Freedman was the brokerage house's foreign representative, based in Monaco.

How Miss Freedman came into this position was described by Bernard Dishy:

"Miss Freedman was a barrister, I believe, in England.** She was working there for a large law firm. My partner, Mr.

---

*Dishy, Easton also handled personal brokerage accounts for Riordan and Goldblum in addition to its EFCA business.

†Ralph Seligman told the authors he was not yet licensed to do legal business in the Bahamas when Riordan asked him to look into international banking contacts for EFCA, so that give-up fees in payment for this work had to be directed to his wife, who did the work, he said.

**Miss Freedman told the authors she was neither a British solicitor nor a barrister.

Easton, met her socially. She said she was unhappy doing, you know, a barrister's work and not being compensated for it. Her family lives in London.

"She preferred to live on the Continent. And she would be very happy do do anything for us in Europe that could possibly be done. She is a very bright girl; so we decided to train her [in 1967] as a registered representative and have her represent us."

Dishy was shown a photostatic copy of a document which stated under his firm's letterhead: "Commission statement —Marlene Freedman." The bottom line read: "Commission 60% = $14,281.20."

Dishy explained the significance of the commission:

"At that particular time we were looking for loans for Equity Funding. Miss Freedman made an original contact with a bank in Paris to obtain a line of credit for Equity Funding. Mr. Easton went over to Paris and subsequently established a line of credit as an opening. And for this, Equity Funding directed the New York Stock Exchange brokerage [business] to our firm. We apportioned this amount to Marlene Freedman as her share, and it was subsequently paid to her.

"As [Equity Funding's] sales have increased, they have been endeavoring to increase [their] lines of credit, and our major service to them has been obtaining for them lines of credit . . . ," Dishy added.

Dishy, Easton also had another arrangement with Miss Freedman. All foreign bank arbitrage accounts with Dishy, Easton would be credited to her. These accounts included the following money on deposit with Dishy, Easton: Salik Bank in Basel, $250,000; Banque du Rhône in Paris, $50,000; and Bishop's Bank, $180,000.

An exhibit was then introduced showing that Miss Freedman received $29,390 in net commissions on these arbitrage accounts from September, 1967, to May, 1968.

Interestingly enough, the SEC testimony brought out that Dishy, Easton also had a give-up arrangement with the

Republic Technology Fund, which had the Salik Management Company as its principal advisory firm. Charles E. Salik, of San Diego, was the president of the fund which he was later forced to sell by the SEC and which was acquired by EFCA. He also was the principal owner of the Salik Bank in Basel, in which United California Bank purchased a controlling stock interest in May, 1969. The bank had approximately $60 million in assets and performed commercial, investment, and merchant banking functions.

Republic Technology was purchased in 1968 and became one of three mutual fund subsidiaries of Equity Funding Corporation of America. Through this deal, Salik established a business association with Equity Funding. This relationship was being explored by investigators combing through the EFCA scandal, attempting to determine if Salik's Basel bank became a depository for any siphoned EFCA cash. A source familiar with Salik's Basel operations told one of the authors there was no EFCA—or Goldblum —cash in that bank.*

Now, to continue with the saga of the women receiving Equity Funding-directed give-ups: All three were trained by Dishy, Easton.

Within the confines of the give-up procedures of the late 1960's, the SEC could find nothing wrong with the fees being received by the three women. Indeed, it simply was payment for services rendered, testified Dishy. Nor did the SEC come up with any complaints against Dishy, Easton or EFCA for the way the give-ups were handled.

The case appeared closed.

But SEC investigators were still suspicious of the EFCA-Dishy, Easton-Marlene Freedman link and requested the

---

*In 1970 United California Bank, which by that time had purchased Salik's bank, suddenly found itself in the midst of a massive cocoa futures scandal involving its new Basel UCB operation. The Basel bank collapsed and UCB lost $40 million in one of the biggest scandals in Swiss banking history. Several officials were arrested by the Swiss and charged with unauthorized futures trading.

Internal Revenue Service to take up the probe. Primarily at issue was whether EFCA was somehow channeling money out of the country to avoid U.S. taxes.

The IRS investigation began in November, 1968, and involved several agents from its Intelligence Division. A painstaking search was mounted in Wall Street, Los Angeles, Boston (home of Keystone), and Washington. Mountains of brokerage records were examined for possible clues to where the give-ups were ultimately ending up.

Riordan and Goldblum appeared to be cooperating 100 percent with the IRS. Truckloads of EFCA records were turned over to the agents. The trouble was—whether intentional or not—the company's internal record keeping was a mess reflecting little organization. Even worse, records were missing.

The IRS determined that Riordan and Goldblum were directing some give-ups to either Dishy, Easton or to Miss Freedman. In the latter case, the commission fee would be sent to Miss Freedman through the Dishy, Easton firm.

Although the IRS doggedly pursued various channels after Miss Freedman got her money, they couldn't get to the end of the maze to see where the cash was finally dropped. No one at the IRS believed that Miss Freedman kept all of it.

But the IRS investigators kept prodding, spurred on by private information received from individuals close to EFCA that Riordan and Goldblum had pocketed hundreds of thousands of dollars through the give-up arrangement with Miss Freedman. Equity Funding records ultimately documented that much of the give-up money handled by Miss Freedman went to her in the Bahamas (like her two female colleagues), as well as to her European office, although she did not claim the Bahamas as her permanent domicile. Mike and Stan were said to have made frequent trips to the Bahamas in those years—presumably on business involving Bishop's Bank.*

---

*Goldblum told the authors he had visited the Bahamas only once.

"I think Mike and Stan pocketed half a million dollars in three years through a contact woman," said one IRS investigator. "But I had no proof whatever."

Another individual close to the IRS investigation, but not directly involved, estimated that "probably well over a million dollars" of Equity Funding money was siphoned out of the United States and into "travel accounts" in Swiss banks.

Miss Freedman was found in Manhattan living just off lower Fifth Avenue. She refused to see either of the authors but did grant a telephone interview.

She categorically denied that she deposited any EFCA or Dishy, Easton money in foreign banks. She said she certainly was not a contact woman for any EFCA cash leaving the United States.

The thirty-four-year-old Miss Freedman said she hadn't worked as a stockbroker since 1969. When in the securities business, however, she said she was an international broker who represented Dishy, Easton interests in Europe.

Miss Freedman, born in London on March 8, 1939, attended the City of London College. Between 1964 and 1967 she did secretarial work for the prominent New York law firm of Simpson, Thatcher and Bartlett. Her employment at Dishy, Easton began in March, 1967, and ended in April, 1970.

At the high point of her brokerage career the attractive redhaired (it was now brown) Miss Freedman said she worked out of her combination home and office at Five Avenue Princess Alice in Monte Carlo. She said she couldn't remember a great deal about those years because "I have a lousy memory."

"It was a residency office for Dishy, Easton," said Miss Freedman. "But I wasn't permitted to do any business in Monte Carlo by the French government. I used to do most of my business in Switzerland and some in Belgium."

The once-married Miss Freedman maintained that although she knew Mike Riordan ("A very nice guy"), she wasn't really involved with Equity Funding. She declared that her primary mission was acting as a broker for a number of Swiss banks which were her customers. She claimed she received commissions on bank-stock transactions made through Dishy, Easton.

"I never wrote a check or gave money or anything like that back [to the banks]," emphasized Miss Freedman. She later said, however, she had trouble remembering all the details of her business in Switzerland. "You must remember that this was 1968 and I often have trouble remembering what happened yesterday afternoon," Miss Freedman said.

In fact, she said, it wasn't necessary for give-ups to be directed back to the Swiss banks in exchange for the business they were giving Dishy, Easton because the banks were, in turn, charging their customers one and one-half times the commission rate.

Moreover, claimed Miss Freedman, her only real business contact with Equity Funding came in the late 1960's when Stan Easton asked her to sound out her bank customers on a bond issue EFCA wanted to float (which was referred to in the SEC hearings).

Was there any way that Miss Freedman could have been used without her knowledge to drop money in European banks? "No, I would have to have known," she replied. "I mean, I'm not that dumb."

Miss Freedman confirmed making frequent visits to Bishop's Bank at a time when Dishy, Easton had an interest in the bank.

At that time, she said, the Bishop's deal was "tremendously exciting to everybody because they [Wall Street] would say Dishy, Easton's got a Bahamian Bank and it must be doing all sorts of things. But in fact they [Dishy, Easton] never got around to doing anything with it. And then they sold it to Equity Funding."

Miss Freedman helped keep the books for tiny Bishop's, which she said used to be called a piggy bank because of its size.

Miss Freedman admitted she knew she was under investigation by the IRS in 1968 because she was aware the IRS was looking at Dishy, Easton. "I assumed that somewhere in there they had a look at me." But she said she was never contacted by IRS agents.

Rumors about her international activities have surfaced from time to time, Miss Freedman suggested, but they're all nonsense. "I've been accused of going to bed with almost everyone. I just couldn't have had the time. But rumors are lovely. I rather enjoyed them."

Miss Freedman said her business began to fall apart in 1969 when the American stock market hit the skids and that she currently worked as a secretary.

Finally, the IRS threw in the towel. When Goldblum, upset over the probe by the tax agents in the first place, heard that it was being called off, he quipped to one of the investigators: "You must not have found our Swiss bank account."

On June 1, 1968, Goldblum hired forty-three-year-old Israeli-born Dov Amir, a petroleum engineering specialist who lived about a block and a half from EFCA's offices. Amir, an intense-looking person who speaks with a touch of old-world inflection, had made somewhat of a reputation for himself with a Los Angeles firm called Sunset International Petroleum.

Amir's responsibility was to develop tax shelter-oriented oil and gas programs.

"We have five thousand salesmen," Goldblum told Amir. "You just make sure that we drill in the right places."

About three months later, Mike Riordan told Amir he wanted EFCA to go beyond simply setting up investor tax shelters. Instead, said the internationally minded Riordan, EFCA, through its new subsidiary, should invest money in developing a group of mineral exploration companies with interests around the world.

Riordan's proposal substantially changed EFCA's game plan. Amir had been originally hired to establish programs that would enable the company's salesmen to sell limited partnerships. Now, Riordan was proposing that the company take a piece of the action utilizing EFCA's—not the public's—money.

Amir was enthusiastic. Suddenly, EFCA found itself with commitments to international consortiums exploring for oil off Ecuador ("My analysis as a geologist was that it was very favorable," Amir told one of the authors), Israel, and Ethiopia. Two international subsidiaries were established under Equitex: Traserco, Inc. to handle Ecuador; and Equitex Petroleum Corporation to take care of Ethiopia, Israel, and, eventually, Zambia.

Early in 1969, while Amir was attending a meeting in Tel Aviv on the Israeli oil drilling project, he got a middle-of-the-night phone call from Goldblum.

"What do you know about Zambia?" came the faint but distinguishable voice of Amir's boss on the other side of the world.

Goldblum told Amir to get in touch with one Joseph Golan in Rome who would introduce Amir to Kenneth David Kaunda, the President of Zambia.

"I went along because it was my naïve belief that I was really going to be given the chance to build a natural resources company," Amir recalled. He subsequently made several trips to Zambia and became friends with its President.

Amir concluded from his exploration of Zambia that EFCA had "a fantastic opportunity for mining and exploration" and at once filed applications for concessions there. At the same time, Amir concluded a similar deal with a French company in West Africa and in Trinidad.

In a short time, Amir had indeed set up a globe-girdling oil and gas exploration network—utilizing some $10 million in EFCA capital. Additionally, Amir was setting up programs with several European governments for more exploration projects.

Meanwhile, Goldblum and Golan had gotten together for

an even more spectacular project. Using Golan's high government contacts in Senegal, Goldblum entered into an agreement with the Hyatt Corporation, the hotel organization, to build a convention center-hotel-sports complex in Dakar, Senegal, which was to be a showcase for all of Africa. The project was planned as a joint venture between EFCA and Hyatt, with the materials and financing to come from Italy. Goldblum was enthusiastic about the project and quick to show his colleagues a model and plans he kept in his office. Others in the EFCA hierarchy weren't quite as enthusiastic about the deal, however, and dubbed the project "the Halfwit Hyatt." Eventually, EFCA and Hyatt hit an impasse and the deal fell apart.

At the same time Golan plodded on, providing entrée for EFCA in several other African nations where EFCA might, for example, enter into a beef and cattle operation in Madagascar or buy and sell industrial goods and commodities in any one of a number of African countries.

A case in point was Fernando Po.

Fernando Po, an island off the west coast of Africa, directly west of Cameroon and less than five degrees north of the equator, is owned by the African nation of Equatorial Guinea. It was Golan's proposal to have EFCA organize the Bank of Fernando Po into a national bank for Equatorial Guinea. Golan and Herb Glaser also looked into ways to help the country finance its cocoa crop to make it a money-producing export.

EFCA executive Glaser recalled flying to Fernando Po with Golan in 1969 to look over the deal. The two first flew to Cameroon, where Golan was interested in setting up a ceramics factory, and then took a hop over to Santa Isabel, the island's principal town and port on its north coast. Unfortunately, Santa Isabel's one modest hotel was full, and the two corporate adventurers had to spend the night on the second floor of the Bank of Fernando Po, where they put together makeshift beds. The next day they met with

Fernando Po's President. But, like most of the other international deals it never got off the ground.

Meanwhile, Arkus-Duntov was growing decidedly cool to Golan's wheeling and dealing and felt that not only was the company becoming overextended but it simply had no business entering into some of the ventures Golan was promoting.

"Suddenly we were involved in a hotel in Senegal, some possibility of copper mines in Zambia, cattle in Madagascar, and above all this damn spaghetti factory in Rome," Arkus-Duntov said, recalling how he complained to Goldblum.

The chairman finally decided to heed Arkus-Duntov's advice. That spelled the end for Joseph Golan and Dov Amir as far as EFCA was concerned.

Amir, like Golan, later complained that Goldblum was only interested in turning a quick profit and had no concept of the time needed to gain a return on investment.

"Dov," said Goldblum in late 1970, "this is really not our business. We're making a lot of money and good earnings on insurance and financial operations. We cannot tie up our income."

Amir attempted to explain to Goldblum that the Zambian copper project could mean rich rewards. Amir said that in five to ten years, EFCA could be turning a tidy profit from Zambian copper.

"I don't want to wait that long," replied Goldblum. "I want it [the profits] now." Goldblum explained that when one of his salesmen sold an insurance policy, EFCA reaped the profit within thirty days. It was an argument that Amir couldn't counter.

Amir was no doubt bitter as he prepared to dismantle his empire. Looking back, he felt that if EFCA had stuck it out, some of his proposals—for drilling in the North Sea, for example—would have paid off handsomely, recapturing

EFCA's $10 million investment in the ventures many times over.*

Golan, like Amir, looks painfully back on his EFCA adventures. "They [EFCA] can say what they want, I have my reputation all over the world," Golan declared. "I have a position that has nothing to do with . . . the shady characters . . . of Equity Funding."

Sifting through the wreckage of Golan's company, BEDEC International, investigators found evidence of at least four bank accounts in Europe. As this book went to press they were ready to attempt an investigation of those accounts to see if any EFCA money was in them.

Golan's work for EFCA generally appeared to have remained within the law. At the most, until authorities can prove otherwise, it appeared he was used by Goldblum as a European business contact for a series of misguided adventures.

One of those adventures involved a complex chain of international transactions designed to camouflage the creation of $13.5 million in fictitious assets. It clearly illustrated the mind-boggling lengths to which the conspirators would go to fraudulently inflate Equity Funding's net worth and, in turn, inflate the company's stock.

The episode began in January, 1969, when EFCA

---

*Not all of Amir's work could be immediately dismantled. Traserco's concessions covered approximately 2,147,000 acres in the Gulf of Guayaquil off the coast of Ecuador. Traserco and the consortium of oil companies drilling there subsequently reported substantial finds of natural gas. EFCA's trustee was attempting to negotiate with one of the members of the consortium, Ada Oil Company, to take over Traserco's interest in the consortium in exchange for a future production interest.

Amir also had negotiated for a 10 percent interest in nine offshore oil and gas licenses from Israel. Seven test wells were drilled and none came through. A 25 percent interest in an offshore oil and gas concession from Ethiopia met with a similar fate.

acquired substantially all of the domestic assets of Investors Planning Corporation of America (IPC), primarily owned by Cornfeld's Investors Overseas Services, for approximately $8.5 million plus 27,367 shares of EFCA stock. The total deal came to approximately $12 million, far too high a price, according to some observers.

The SEC had forced Cornfeld to look for a buyer for the big mutual fund sales organization which had twenty-nine offices in twenty-one states, primarily in the East, and some 2,000 sales representatives. Equity Funding hoped that the PIC organization would complement its own Western sales force.

Along with Investors Planning, Equity Funding purchased the right to receive certain future sales commissions generated by the IPC contractual plan—in which investors would periodically remit money for the purchase of mutual fund shares.

According to the United States Attorney's office in Los Angeles, Goldblum and Lowell calculated what the IPC plans and commissions would bring to EFCA over several years and claimed all of this as income for the year 1969.* The commission rights were considered highly speculative because fund buyers could terminate their share purchases at will, thus making it difficult to set an absolute value on them.

Then in 1970, according to the government's information, Goldblum and Lowell concocted a plan to justify this bit of bookkeeping sleight-of-hand by constructing a fictitious sale

*Commission Rogatory for International Judicial Assistance, a request by the United States District Court for the Central District of California to Switzerland for authority to investigate account number 001–1–821–774 of the Cifico-Leumi Bank of Geneva, filed January 18, 1974.

Cornfeld told one of the authors that it was Riordan who actually closed the IPC deal.

"He was the brightest and strongest element in that company," said Cornfeld of Riordan, whom he had known for years. Cornfeld added that Riordan wanted to use IPC as a springboard to put Equity Funding into Europe since IPC had been dealing with U.S. military forces stationed on the Continent.

of these future IPC mutual fund commission rights to Compañía de Estudios y Asuntos for $13.5 million. Estudios was a shell—or nonoperating—Panamanian corporation formed in 1949 and bought by Pavia & Harcourt, a law firm with offices in New York, Rome, and Milan. Thus the proceeds from selling the rights could then be counted as a legitimate asset.

But federal investigators also discovered that the real owner of Estudios was Equity Funding. It seems that in 1970 Golan, claiming he was acting on behalf of Equity Funding, purchased Estudios from Pavia & Harcourt. The EFCA purchase was made through Etablissement Grandson,* another shell corporation Equity Funding set up in 1969 in Liechtenstein through Dr. Rupert Ritter, a Liechtenstein attorney.† Placed in charge of Etablissement Grandson was a Heinrich Wangerhof.

The skeleton was constructed for an intriguing game of international chicanery that still wasn't fully resolved as this book went to press.**

*Golan told investigators that in his dealings with Etablissement Grandson he was simply handling paperwork on orders from EFCA's management.

†Parenthetically, in September, 1973, Ritter wrote EFCA's trustee asking for a fee for his services in setting up the corporation, which, like Estudios, had not been active and was therefore believed to have been a shell up to the time EFCA began using it. EFCA officials replied in a letter to Ritter's office in Vaduz, Liechtenstein, inquiring into who had been paying Etablissement Grandson's bills and taxes up to that time. There was no immediate response from Ritter.

At publication of this book, federal authorities were preparing to go to Europe to further interrogate Golan and to try to question Ritter about the little-known operations of the Liechtenstein shell. This was a difficult task, since Liechtenstein's laws—like Switzerland's secret banking laws—sharply limit the questions authorities from another country can ask about corporations domiciled there.

**This is not to be construed in any way as casting an aspersion on Compañiá de Estudios y Asuntos or on Pavia & Harcourt. In the authors' opinion, neither were guilty of any wrongdoing in connection with the Equity Funding Case. Indeed, neither has ever been accused of any wrongdoing.

On May 19, 1970, charges the United States Attorney, Goldblum signed a contract for the sale of the IPC commission rights to Estudios for $13.5 million. Signing on behalf of Estudios was an Alfonso Pérez deSilva. Investigators said the deal was notarized in New York City.

Before any money changed hands, the contract for the "sale" to the Panamanian corporation (which EFCA actually owned) was amended on October 19, 1970, to provide for a reduced down payment to $2 million from $5 million. Estudios was then to pay off the balance of $11.5 million in installment payments.

To show the down payment, Lowell, according to the United States Attorney, then directed that $2 million be transferred out of Equity Funding Capital Corporation, N.V., a Netherlands Antilles corporation which EFCA used as a foreign financing vehicle and which owned all of the stock of Bishop's Bank. The $2 million went to an account at Franklin National Bank of New York (which in 1972 was to become a member of a four-bank consortium authorizing a $75 million revolving credit arrangement for EFCA) in the name of Bishop's Bank.

Then, say the government's prosecutors, under Lowell's direction, the $2 million found its way through the series of transfers from Bishop's to Account Number 001-1-821-774 at the Cifico-Leumi Bank of Geneva, Switzerland, the account of Etablissement Grandson.

A few days later, on October 21, 1970, there suddenly appeared on the books of the parent EFCA in Los Angeles the $2 million down payment from Estudios for the future commission rights of IPC. "The payment is reflected as having come from Cifico Bank, Geneva, through Chase Manhattan Bank to Equity Funding's account at United California Bank (UCB) in Los Angeles. . . ." noted federal authorities in the request for further assistance from the Swiss government.*

*Commission Rogatory, p. 10.

To cover up the $2 million note outstanding on the books of Bishop's Bank, federal authorities allege Lowell transferred the liability to the parent EFCA's books. To make it look legitimate, say authorities, Lowell designed a fictitious commercial paper transaction so that it appeared as if Bishop's had bought $2 million worth of commercial paper (corporate IOU's) from Apatinska Tekstilna Industrija, a textile manufacturer near Belgrade, Yugoslavia, which had the cable name "Apatex." Lowell was aware that Bishop's bought legitimate commercial paper in Eastern Europe and that the bank in fact held some real Apatex commercial paper.

Coe, the president of Bishop's, felt uncertain about the cover-up and passed on the job of actually signing for the phony commercial paper to one of his underlings. Coe would have no part of this.

After several months of dissection of this complex scheme to cover up $13.5 million in phony assets on EFCA's books, federal investigators concluded that "Heinrich Wangerhof" was as phony as the rest of the transaction. "A co-defendant told investigators that Lowell may have signed the name Heinrich Wangerhof," according to the government's request to Switzerland.* Another investigator who had seen the signature said it had "a European flair or flourish." Another theory was that it was Goldblum's handwriting. Goldblum said, however, he knew no one by that name. Wangerhof's signature also appeared on other documents involving the Liechtenstein corporation.

"Another co-defendant stated that Lowell kept the Grandson seal in his office and indicated that he could execute documents for Grandson," the same government brief to Swiss authorities stated.*

Authorities also ran up against a brick wall with "Alfonso Pérez deSilva." There was a strong feeling as this book was

---

*Ibid.

being completed that he also was a figment of the creative imagination of an Equity Funding conspirator.

In summing up this international mirage, the United States Attorney concluded: ". . . the sale [of the IPC mutual fund commissions] was therefore a sham and a part of the scheme to defraud designed to help deceive persons about the financial condition of Equity Funding, and thereby to encourage various banks to loan Equity Funding large amounts of money."*

Federal authorities were hopeful that the Geneva-based bank would be able to fill in the myriad of questions raised by this "pass-through" bank account through which money bounced from Bishop's to EFCA. Were there other fraudulent international transactions that made use of this secret Swiss account? Was there any EFCA or personal money in the account belonging to EFCA management that no one knew about?

Meanwhile, Bishop's continued to prosper.† Coe, an American, had good banking contacts in the United States and was making money for EFCA through commercial paper deals in both Eastern Europe and, particularly, in South and Central America. Coe would, for example, negotiate a line of credit with a big New York bank and then purchase short- and medium-term corporate notes from various Latin American companies. The lines of credit would be rolled over as the corporate loans were paid off, with Bishop's making a tidy profit on the interest rate.

---

*Ibid., p. 13.

†Immediately after bankruptcy proceedings began, Bishop's almost collapsed. A British bank called $5 million in loans to Bishop's and the Bahamian bank was unable to get any new lines of credit to pay it off. "Roy West"—comprised of the Royal Bank of Canada International and Roy West Banking Corporation Limited—came to the rescue, however. The latter was a corporation jointly owned by The Royal Bank of Canada and the National Westminster Bank of the United Kingdom. Bishop's was subsequently sold to this group in 1973 for $13.4 million.

Bishop's was a merchant or corporate bank, not a commercial bank. It didn't take deposits, although certain certificates of deposit were issued. In addition to purchasing commercial paper or debt obligations of corporations, banks and governments, it had outstanding several loans, including two on construction projects in Venezuela and Jamaica. On December 31, 1972, Bishop's inventory of these debt obligations stood at $31 million but dropped to $15 million by August 31, 1973.

Lowell had always viewed Bishop's as EFCA's financial pipeline to the rest of the world, from which an international financial conglomerate could take root. "We continue to review the feasibility of Bishop's functioning as a true Eurodollar bank," Lowell reported to the EFCA executive planning committee as early as December 30, 1970. He declared it was not his intention "to restrict Bishop's role to that of a captive financial subsidiary." And in April, 1972, Lowell reported to the executive committee that Bishop's would have its own full-time London representative.*

There was suspicion among the IRS investigators in 1968 and the federal investigators that took over after the EFCA scandal surfaced in 1973, that Bishop's might have been used as a conduit for illegal financial deals. But no hard evidence was forthcoming to support this theory. Furthermore, authorities could find no personal deposits by EFCA officials at Bishop's.

Coe stayed on after EFCA went into bankruptcy proceedings. He refused to discuss any aspect of the case.

EFCA incurred heavy foreign financial debt in 1969, presumably to finance acquisitions and provide the corporation with working capital. More than $40 million was obtained through public and private placement of Eurodollar and Swiss franc notes. Loeb Rhoades' international arm

---

*A Frank Griffith Dawson was hired to represent Bishop's in London on July 1, 1972.

and a French financial group called Paribas (a shortened name for Compagnie Financière de Paris and de Pays Bas) handled some of the placements during this period.* Dishy, Easton helped arrange some of the contacts.

In January, 1969, for example, EFCA, through Equity Funding Capital Corporation, N.V. raised $25 million through a Eurodollar public offering involving 5¼ percent guaranteed subordinated debentures due in 1989.

In November, 1969, EFCA, again through "N.V.," raised $10 million through a Eurodollar private placement of 7½ percent guaranteed subordinated notes due in 1974, which offered EFCA common stock purchase warrants as the sweetener.†

Federal and state investigators reviewing EFCA's books after the corporation was placed under a trustee, felt this was far more cash than EFCA's activities in 1969 warranted. Because the company's bookkeeping procedures were so chaotic, however, efforts to trace where all of this money ended up were fruitless.

EFCA's interests in South America also have come under close scrutiny.

Anonymous telephone calls claiming EFCA officials had

---

*Another loan arrangement occurred on December 31, 1971, when Dow Banking Corporation, the Swiss banking subsidiary of Dow Chemical Company of Midland, Michigan, acting for itself and several other European banks, loaned 20 million Swiss francs to "N.V.," the equivalent of $5 million and worth about $6.5 million when this book went to press. The loan was later secured by an EFCA pledge of certain mutual fund shares. On February 18, 1972, "N.V." borrowed an additional 19.2 million Swiss francs from Dow. This time the loan was unsecured. After EFCA went into bankruptcy proceedings, a Dow official said the two note issues represented only a tiny portion of the assets of Dow Banking and that its Swiss bank subsidiary could sustain any EFCA loss without difficulty.

†Federal authorities also discovered that EFCA—with the help of Dishy, Easton acting as a finder—was selling commercial paper in Europe and was counting the proceeds as assets instead of liabilities.

siphoned company money into personal accounts in certain South American banks were received by investigators. At this writing, nothing could be found to substantiate those reports. The extent of EFCA's business in South America appeared to have been legally conducted through Bishop's commercial paper operations.

South America presented a difficult problem because the United States had no reciprocal banking treaties under which investigators could inquire into personal banking accounts of United States citizens under criminal indictment.

In Switzerland it was another story. Following the indictments, John Newman, the United States Attorney who put together the federal case in Los Angeles, opened negotiations through the United States Justice and State Departments with Swiss banking authorities to determine what corporate and/or personal funds of EFCA officials might have been sequestered in Swiss banks. Despite recent negotiations between the United States and the Swiss to hammer out a treaty that would allow U.S. officials to lift the lid on secret Swiss bank accounts when a person has been indicted, the Swiss jealously guard the traditional secrecy of their numbered bank accounts and the negotiations were expected to take time.

Whether Golan had the "power of signature" to open up any of the Swiss or other EFCA bank accounts scattered about Europe was a matter of conjecture. Whether any EFCA funds were intermingled in these accounts also was not immediately known.

Lowell's and Levin's frequent European trips and the banks and bankers whom they met on their journeys were also scrutinized. On one trip Lowell and Levin reportedly met with five German bankers in five days. What EFCA business transpired? Was there any private reason for these trips, which produced no apparent loan activity or led to any business ventures?

The maze appears endless.

At this writing, millions in loans, much of it from abroad, cannot be accounted for. Perhaps some of the cash sits in secret numbered Swiss accounts. Most may be lost forever in the corporate flimflam that was known as Equity Funding Corporation of America.

VIII
The Atmosphere, *or*, What It's Like to Work for a Winner in Glamorous Century City

CENTURY City is a collection of shimmering, high-rise steel, aluminum, and glass office buildings, shops, restaurants, theaters, and cozy bars on the chic West Side of Los Angeles, near superaffluent Beverly Hills. The land was once owned by the 20th Century Fox film company, which still retains a small corner of Century City for its own studios.

Century City exudes its own brand of innovation and corporate élan free from the oppressive tension of Manhattan's canyons. It was the kind of atmosphere where a sleek outfit like Equity Funding could feel at home.

Prestige and wealth are a Century City way of life. From the insurance, banking, securities, and computer industry executives, to the healthy-looking, miniskirted California secretaries, there is a "with it" atmosphere generated there. It is indeed a free spirit where companies that have some tradition can rub elbows with the Johnny-come-latelies who are making their speculative fortunes overnight.

Equity Funding fell into the latter category, a hot stock that was driving Wall Street into ecstasy daily. And, to the 650 EFCA staffers who worked in the 1900 Avenue of the

Stars building,* it was certainly a "with it" company, a generally happy place to work, where a majority of the employees appeared interested in the welfare of their company.

"One of the things I liked about the place was that everyone did things to make life easier for other people," recalled one former employee. At least among middle management, he said, there were no power struggles because "everyone was too busy."

The protocol among middle management certainly was relaxed. Department underlings could communicate and meet with their counterparts in other sectors of the company without formally going through a chain of command.

Part of the reason for such a high level of esprit de corps was that there were so many young people working there. Moreover, those individuals over thirty-five were friendly toward the younger employees, possibly because they, too, were caught up in the mystique of a company which was considered to be one of the most dynamic financial conglomerates of its day. The workers actually believed in what they were doing and that, perhaps, they were the corporate wave of the future.

At least that was the general feeling on floors three, four, five and six—where middle management and lower-echelon employees worked.

The twenty-eighth, or executive floor, was another story. Some of the workers on the lower floors maintained that the gap between six and twenty-eight was designed purposefully by EFCA's hierarchy to symbolize the great gap in position between upper management and the rest of the company.

It wasn't necessary to notice that management was several floors and a different set of elevators away from the rest of the EFCA crew. All one really had to do was contrast the

*Even the address Avenue of the Stars had a certain mystique. But given the immensity of the EFCA scandal and the fact that several other corporations had gone bankrupt on that regal avenue in recent years, one wag quipped it should be renamed "Avenue of the Fallen Stars."

million-dollar interior-decorating job Goldblum had authorized for the twenty-eighth floor against the more "normal" office environment of the lower floors to come to the conclusion that there was a tremendous gap between upper and middle management—a vast difference in the two worlds of EFCA which also created a caste system with less-than-complete communication between the two segments.

Goldblum, Levin and Lowell seldom visited the lower floors and were difficult to approach by lower-level staffers. At times even upper-management personnel felt EFCA's troika was almost cliquish and found it difficult to establish a strong line of communication with the three. Moreover, as might be expected, the atmosphere on "twenty-eight" was a bit more formal than below. One simply did not trot into an EFCA executive's office to expound on new ideas.

And, even as enthusiastic as everyone tried to be on the lower floors, in a way there was always a demoralizing cloud hanging over Equity Funding. Except for the chosen few, EFCA was exceptionally stingy when granting pay increases to its nonexecutive staff. One middle manager recalled that "You couldn't get a raise for a secretary." But, he said there was a great paradox because the company would think nothing of spending several hundreds of dollars to air-freight new prospectuses around the country. This led to a feeling among some staffers that upper management was quite impersonal toward employees.

But there were a few bright "young Turks" on the middle level who were extremely well paid. In fact, perhaps in no other company was youth so magnificently rewarded—at least for those chosen few.

Jim Smith, for example, joined EFCA in November, 1968, from Minneapolis National Life and at the age of thirty-four became a vice-president of Equity Funding and chief administrator of its life insurance subsidiaries. For his efforts Smith was getting $118,000 a year in salary and stock bonuses.

Lloyd Edens joined EFCA in September, 1968, at twenty-five, coming from the Los Angeles office of Ernst & Ernst, the accounting firm. Edens became vice-president for financial services with responsibility for accounting in the life insurance companies and handled commissions paid to EFCA's sales force. Edens received $83,000 a year in salary and stock bonuses.

Arthur Lewis was twenty-six when he joined EFCA in the same period and became its chief actuary. Lewis was considered one of the most creative and brilliant of those in middle management and even though Smith was higher on the company chart, Lewis commanded greater attention on the twenty-eighth floor. Lewis drew the same salary and stock bonus total as Edens.

Of course, these sky-high wages were still pittances compared to what the troika was pulling down. By 1973, Goldblum, at forty-six, was making $125,000.08 a year, plus stock bonuses worth another $247,500, plus another $3,000 a month in entertainment expenses (curiously increased during an austerity program he began pushing in January, 1973). Levin, thirty-five, and Lowell, thirty-three, were making $80,000.16 in wages, plus $198,000 in stock bonuses, plus $1,000 a month for entertainment expenses.

Apparently these salaries were fairly well guarded secrets. One middle-management type said he was "shocked" when he read about them in the press.

The disparity in salaries among middle management was appalling. Pat Hopper, for example, was vice-president in charge of investments at EFCA's Banker's National Life subsidiary in New Jersey, and was earning a salary in the middle-$20,000 range.

The innovative environment at the company also apparently led to innovative thinking on how to commit fraud. Dr. Edward Stainbrook, chairman of the human behavior department at the University of Southern California, said in an interview with Harry Anderson, a reporter for the Los

Angeles *Times,* that the very brightness of the young EFCA management may have contributed toward the fraud.

"The more intelligent and shrewd the individual is, the easier it is for him to convince himself that what he is doing really isn't illegal or unethical," said Dr. Stainbrook. "He may rationalize alternatively that even though the act is wrong, if he is smart enough or clever enough, he won't get caught—or else he'll get out before he gets caught—and that is sufficient to keep him involved."

Dr. Stainbrook's analysis of rationalization is borne out in a 1969 memo from middle to top EFCA management suggesting that the coinsurance, of which two-thirds ultimately turned out to be phony, was comparable to a loan that would be paid back.

Bill Symonds heard the same story.

Symonds, the thirty-four-year-old reinsurance assistant to Art Lewis, both of whom were indicted, said in an interview that he was assured that artificially reviving lapsed insurance was one of the arrangements the company had with the coinsurers. "This is like an interest-free loan—it's a business arrangement," Symonds recalled hearing from his superiors.

Symonds said that he started in the company's life insurance policy service department. He said the phony insurance scheme began with the company giving away free insurance to its own employees.* In the second year,

---

*The February report of the trustee supported Symonds' phony-insurance-thesis statement:

"A prelude to the creation of bogus insurance occurred following the termination of the general agency contract between EFCA and Pennsylvania Life Insurance Company ('Penn'). After acquiring EFLIC in 1967, EFCA desired to sell EFLIC policies in lieu of the Penn policies it was required to sell under its exclusive agency agreement. In connection with the termination of this obligation in 1968, EFCA agreed to place $250 million of insurance with Penn through 1970, either by selling Penn policies or by reinsuring EFLIC policies with Penn. EFCA found itself unable to sell enough policies to meet the commitment; to make up the shortfall, 'special class' insurance was instituted. This involved EFLIC policies with minimal or no first-year

however, a lot of this insurance lapsed and Symonds said that Lewis and Edens, the EFCA vice-president for financial services, asked him to put the lapsed policies back in force. Symonds said Lewis assured him there was nothing illegal about it. "I just did what I was told," he said. "I wanted to please."

The "borrowing" theory also is explored by Professor Donald R. Cressey of the University of California at Santa Barbara, who has made an international name for himself in the study of white-collar crime. Declared Professor Cressey:

"By conceiving of himself as a borrower (not a thief) the violator cuts himself off from the influences of a social order which otherwise would deter him, and before he gets in too deep he is not fully cognizant of the social attitudes which later induce him to behave like a criminal. While he is able to look upon his behavior as borrowing, his desire is to repay

> premiums which were issued to EFCA employees and their families and then reinsured with Penn. When a substantial number of the employees let the policies lapse rather than pay the renewal premiums in the second year, EFCA itself made many of the payments to Penn to reduce the apparent policy lapse rate. . . .
>
> ". . . Although EFLIC inflated its profits by creating and coinsuring bogus insurance, it had to vastly increase its real sales of new policies, which it did not do, or create even more bogus policies with every passing year in order to record increasing earnings. Furthermore, although it profited from the coinsurance of bogus policies in the year in which they were sold, the required payments to the coinsurer on account of renewal premiums in subsequent years were total losses, and persistency guarantees in the coinsurance treaties left EFLIC no alternative but to pay them. To generate the cash needed to pay these amounts, ever more bogus policies had to be created and sold. Thus, as in a pyramid scheme, once EFLIC began to create and coinsure bogus insurance policies, the size of the manipulations had to increase exponentially to show continued growth.
>
> "Again, the purpose and effect of these various devices was to inflate EFCA's earnings and assets so as to support EFCA's borrowings and to maintain EFCA's image as a growth company and to sustain the price of its stock—the key to its expansion plans and compensation structure. The fraud fed on itself, requiring ever greater exaggerations in order to cover prior fraudulent transactions."
>
> *Report of the Trustee of Equity Funding Corporation of America*, February 22, 1974, pp. 33–34.

the money borrowed and not, as may be the case later, to avoid being caught and sent to prison . . . trust violators who take funds over a period of time by rationalizing that they are borrowing the money become criminals without intending to do so."*

Aside from the rationalization of borrowing from the coinsurers, there was also a great deal of decay in EFCA's middle management in the form of outright fraud.

There was, for example, the "Insurance Club"—a secret bank account holding hundreds of thousands of dollars which was discovered by the IRS. These were funds siphoned off from the company for the use of a privileged few in middle management.

Another middle-management employee was involved in the embezzlement of phony death claims. These claims were an important part of the fraud, and were perpetrated so that the phony insurance would appear to the reinsurers to have real owners. Normally, the death-claim checks received by EFCA from the reinsurers would be banked. This particular embezzler, however, pocketed about $25,000 worth of the phony death claims over a year's time.

Other forms of embezzlement also were discovered by federal and state investigators who moved in on the company after the scandal surfaced. One involved the brother of a high official of the parent company who was splitting commission checks, each for less than $1,000, every few weeks, with an individual in the company's commission payout section—commissions that this individual didn't earn.

Just how penny ante some of the fraud was could be observed in the method used to profiteer from phony expense accounts. Ron Secrist, the Bankers National Life Insurance Company executive who helped expose the scandal, told the authors about EFCA executives "triple charging" their expense accounts. Certain EFCA officers,

---

*Donald R. Cressey, *Other People's Money, a Study in the Social Psychology of Embezzlement* (Glencoe, Illinois, The Free Press, 1953), p. 121.

said Secrist, would go to a restaurant for dinner, for example, near Parsippany, New Jersey, where Bankers was located and where the subsidiary had a charge account. Secrist recalled the executives would run up a bill of $100 or so and the restaurant would, in turn, bill Bankers. The officers, however, also would put the dinner on their own expense account and be reimbursed by Bankers. Finally, when they returned to Los Angeles, they also would bill the parent company. Thus, reconstructed Secrist, EFCA got hit three times for the same dinner—and it happened several times. Certain EFCA officers, said Secrist, "just spent money like it was going out of style."

What about the men at the top?

USC's Dr. Stainbrook attempted to psychoanalyze top-echelon executives who commit white-collar crime:

"It comes down to a desire for power that stems from very personal needs—perhaps a need to become powerful that has never been satisfied despite legitimate triumphs and attainment of position. That mentality might lead a man to require constant reassurance of his power, to act out fantasy and indeed to succeed in acting out fantasy."

It was indeed a fantasyland, a bubble that would burst and spray the innocent as well as the guilty.

Those who tried to start their lives anew repeatedly found industry doors slammed in their face. Symonds was forced to work as a security guard. Another middle-management individual was reported to be driving a cab. The computer employees were particularly hard hit. The job reference "Equity Funding" almost always poisoned an employment application. Exaggerated press reports of employees giggling in company corridors over the fraud—which was nonsense—stuck in outside employers' minds. It was a classic case of guilt by association. Hundreds of shattered lives were strewn on the EFCA battlefield.

(In another chapter, we'll discuss a group of individuals hard hit by the fraud and subsequent collapse of Equity Funding, the most tragic group of all—the shareholders.)

IX
The Computer Game
(And the Maple Drive Gang)

THE camouflage for the fraud was provided by sophisticated computer technology. It allowed the perpetrators at the Equity Funding Life Insurance Company to get away with their incredible plan for over three years. In the end they had created some 56,000 life insurance policies (of 97,000 total policies) out of thin air and caused, at least on paper, a $2-billion loss for the reinsurance companies that bought the fake policies.*

The case constituted fraud on an unprecedented scale, in which the microsecond speed of the computer age was effectively used to cover up a crime. The instigators also knew how to manipulate computer programs—that which is designed for feeding into the actual computer hardware or equipment.

In EFLIC's case, individuals outside the company's electronic data processing department (EDP) designed the scope of the fraud through their knowledge of computer programming. Art Lewis, in particular, was not only

---

*This worked out to only a loss of over $10 million for the reinsurers, however, because they had been getting annual payments from EFCA beginning with the second year of a reinsured policy that amounted to 90 percent of the premium. What the reinsurers didn't know, of course, was that the money came from other phony policies sold to other reinsurers who were making big cash payments to EFCA for the privilege of getting the insurance business.

extremely bright in his role as EFLIC chief actuary, but knew the programming side of computer technology and the capability of the company's equipment (an average-sized computer operation with the equipment rented from International Business Machines for $30,000 a month.)* Lewis, Smith, and Edens would arrange with William Gootnick, the head of computer programming and its eighty employees, "to make alterations in computer records," according to the Federal Grand Jury indictment.

The phony policies were programmed, inserted onto master computer tapes, and were given the code name "99." Among some of the perpetrators, these phony policies were also referred to as the "Y" business.†

The term "99" came from EFLIC's policy of filing different categories of insurance by code number—such as 65 for a policy given to an EFLIC employee, 35 for a union group contract, and so on. The "99" business was generally defined as group business which involved no direct billing. Blocks of this business were then sold to the reinsurers, including such substantial companies as Ranger National Life Insurance Company of Dallas, which bought the largest amount of EFLIC's policies; as well as Connecticut General Life Insurance and Phoenix Mutual Life Insurance companies, both of Hartford. Under the reinsurance system, all EFLIC had to do to make a hefty 80 to 90 percent profit on each phony policy was to sell blocks of policy numbers to the reinsurers without physically transferring the policy records

---

*EFCA maintained at its home office a costly data-processing center, which was used to assist the administration of the marketing organization as well as other business activities. Over a hundred programmers, computer operators, and other employees worked in the data-processing center; the cost of operating the center amounted to substantially over $2 million in 1972. Controls over utilization of the data-processing center were not only inadequate, but virtually nonexistent. *Report of the Trustee of Equity Funding Corporation of America*, February, 1974, p. 26.

†At the same time, the $62.5 million in phony funded-loan assets had the code designation "R," which was believed to have once stood for "reciprocals."

The Computer Game (and the Maple Drive Gang)

off the EFLIC premises. That's why in succeeding years, under the reinsurance agreement, EFLIC was to still retain a small percentage of the insurance premium (with the bulk of the premium going to the reinsurer) to perform the bookkeeping and storage functions for the reinsurance companies. Apparently, the "good faith" policy system of the insurance industry precluded the reinsurers from performing a physical inventory of the policies EFLIC claimed on its books.

To make the whole scheme appear realistic, a system of checks and balances was established.

To keep the reinsurers from becoming suspicious, some of the nonexistent policyholders had to die from time to time at a rate comparable to a real death rate.

The Federal Grand Jury indictment stated that James Smith, the head of EFCA's insurance operations, instructed an EFLIC lawyer, James Banks, that he (Banks) "would be expected to make death claims on various fictitious insurance policies." But as bright as the perpetrators were, there had to be a liaison with EDP—a programmer who could get to the hardware. That's where Alan Lewis Green, the bearded, likable young man who had aspired to be an actuary, came in.

Green joined EFCA in 1969 and had passed three of the ten examinations needed to become a full-fledged fellow in the Society of Actuaries—the profession of those who compute the nuts and bolts of a life insurance policy. But the soft-spoken Green became bored with his work and wanted a change within the company—perhaps into computer programming.

Green was popular among his colleagues. He was also one of about ten young employees in the sixth-floor insurance section who would go out to one of the grassy areas around sprawling Century City on their lunch hour and get stoned on marijuana.

Early in 1972 Art Lewis invited Green to his suburban Toluca Lake home.

Green described the encounter:

As the two were walking around the pool, Lewis, in a very casual way, told Green about the phony policies and inquired if Green was willing to join the team.

Green wasn't surprised. He had learned of the "policy parties" a year earlier, anyway.

"Lewis said that they were manufacturing policies, but didn't mention names," recalled Green.

With a degree in mathematics, Green was well equipped to take the new job.

Declared Green: "Lewis said the main reason for it all was power. They would manufacture the policies and sell them to reinsurers and this would increase Equity Funding's earnings and then Equity Life would become bigger within the parent corporation. He [Lewis] would then become more powerful within the corporate structure. It was understood that I should keep a tight lid on what I was doing.

"The job for me was a great thing because I love programming," Green said. "I hadn't had a chance to do any [programming]. That was my chance. I was motivated by being able to do work that I would enjoy.

"I knew I was committing fraud. I really didn't think it would ever blow up for one thing. It just seemed like a pretty foolproof thing."

Shortly after his secret meeting with Lewis, in March, 1972, Green took over the job, which he described as writing "all the computer programs that would manufacture the policies."

Constructing the computer programs was just the first step in the phony policy process. After the main set of programs was completed, which took only a few months, the procedure became almost automatic. Green said EFLIC could produce "as many phony policies as were needed for any period of time." In other words, the phony program skeleton had been created and was ready to be fleshed out.

How did Green construct the fictitious computer programs?

The Computer Game (and the Maple Drive Gang)

He said he was trained to inject certain basic phony data into the computers, such as the dates and face amounts of the policies. "The amount was just a rotating thing. I'd start with maybe ten thousand dollars and just to confuse the issue I would multiply it by 1.2 and the next [phony] policy by 1.3," and so on, "so that it would look authentic." A policy premium was computed in a similar random manner.

Green would also feed in the type of life insurance policy and the name of the policyholder. Only the names of policyholders were duplicated—all of the other data was fabricated—with the names initially taken from policies held by Pennsylvania Life Insurance Company of Los Angeles (for which EFCA had been an agent before acquiring EFLIC) and later from policies of the Bankers and the Northern life insurance companies.

"I knew what type of reinsurance Ranger and other reinsurers would accept—they wouldn't take everything— and I would plug in specific plans of insurance that they would accept," said Green.

When a fraudulent computer tape was completed, it was returned to EFLIC's data-processing library for safekeeping.

The perpetrators had one other major problem. A phony loan had to be created with each insurance policy (since the policyholder was borrowing to pay his premiums by using his mutual fund shares as collateral). That's why some $62.3 million of $117 million of loan assets on EFCA's books simply didn't exist.

Green said that a "cash receipt check-and-balance system" was also created through the manipulation of the computer program. "With every policy that I created, there had to [also] be a cash receipt generated and then merged into all of the real cash receipts," said Green.

The phony cash-receipts flow took into account, for example, the premiums taken in by EFLIC on the policies and the phony commissions paid out to the salesmen. "And in the final analysis," said Green, "you could look at the end of the year at all the premiums coming into the company and all of the real and phony [cash receipts] would be mixed up and everything would look real."

The auditors—first, Wolfson & Weiner and then Seidman & Seidman—were apparently ill-prepared to double-check the computer records. Part of the reason was that the actual computer printout would produce reams and reams of paper and might take months to check out. The personnel of these auditing firms could therefore only random-check the policies.

So what happened when the auditors asked to see a random sample of policy files? Therein lies one of the most fascinating stories of the fraud.

The actual creation of a phony life insurance policy file was a time-consuming process which included construction of an individual's personal and medical history—in short, the same detailed information found on a real life insurance policy.

The real sub-rosa operation was done by the infamous Maple Drive Gang, a group known only to the handful of Equity Funding individuals who were in on the fraud scheme. To others who had heard of "that other office" it had been referred to as the "mass marketing" division.

Located in a one-story, red-brick building at 341 North Maple Drive in Beverly Hills, the office (actually four rooms) had been functioning at least since 1971.

The building itself was situated across the street from the Beverly Hills Tennis Club and was wedged between an office supply company and a metaphysical institute—about two miles from Century City, far enough away to conduct the covert operations.

Twenty-five-year-old Mark Lewis, the younger brother of Art Lewis, was ultimately put in charge of the Maple Drive Gang—which consisted of a dozen young women who were the unknowing dupes in the fraud.

In fact, as Mark Lewis later confessed in an interview, he didn't really have the full picture himself. "I didn't know the total picture of what was going on but I knew something was wrong," declared Lewis, a University of Bridgeport (Connecticut) graduate who, like his brother, grew up in New York City, and who started working at the Maple Drive office in December, 1971.

But whether Mark Lewis knew it or not, the Maple Drive operation was absolutely essential to the fraud.

The annual EFLIC audit was the "busiest" time of the year at Maple Drive. That's when the auditors selected life insurance policies at random, off computer tapes. Those with the "99" designation were fakes and, of course, had no corresponding policy files.

As many as seventy policies might be selected for study by the auditors. The auditors would then take these numbers to Lloyd Edens, who in turn would give them to Bill Symonds. According to Mark Lewis, Symonds, to whom Lewis reported, then drove over to the Maple Drive office and gave Lewis his orders on how many files to create. That's where the dozen young women came in.

Starting from scratch, they would use a manual that gave them choices of answers to the dozens of policy application questions. "Like a urine analysis," said Mark Lewis, "it [the manual] would say, 'Fill in one of the four,' and it didn't matter which one . . . the manual showed us how to complete the policies."

So it went, from medical to job history, with each woman given a specific jurisdiction for each phony policy. "On a very good day we could manufacture between fifteen and twenty policies," said Mark Lewis. "It was like an assembly line."

Mark Lewis would then deliver the manufactured files to Edens, who would merge them with the real files. The entire package—containing both real and fake policies—would then be turned over to the auditors. (If the auditors had heard of the Maple Drive office, they never visited it.)

"The work was strange," Mark Lewis asserted. "We either had to have one hundred policies out in a week or there was nothing to do for months."

To liven things up in that drab, windowless office where the air conditioning constantly broke down and the roof leaked, Lewis and the girls would hold parties at the drop of a hat. Certainly, a woman's birthday was a good excuse, and instead of bringing lunch that day, one of the girls would cook for the entire office and everyone would break open champagne. Sometimes the group, which ranged in age from eighteen to twenty-four years, would get drunk, Lewis remembered.

And, of course, after each policy-manufacturing project, Mark Lewis and his girls would celebrate with an all-day party.

And in between projects and parties some girls even knitted blankets. There was plenty of time since there would be gaps of several months without work and time weighed heavily on their hands.

Strange relationships developed. With so much time on their hands, the women began confiding in each other about their personal lives. For example, one of the girls described for the entire office how a new interuterine device worked. Apparently her sales pitch was so successful that the other girls went out and bought it.

Pills also were popular at Maple Drive, especially the pill called Quaalude, a sedative, which Lewis said made the girls "relaxed" at the Maple Drive happenings.

"And it got crazy," said Lewis. "You'd just come into an office because you'd have to be there . . . and sitting there with no work drove me nuts after awhile."

Some who have closely investigated the case can't see how any of the Maple Drive women could be held responsible for what they were doing. They were performing the same paperwork performed by thousands of other clerks in other companies. And, to be sure, none were mentioned in the indictment. Mark Lewis, however, was indicted.

The week before the April 2 blowup, Mark Lewis said he was told by his brother, Art, by Larry Collins, vice-president of EFLIC, and by Symonds to pack up everything in the office, including a "library" of partially filled out life insurance policies that were never used. "Collins came with his camper and took some of the boxes and Symonds packed some up in a truck," said Lewis.

According to the Federal Grand Jury indictment: "On or about March 23, 1973 . . . Collins . . . Symonds and Mark Lewis, at the instructions of . . . Smith . . . removed all documents relating to the creation of insurance files from 341 North Maple Drive. . . ." Authorities later were able to recover most of the evidence.

To be sure, not all of the phony insurance was manufactured at the Maple Drive office. Secrist recalled that before he joined Bankers National Life, he attended a middle-management "manufacturing party" early in 1971 in EFCA's sixth-floor conference room. Secrist recalled the "party" lasted from around 6 P.M. to 10 P.M. He said he was told by his middle-management colleagues who took part that the phony policies were needed to fool the auditors and that since he knew a lot about the medical area, he was asked to make up the medical exams section of each policy.

Secrist recalled a party atmosphere with lots of laughs over such things as making up funny names for the fictitious doctors whose names were forged on the insurance forms. People casually wandered in and out of the party during the course of the evening, Secrist remembered.

To make the documents look real, Secrist said a "manufacturing kit" was used, consisting of office forms, rubber stamps, different-colored pencils (to make it look as if the forms had been signed at different times), and various other office equipment.

It may have been the mystique of the computer that accomplished the massive fraud. Frank Hyman, who took over the computer operation from William Gootnick, analyzed it this way:

"The computer just spews it out and the average person tends to accept computer output without question. If it comes off the computer it's got to be right. The possibilities for computer fraud are immense."

Separately, Green added that "the funny thing about it was

that the auditors would take a computer listing and accept it as the truth."

Hyman said he doubted that the Equity Funding fraud could have happened on such a large scale twenty years ago, for the very reason of the existence of computer technology. The computer, he concluded, certainly speeded up and covered up the fraud to a degree impossible for human hands to duplicate.

Donn B. Parker, a member of the staff of the Stanford Research Institute, who claims to be the only full-time computer fraud expert in the United States, said in an interview that the EFCA case had some similarities to other computer fraud cases he had studied where there was "an open-shop computer operation" which allowed the primary fraud techniques to be designed outside of the EDP area.

In a major study entitled "Computer Abuse," which Parker helped write for the Stanford Research Institute, he concluded that even though the federal government and major computer manufacturers have programs underway to meet the challenge of computer fraud, "effective levels of computer security and of auditing of computer systems and applications are several years away from general realization."

This was one of the facts that frightened authorities about the Equity Funding case. How many other Equity Fundings are lurking in the corporate wastelands? No one knows for sure. But authorities are convinced that even though there may never be another example of massive fraud turning on manipulation of computers on the scale of Equity Funding, there are computer-crime brushfires breaking out with greater frequency.

This has given rise to a new breed of criminal who is using an electronic brain. Individuals can steal millions from their company if they know the capability of their firm's computer system and how to cover their tracks.

In terms of what they can steal, most law enforcement experts are beginning to consider computer crooks more dangerous than bank robbers or other more visible, violence-oriented criminals. Computer crooks may not physically harm anyone, but the scope of their crime may be enormous in terms of monetary damage—such as that suffered by the stockholders of Equity Funding.

"Business has probably never been so vulnerable to fraud," said one computer expert. "Many firms are losing millions without realizing it."

To put the EFCA case into perspective and to gain an additional insight into that unique product of the Age of Automation—the computer thief—it is worthwhile to digress for a moment and look at some lesser computer crimes of recent vintage.

One of them, the Roswell Steffens case, broke about the same time the EFCA drama exploded.

Roswell Steffens lived a quiet life in a $275-a-month apartment in a New York City suburb. Each day he traveled an hour by bus to his Manhattan job as supervisor of tellers in a branch of the Union Dime Savings Bank.

At about the same time that the authorities were confronting Goldblum, Levin, and their colleagues in the swank Century City executive suite, New York City detectives 3,000 miles away were running down Steffens.

The one thing the Equity Funding people and the New York bank teller had in common was that they stood accused of perpetrating massive frauds using the computer as their silent accomplice.

In Steffens' case, his crimes were caused by a habit that spun out of control: heavy betting on the ponies and professional basketball games. His primary problem was that the gambling seldom paid off.

When the teller needed more money for his bookmaker, he put his hands in the till at the bank. To cover up his thievery, Steffens simply registered withdrawals on the accounts of some unsuspecting depositors (usually ones whose accounts were not very active) so that the bank's balance sheets appeared normal. When quarterly interest payments time came around, he'd feed false information into the computers so that a brief correction would be made on all accounts.

According to the authorities, Steffens got away with his scheme for three years. He might never have been caught, had he not run into a bit of bad luck, when his bookie joint was raided. In their search for big bettors, the police came across the bank teller's name as one who wagered upwards of $30,000 in a single day. They traced him right to the bank.

Steffens, like most other computer crooks who *are* uncovered, was caught by mistake.

"I have studied more than one hundred thirty cases of computer crime," said Stanford's Parker. "If all we're doing up to now is accidentally stumbling onto these things, I can't help but wonder what the really smart computer crooks are doing. How much of this criminal activity is going on that never gets detected?"

Besides the fact that computers are making crime harder to detect, the illegal activity is often not brought to the attention of the public because the companies that have been "had" are embarrassed over their lax security precautions. They remain silent.

Parker feels that successful computer fraud schemes soon become bottomless pits from which a "virtually unlimited amount of money can be taken without any increase in the danger of being detected." Computer experts and computer crime sleuths, therefore, predict that still larger and more novel computer frauds are yet to be uncovered.

Not too long ago, a couple of payroll clerks in Brooklyn thought they had a good thing for a while. They kept records of former employees on file and continued to issue their paychecks, changing only the addresses, so that the checks were mailed to themselves.

And a clerk at the Morgan Guaranty Trust Company in New York came up with a similar ploy. He was convicted in 1971 of having directed the bank's computers to issue dividend checks in the names of some former shareholders who had sold their stock in corporations for which the bank served as a transfer agent. The checks were sent to the address of an accomplice, who deposited them. Afterward the computer went to work once again to erase all records of the dividend checks ever having been issued.

One problem of detection is that traditional bookkeeping methods that used to trip up swindlers don't really apply to computers. Thus a computer programmer can manipulate the machines and stand a reasonable chance of getting away with the crime.

The programmer—such as Equity Funding's Green—writes a series of instructions that, when fed into the computer, causes it to perform certain operations—be it ordering merchandise, writing checks, or producing phony insurance policies. The computer operator, however, is usually a separate individual. But, according to computer fraud specialists, in too many instances the computer programmer and the operator are the same person, making it harder to detect the fraud and—the other side of the coin—making it easier to commit.

Computers leave printed records, called printouts, of their activities. Can't these records be properly audited? Critics of the computer complain that too few auditors are knowledgeable about the electronic apparatus and how it can be manipulated. Moreover, computer systems are becoming more sophisticated, telescoping several operations into one. And much of what goes on inside a "mechanical mind" can be prevented from appearing on the printout by a cunning computer con artist. What has perplexed auditors and computer experts, however, is that such unlawful uses of the computer can be erased just about as fast as they are programmed, covering up any fraud in microseconds.

In the days preceding the computer era, auditors and company officials could, of course, be kept in the dark about a fraud—at least for a while. But before the computer there were more double checks, more written records of transactions, and more people through whom business records had to pass.

Computer security experts say that many of these double checks have been eliminated. Record keeping has been centralized in the brain of the computer. A criminal simply needs to have the machinery to himself for a few minutes to commit a computer crime.

Computer embezzlement has become so simple, in fact, that Robert V. Jacobson, vice-president of Sentor Security Group, a New York-based consulting firm, figures that some 86 percent of computer crimes go undetected. And banks, brokerage houses, and insurance companies aren't by any means always the victims.

In one large city, an employee, after collecting a fee, altered payroll records during night computer runs and thousands of dollars were lost in fraudulent overpayments.

In another instance, an antipoverty agency was taken for more than $2 million in a few short months when phony payroll checks for a youth program were processed through its computer at the rate of 102 a week.

And the programmer for a board of education managed to steal more than $40,000 in an even shorter period by instructing his equipment to issue checks for teachers no longer employed.

While the computer is the ideal tool for the "inside" crime—the so-called robbing-from-the-boss technique—it has also enabled outsiders to penetrate companies, enabling the theft of goods and valuable secrets.

The means by which the computer crook on the outside gets "into" an electronic brain are difficult but certainly not impossible.

Computers are connected to terminals that have a combination of buttons to activate the computer. The buttons, however, must be pushed in the proper sequence, similar to the combination of a safe.

The lines that connect the terminals to computers are usually telephone wires, so that the computer can be activated by making a simple telephone call. That's why computer phone numbers are unlisted and are in fact kept a big secret by most firms. Only persons who know how to use the apparatus can dial into the machine, by using a two-step procedure. First the caller punches that confidential telephone number. In response, he hears a squeal that lasts for a few seconds.

Next the caller punches in a special number that informs the computer that the individual is authorized to use it. The computer then asks for a password. Once the caller has spelled out that secret word, he has penetrated the system.

Like a thief who has the ability to open a safe without knowing the exact combination, the computer "burglar" can perform a similar act. But there's one big difference. A burglar fooling around at a safe has to do it in the still of the night and then must live in fear of getting caught. A computer thief can work in broad daylight. It's hard to catch someone who can simply hang up.

It was in precisely this manner in 1971 that a young Los Angeles man was able to penetrate the computer system of Pacific Telephone Company, the West Coast affiliate of American Telephone & Telegraph Corporation. The charges were that he stole at least $100,000 and perhaps as much as $1 million worth of telephone equipment and supplies through his scheme.

From a computer specialist's point of view, the method was rather simple. All he needed was a push-button telephone with which he could tap into the telephone company's IBM computer. He would indicate the number and type of supplies to be delivered to one of the company's docking areas in Los Angeles County. The supplies were then placed on shipping platforms between midnight and 2 A.M. After obtaining keys to the docks, he would drive in with a truck to steal the loads before the morning warehouse crews arrived.

The only reason he was caught was because one of his disgruntled employees turned him in. He was sentenced to forty days in jail and put on three years' probation.

In another case, a programmer for University Computer Company of Palo Alto, California, attempted to deal in information and not tangible equipment.

He learned enough code numbers from customers of the competing Information Design Systems of Oakland to enable him to dial a special telephone access code and receive a full printout of the competitor's program, which he apparently intended to market.

The scheme was uncovered by a telephone company tracer and the programmer was given a suspended sentence. A civil jury awarded IDS damages for its loss.

And yet another example of stealing information involved three employees of Encyclopaedia Britannica, who copied the names of three million customers on computerized mailing lists and sold them to a competitor. The publishing firm claimed it lost millions of dollars.

Computer experts feel that police departments have no sophistication whatsoever in catching computer thieves—even when the scheme is pointed out to them. Some law enforcement agencies have recognized this deficiency and have focused greater attention on computer technology and electronic countermeasures. The Los Angeles County Sheriff's offices, for example, initiated a program to handle computer crime investigations. The FBI and some other agencies have followed suit.

Some investigators actually are placing the blame on the computer makers for building products that allow such crimes to be possible.

A group of persons in Los Angeles thinks IBM was at least partially responsible for the Equity Funding scandal because it leased the company computers without warning the public of possible computer fraud. The class action suit filed against IBM in Los Angeles Superior Court asks damages of over $4 billion.

IBM, of course, moved to dismiss the complaint.

"It's like saying that General Motors is negligent in making a Chevy that was used in a bank holdup," said Daniel J.

Ashley, regional counsel for IBM, "or that Royal Typewriters could be negligent for making a typewriter that could type a fraudulent check."

So what can the public expect from law enforcement authorities in the way of protection for their investment in American companies—investment which forms the very foundation of our capitalistic system?

Summed up computer fraud expert Parker:

"In spite of what we do, more major catastrophes similar in seriousness to the recent alleged $2 billion Equity Funding Insurance fraud in Los Angeles will happen."

The Equity Funding case follows in the tradition of great American frauds which rely on making the public believe in something that just isn't there.

In 1962, Billie Sol Estes was arrested by federal and state authorities and charged with fraud stemming from the use of fictitious fertilizer tanks as collateral for $22 million in loans from a dozen finance companies. Most of the fertilizer tanks were never constructed. So Estes, a Texas country boy who exploded onto the nation's front pages in 1962 at the age of thirty-seven, saw his $150-million agricultural empire collapse. Estes' high contacts in the Kennedy Administration made the case a Washington sensation.

Estes had a great line: To be successful, he said, "You have to walk out on a limb to the far end—for that's where the fruit is. If it breaks, you learn how far to go next time."

The Allied Crude Vegetable Oil Refining Corporation scandal which surfaced in December, 1963, is another case of dealing in phantom goods. Major commodities dealers who believed they had soybean, cottonseed, fish, and other commercial oils stored at the company's Bayonne, New Jersey, tank farm got a rude surprise—the oils didn't exist. Several major companies dealing in commodities unknowingly used the phantom oils as collateral to borrow from banks. Final losses reached upwards of $100 million.

Another classic case took place in 1938. An executive with

McKesson & Robbins, the drug manufacturer, inflated the assets of the company to the tune of some $25 million through the creation of false receivables and nonexistent inventories. The case was the sensation of its time and considered the business fraud of the century.

P. T. Barnum said it all. But just think what he could have done if he had had a computer.

X
Storm Clouds

DESPITE rising operating costs and the constant headache of having to create even more phony insurance to support the company's stock, Equity Funding's whiz kids felt that 1973 would be a very good year. Somehow in the Equity fantasyland at Century City there was almost a cosmic feeling that like Jack's beanstalk, Equity Funding's amazing growth record could continue unabated.

As late as November, 1972, Fred Levin was coming up with new sales gimmicks for life insurance sales. Levin said in a confidential executive committee report that he was currently exploring for additional sources of premium income and, as a result, was researching whether Equity Funding Life could sell its product in supermarkets. "We are testing the level of various benefits which can be provided for a two-dollar weekly premium," Levin reported. The appeal was certainly there to a promoter like Levin. ("Jimmy, please run to the store and get me a loaf of bread, a dozen eggs, and an Equity Funding life insurance policy. And don't forget the Green Stamps.")

Because the company's operations appeared to be growing so rapidly, Lowell proposed to the executive panel in December, 1972, the decentralizing of operations with the possibility of acquiring property in the San Fernando Valley that would serve as the base for the home office.

Lowell's proposal that year came in the wake of good news

151

from Levin regarding life insurance sales. In November Levin told the executive committee that life insurance written by branch offices was up 9 percent over September and 40 percent over the previous November. Levin was to report the next month that December showed a 15 percent drop against November but a whopping 43 percent increase over December of 1971.

But the rosy picture being painted by Equity's wunderkinder was a façade for the increasingly nefarious operations going on behind the scenes.

Sometime toward the end of 1972, some of Equity Funding's management became concerned that the firm might come under an intensive audit or investigation by outside authorities, and began to look around for ways to cover up some of the fraud. Of great concern were the $25,300,000 worth of bonds on the books of the Equity Funding Life subsidiary. The public figures (which, of course, also were on file with the California and Illinois insurance departments) showed that Equity Funding was carrying blue chip bonds from the following companies:

American Can Company
Armstrong Cork Company
Burroughs Corporation
Carolina Power & Light Company
Carrier Corporation
Central Hudson Gas & Electric Corporation
Chemetron Corporation
Chesapeake & Potomac Telephone Company of Maryland
Cities Service Company
Coastal States Gas Producing Company
Continental Can Company, Incorporated
Diamond Shamrock Corporation
Dow Chemical Company
The Firestone Tire & Rubber Company

Florida Power & Light Company
FMC Corporation
Fruehauf Corporation
General Mills, Incorporated
Halliburton Company
Harris-Intertype Corporation
Indianapolis Power & Light Company
Iowa Electric Light & Power Company
Kaiser Aluminum & Chemical Corporation
The Kroger Company
Laclede Gas Company
Mountain Fuel Supply Company
New England Telephone & Telegraph Company
Northern Indiana Public Service Company
Northwestern Public Service Company
Owens-Illinois, Incorporated
Packaging Corporation of America
PPG Industries, Incorporated
Ralston Purina Company
R. J. Reynolds Tobacco Company
Schlitz (Jos.) Brewing Company
SCM Corporation
Siegel (Henry I.) Company, Incorporated
Signal Companies, Incorporated
Norton Simon, Incorporated
Southwestern Bell Telephone Company
Teleregister Corporation
Tenneco, Incorporated
Texaco, Incorporated
Texas Eastern Transmission Corporation
Texas Oil & Gas Corporation
Transcontinental Gas Pipe Line Corporation
Wilson & Company
F. W. Woolworth Company

All the bonds were reported to have been purchased in

1972 and they certainly represented a cross-section of some of the finest corporate issues to be found anywhere.

The trouble was they were all phony bookkeeping entries. Every last one was a fabrication. No wonder some worry was expressed. A painstaking audit would spell trouble.

The Federal Grand Jury indictment accused Goldblum, Levin, Smith, Sultan, Lewis, and Edens of arranging through Gary S. Beckerman, the company's advertising manager, for the printing of counterfeit bonds to cover up the fraud, in case auditors asked for physical evidence of the securities.

These long-term corporate bonds made up the entire securities portfolio of Equity Funding Life at the end of 1972. Equity Funding Life, in reporting these holdings to state insurance regulators, claimed to have purchased the bonds from United California Bank of Los Angeles. But UCB could (of course) never trace the transactions. And American National Bank & Trust in Chicago, which was first thought by investigators to be keeping the securities for Equity Funding Life, knew nothing about them.

The reason American National expressed ignorance was that "American National Trust Company" of 1866 Sheridan Road in the North Chicago suburb of Highland Park was supposed to have the bonds. The "bank" consisted of a single office with no furniture, rented by Levin, who knew that the real American National Bank didn't have the bonds (which indeed never existed). So a phony repository had to be created.

Levin's motivation apparently was a fear that Seidman & Seidman, EFCA's accounting firm, might indeed insist on knowing the whereabouts of the bonds in its 1972 audit.

The deception would be tried later, both on the auditors and on the examiners from the Illinois Insurance Department.

But first some counterfeit bonds would have to be created. The counterfeiting affair began about the first week in December, 1972. Robert Ochoa, the twenty-eight-year-old manager of Equity Funding's printshop in nearby Santa Monica, was told by Levin and his colleagues that the company needed the bonds "for trading purposes."

Levin, Beckerman, and some of their colleagues visited the plant that first night to run off initial proofs to study the quality of the forgeries. They had hopes of eventually using some $100 million in counterfeit bonds to placate the auditors and any investigators who harbored doubts about the company's assets. Various members of the forgery crew would go to the plant at intervals of a few days, stopping by at closing time, telling Ochoa what they needed, going out to eat, and then returning later in the evening to study the results.

Ochoa apparently thought his work was pretty good, although he wasn't quite sure what it was going to be used for, nor whether the strange request was kosher. But Levin and his cronies disagreed with Ochoa's assessment and were disappointed with the print job. Thus, the counterfeit bonds were never used.

The Equity Funding executive crew felt bad about the bond fiasco. It should have been a success. After all, they had had vast experience in other counterfeiting operations over the years, including the counterfeiting of phony bank deposit slips, legal stationery, and other documents.

While that behind-the-scenes melodrama was unfolding, Equity Funding was still a bright star on Wall Street. On December 12, 1972, Standard & Poor's Corporation's Stock Reports contained the following recommendation:

"With earning in a long-term uptrend, the shares appear to have above-average appreciation potential, although they may appeal mostly to the aggressive investor in view of their wide market swings."

The financial analysis predicted that 1973 insurance operations of Equity Funding would constitute the largest source of its revenues and profits. Moreover, it forecast increased insurance volume in the New York, New Jersey, and Connecticut markets as a result of the Bankers National Life acquisition. Overall earnings for 1973 were projected to stage another advance. And as for its long-term appraisal, the analysis said that increasing emphasis on life insurance would augment the company's ability to maintain "steady, long-term growth."

XI
Holes in the Dike

STAN Goldblum was in his element on January 22, 1973. Standing at the podium, he looked like the stereotype of the American capitalist—impeccably dressed, self-assured; an imposing giant of a man. It was the weekly session of the New York Society of Security Analysts, in their drab second-floor meeting hall at the corner of William and Beaver streets in the heart of Wall Street.

Goldblum recalled that the last time he had appeared there was in 1968. "Since that time, the company has grown, matured, and has made some important acquisitions," he told his enraptured audience, which represented some highly regarded brokerage houses.

Equity Funding's great strength, said the chairman, was as a life insurance marketing company. Goldblum then added:

"We have succeeded in identifying unfilled needs in the financial services area, and have the technical capability to develop new products to satisfy those needs. Finally, we have the organization, manpower, and know-how to effectively market those products. . . .

"Our total insurance in force at the end of 1972 was over $6.5 billion. In the past year our individual insurance in force has been rising at an average of two percent a month, approximately three times the average for all life insurance companies."

This is what the analysts came to hear. Their baby was

healthy and growing. Visions of buy recommendations swirled in their heads.

Goldblum continued:

"During 1971, only one publicly owned life insurance company exceeded the $1.2 billion gain of insurance in force which we achieved, independent of the effect of acquisitions."

At Goldblum's elbow was his financial manager, Sam Lowell. Anticipating questions on the troubles of the mutual fund industry and the fact that mutual fund customers were redeeming their shares faster than they were buying them, Lowell said that wasn't something Equity Funding was worried about. Lowell declared that Equity Funding's group of three mutual funds had never had net redemptions mainly because of the success of the insurance-mutual fund package the company was marketing.

It was obviously a smash of a presentation. Among those recommending Equity Funding stock shortly afterward were Smith, Barney & Company; Cowen & Company; Hayden Stone & Company; Burnham & Company; and Edwards & Hanly.

But the dike was beginning to spring leaks.

Thirty-six-year-old William Donald Gootnick had joined Equity Funding in February of 1971 after Publishers Computer Systems of Los Angeles, of which Gootnick was general manager, went bankrupt. William Mercado, EFCA's computer manager, had needed someone to clean up the ever-complicating mess of Equity Funding's computer system. Actually, Lowell had asked Gootnick to straighten the mess out—one caused partly by Mercado's conflicts with some employees and partly by the fact that Equity Funding's personnel weren't properly using the International Business Machine computer system.

Gootnick had seen some curious things during his brief period with the company, but nothing that really added up. Shortly after joining the company, for example, he noticed

B & G International Photos.

Mike Riordan when he headed Equity Funding.

Tommy Weber.

Equity Funding admitted for listing on the American Stock Exchange in 1966. Left to right: John C. Turner, then an Amex floor official; Stan Goldblum; and Mike Riordan.

Jim Collison.

Lowell and prize bulls at Equity's Ankony cattle subsidiary in Colorado.

Equity Funding makes the big time, October 19, 1970: listing day on the New York Stock Exchange. Left to right: Loeb, Lowell, Goldblum, Merle S. Wick, a Big Board vice-president, Arkus-Duntov, Kroll, and Dov Amir.

Goldblum on a happier day: the company's first annual picnic in 1971. Behind him Lowell and Loeb.

Company Archives.

Company Archives.

Levin and wife Carol during a business trip to Spain in 1972.

Herbert Kravitz.

Rod Loeb, general counsel then and now.

Robert E. Dallos.

The man who blew the whistle, Ron Secrist outside his home in Atlanta, where he now lives.

that there was more insurance than there were actual name and address records.

But it was the system itself that had a computer expert like Gootnick mystified. The system couldn't efficiently handle the large blocks of reinsurance and every time Gootnick attempted to propose a new design, roadblocks were thrown in front of him at management meetings.

Gootnick told the middle-management meetings—attended by Smith, Edens, and Lewis, among others—that there were times when he put five transactions in the front end of the computer system and only two would come out the back end. Moreover, Gootnick remembered that every time he would bring up the subject of reinsurance, there were "snickers" among several attending the meetings.

Finally, Gootnick had had it. He wasn't getting anywhere with the present computer system, so in 1972 he dug up an old proposal by International Business Machines which had the project name ECLIPSE (Equity Consolidated Life Insurance Processing System) and was designed to institute a massive five-year overhaul of the entire Equity Funding computer complex. Gootnick tried to sell top management on the project.

After a presentation on the merits of the IBM system to Goldblum, the chairman, Smith and Lewis told Gootnick to drop the proposal. "Things are too tough and we're in the midst of an austerity program," Goldblum admonished the affable Gootnick.

With 20-20 hindsight, Gootnick recalled for an interviewer that the ECLIPSE system would have clamped too many controls on the computer section and might have greatly slowed the phony-insurance assembly line.

Another leak in the Equity Funding dike was sprung on January 8, 1973.

"I'll never forget that day," said David Capo. "I caught the flu, I stopped smoking, and I quit Equity Funding."

Sam Lowell and Fred Levin tried for ninety minutes to

keep Capo from resigning. The twenty-nine-year-old former Haskins & Sells accountant had been Sultan's top aide in taking care of the real and phony loan program. The loan receivables stemmed from the loans Equity Funding Life made to its policyholders to enable them to buy the insurance-mutual fund package.

Obviously, EFCA's hierarchy was disturbed over the possibility of a leak to the authorities. They knew, however, that their system of strictly departmentalizing the company into "cells" so that few individuals had a complete picture of what was happening with respect to the fraud, would make it extremely difficult for someone on Capo's level to spill the beans. Nevertheless, they were uneasy over the circumstances surrounding Capo's resignation decision.

Capo, who had worked in the funded loan section for four years, felt he had been sucked into something he didn't quite understand but which he felt was bad. In short, Capo, who had once worked with Lowell at Dart Industries, sensed he had become an accomplice to fraud.

Finally, Lowell and Levin convinced Capo that he should see Goldblum before he turned in his official resignation.

"I can't live with this anymore," Capo told Goldblum in the chairman's twenty-eighth-floor office. "I know something's not right."

"You're acting like a schmuck," replied Goldblum. "It's all in your head."

"I can't face myself when I look in the mirror in the morning," Capo blurted.

Goldblum called Capo back to his office on January 22. "I know you're not going to be happy resigning," Goldblum admonished.

Capo left anyway. David Jack Capo was later indicted along with Goldblum and twenty others for complicity in the fraud.

In early February, 1973, Ronald H. Secrist, thirty-seven,

and Patrick W. Hopper, thirty-four, had dinner at a restaurant in Pasadena called Hutch's Barbecue.

"I was fired in a personnel cutback," declared Secrist, who had risen to a $24,000-a-year assistant vice-president's post at Equity Funding Life. "I'm going to come out with the story now."

The "story" was that the slender, balding, five-foot-ten-inch Secrist knew Equity Life was manufacturing phony assets and had even sat in on some of the "manufacturing parties."

Secrist and Hopper were good friends. The taciturn Hopper had studied economics at California State College at Los Angeles and had then worked in the insurance industry for ten years. He was an expert at money management, as demonstrated by his own portfolio, which had already made him a wealthy man.

Hopper was a principal in a company that Equity Funding acquired in 1970, called Independent Securities Corporation of Pasadena. As part of the deal, he had gone to work for Equity Funding. In October, 1971, Hopper was notified by Levin that he had suddenly been made vice-president of the newly acquired Bankers Life in the wake of a wholesale housecleaning of executive personnel at the New Jersey-based insurance company. Bankers had assets of approximately $170 million and Hopper took over its portfolio management.

Hopper, now sitting with Secrist in the Pasadena restaurant, recalled how Secrist had told him in September, 1971, that something was amiss at Equity.

That first admission had come one evening after dinner at Secrist's home in the San Fernando Valley community of Tarzana. The three were relaxing after another spareribs dinner—Hopper, Secrist, and Secrist's wife, Marilyn—when Secrist opened up.

"My jaw dropped when Secrist told me the story," Hopper remembered.

Secrist joined Equity Funding in Los Angeles in August, 1970, after working for several years on the West Coast with other insurance companies. In October, 1971, he was transferred to Bankers Life in New Jersey.

That night in Tarzana, Secrist told Hopper of the "manufacturing party" he had attended early in 1971 during which he made up insurance files with other Equity Funding employees to fool the auditors. Hopper was astounded and attempted to check out the story with Frank Majerus, the Equity Life comptroller. On October 19, 1971, Majerus told an amazed Hopper essentially the same story—that is, that Equity Funding was carrying phony life insurance on its books.

Majerus was obviously upset and was looking for another job.

The Majerus admission came while Hopper was riding in a cab with the Equity Life comptroller. Majerus was visibly nervous about the situation. He told Hopper he had been ordered to doctor the figures of the life company and, as a result, had resigned. But he reconsidered a few days later and went back with the company. He finally quit for good at the end of 1971 and joined Beneficial Standard Insurance Company.

But back in 1971, Hopper felt he still didn't have a complete picture of what was going on—there was just too much hearsay with not enough hard evidence. And, to be sure, he still enjoyed working for Levin.

That didn't last long, however. Immediately after Hopper arrived at Bankers in October, 1971, Levin began suggesting that Hopper start moving assets around. Levin kept after Hopper to send portfolio securities out of the state so that they could be intermingled with the parent company's holdings.

One day Levin inquired into about $28 million worth of bearer bonds which could be easily negotiated. The bonds were in Bankers' portfolio and Levin asked Hopper if he could mail them to the parent company in California.

"Under no circumstances," replied Hopper.

Then there was the December 31, 1971, request from Lloyd Edens to transfer $3 million to the United California Bank, one of the parent company's corporate banks. Edens had promised to ship the $3 million back "in three hours."

"No," was Hopper's blunt reply.

Early in 1972 Levin asked Hopper to open a $3-million demand-deposit account with First National City Bank of New York, another institution with which the parent did business.

Again, Hopper resisted sending Bankers' money out of New Jersey.

Meanwhile, Lowell kept pressing Hopper to invest Bankers National Life money through EFCA's Bishop's Bank subsidiary in the Bahamas. Since Bishop's bought foreign issues, Lowell wanted Bankers National Life money for investment in Brazilian and Mexican bonds. Additionally, Lowell urged that Bankers money be dropped into demand deposits around the country.

Even Goldblum asked Hopper to buy $1 million worth of Israeli bonds. Again, Hopper said no, not because he had anything against Israeli bonds, but because the yield wasn't more than 4.5 percent and Hopper said he could get a better deal investing Bankers' money elsewhere.

To fend off the assaults, Hopper kept quoting an agreement which Equity Funding signed with the New Jersey Insurance Commission upon its acquisition of Bankers, which declared that the parent couldn't take any money out of the state without the approval of the commission. "I'd bring this agreement up all the time and they'd say, 'Oh, okay,'" Hopper recalled. But still the requests continued.

By December 14, 1971, Hopper had had it, and informed Levin he would be leaving the company. Hopper figured there had been just too many conversations with Levin about Levin's philosophy of "moving things around" and doing "creative accounting." Hopper felt he couldn't continue fighting the assaults on the portfolio of Bankers. Yet, he couldn't go to the New Jersey Insurance Commission because he had no hard evidence of fraud.

On December 13, 1971, at 4 P.M., Hopper met with Levin at Bankers and submitted his resignation. Levin read Hopper's letter:

"I hereby submit my resignation . . . to take effect . . . not later than January 15, 1972. I am taking this step because of what I believe to be a lack of opportunity for adequate compensation. . . . I am taking this action with no malice or regrets from having spent the last 16 months with Equity Funding. . . ."

Levin read the letter and looked up. He asked Hopper if he wanted more money—if that was the only reason for Hopper's resignation.

"No," said Hopper. "I'm concerned about the kinds of things you're planning to do."

Levin then accepted Hopper's resignation and declared he respected Hopper's stand on creative accounting.

"I'm trapped into doing the things I'm doing," said Levin. "I wish I had met you before I started doing things under the table."

All these events flashed before Hopper's mind as he once again listened to his friend Secrist that February night at Hutch's in 1973. As they finished their meal they began talking about where to channel the information which Hopper finally believed should be publicized.

Neither Secrist nor Hopper felt that the California Insurance Department had direct responsibility for the case because Equity Funding Life was still regulated by Illinois. And they didn't want to go to the Illinois Insurance Department because they felt Levin might still have some clout there and, moreover, neither felt the Illinois department had a good reputation in the field of enforcement. The Securities and Exchange Commission was out, they concluded, because the agency didn't have direct control over the insurance industry.

"Why not Ray Dirks?" asked Hopper.

Hopper had been impressed with Dirks' analysis in 1970 of the International Telephone and Telegraph Corporation takeover of Hartford Fire Insurance Company, up to then the biggest merger in United States corporate history. Dirks, a Wall Street insurance analyst, had sharply criticized the merger, and his comments had appeared in *The Wall Street Journal*. In October, 1970, Hopper, while visiting a brother who lived in New Jersey, decided to see Dirks, who by then had formed a firm with his brother called Dirks Brothers, Ltd.

Hopper and Dirks immediately hit it off because they both had a great deal in common—they could talk for hours and with great knowledge about the insurance industry. Hopper and Dirks kept in touch after that initial meeting, Dirks sending Hopper his research material from time to time.

Yes, agreed Secrist, someone with good insurance contacts like Dirks should be the one to hear his unbelievable story.

Raymond Louis Dirks was the man to call.

XII
Dirks

AMONG his Wall Street friends, Ray Dirks was always viewed as something of a nonconformist. Following the Equity Funding fraud disclosures, Dirks' fellow Wall Street analysts avoided him like the plague. The reason was that after uncovering what may be the largest business fraud in United States history, Dirks notified his own insurance clients before going to law enforcement authorities. For this decision, Dirks was subsequently charged by the New York Stock Exchange with passing on insider information, spreading rumors, failing to practice "just and equitable principles of trade," and violating "good business practice."

The Securities and Exchange Commission also investigated the insurance stock analyst. At this writing, however, no action had been taken by either the NYSE or the SEC against Dirks.

In an interview Dirks noted with some bitterness that his security analyst colleagues wouldn't back him up. "I think this is ridiculous," said Dirks, "because the NYSE and SEC investigations are directed at the very existence of an analyst and what he does." Moreover, added Dirks, "There is some professional jealousy."

And rightly so. Because Dirks, practically single-handedly at first, dug for the facts and substantially contributed toward blowing the lid off the Equity Funding case. What Dirks should have done with the information he unearthed is a matter of controversy: whether to put it at the feet of his paying clients, as he did, or to run to the cops on the beat, the NYSE and the SEC.

Dirks himself is hardly the most self-effacing person in the world. He almost revels in his Equity Funding martyrdom and enjoys hearing himself referred to as "the Ralph Nader of Wall Street."

Just who is Ray Dirks, anyway?

Dirks is a Hoosier, born in Fort Wayne, Indiana, in 1934, the son of Raymond and Virginia Dirks. A brother, Lee, is two years younger. Shortly after World War II broke out, Dirks' father enlisted in the Army, which was to lead to a nomadic military life, taking the Dirks family to seven different states.

Ray Dirks always considered himself a "sports nut," and was certainly as much a participant in high school in Needham, Massachusetts, as an observer—winning a letter in tennis.

At DePauw University in Greencastle, Indiana, he began dabbling in the stock market, and without any real knowledge of the market's machinery invested $780 he had saved from a job as a newsboy on the Indianapolis *News*. The stock was Standard Oil Company of Indiana. Shortly after Dirks bought ten shares, the stock split 2 for 1 and rose several points.

"I thought I was a genius," he said in an interview with the New York *Times*.

At the age of nineteen, Dirks felt he was a success and quickly bought and sold several other stocks at a profit. "At this rate, I thought I'd be a billionaire before long," he said in the *Times* interview.

Dirks graduated from De Pauw with honors and held a series of financial positions, including jobs at Bankers Trust Company and Goldman, Sachs and Company, where he became a senior insurance analyst. His first scrape with the Big Board was a minor one in 1964 while with G. A. Saxton and Company, a brokerage house, in which he was privately censured by the NYSE for buying and selling securities without using the facilities of a Big Board member organization or a bank.

In the mid-1960's, Dirks also tried his hand at producing plays. It didn't quite work out, and in 1969 he joined with his brother, Lee, to form Dirks Brothers, Ltd., a stock analysis firm. Lee, also a DePauw graduate (Phi Beta Kappa), had worked as a newspaperman for several years and specialized in newspaper stocks. Ray specialized in insurance stocks and quickly developed a reputation for being a thorn in the side of the clubby securities industry by delighting in finding trouble spots among the companies under his analytical magnifying glass.

Ray Dirks, brought up in a solid, Middlewestern Presbyterian family whose ancestors harken back to the Massachusetts settlers, considered himself an atheist and a nonconformist. (He was also a conscientious objector when he registered for the draft in 1959. The Army refused to grant him the status, but didn't draft him.)

Eventually, Lee, an ex-Army intelligence officer, moved to Rockville, Maryland, near Washington, D.C., where he continued to specialize in newspaper stocks and published a trade newsletter. Ray moved to Delafield, Childs, Inc., a research-oriented investment firm where he became a senior vice-president.

Underscoring his nonconformist attitude was Ray Dirks' life-style in Manhattan's Greenwich Village. His duplex on Barrow Street had a spiral staircase, two telephones, and very little else—with the possible exception of a buffalo head with enormous horns. Dirks said the duplex had been burglarized several times and that thieves made off with TV sets, radios, a leopard skin, a bear rug, and a tiger mat. Somehow, burglars overlooked a cowskin rug.

For someone who was actively athletic as a youth, Dirks let his love of eating good food mold his body in his middle years, and became a roly-poly 5-foot, 6-inches tall. Together with a bespectacled, round face and thick, wavy hair, and his usual out-of-style attire, he came across as anything but the public's image of the Wall Street establishment. Nevertheless, his prowess earned him a position earning well over $40,000 a year (although he professed to being continually broke).

To be sure, Dirks liked the good life.

"I don't lead a Spartan existence," he said. "I like to eat well. I spend whatever money I find."

His legal fees alone must have severely dented his pocketbook because he estimated it cost upwards of $100,000 for counsel representing him in lengthy hearings before both the Big Board and the SEC and in cases involving millions of dollars in lawsuits stemming from his fraud revelations. To help himself out financially he had to borrow substantially from his bank.

Whether he in fact violated insider trading rules is a debate that cuts to the very heart of Wall Street.

Dirks maintained he didn't immediately run to the authorities with his findings on Equity Funding because he harbors a basic distrust of most bureaucratic institutions. He just doesn't trust the regulators. Additionally, the story was so incredible that he didn't think anyone would believe him.

And, he recalled in an interview with *The Wall Street Journal*, after he had dug up enough on Equity Funding to go to the authorities, he still chose not to pull the alarm. "I was in California then seeing headlines on every newsstand that said James McCord was afraid to go to the FBI and the Justice Department about Watergate. Well, I didn't feel very safe about going to the authorities myself."

Dirks was, however, passing on his findings to his blue-chip clients, most of whom—but not all—sold their Equity Funding stock.

Even the Big Board, with its staff of more than sixty-five investigators, couldn't keep up with Dirks on the Equity Funding case. For although the NYSE computer had "kicked out" unusual activity in Equity Funding stock on March 19, and finally halted trading on March 27, the Big Board still hadn't uncovered any specific wrongdoing at the company. But Dirks had.

"This wasn't inside information," Dirks contended. "The guys I would classify as insiders were lying and denying the whole thing. What I had were allegations from people whom I didn't consider to be insiders. They were relaying information which proved upon investigation to constitute a fraud of great proportions."

The free spirit that roams in Dirks was illustrated by one story he told about the day, April 9, 1973, he was to testify before the NYSE on the insider allegations:

"I had a girlfriend in New York and she stayed over with me [at his Greenwich Village duplex] the night of April 8. When I got up the next morning . . . this girl sits up in bed and says, 'What the hell, you haven't even shaved.' And I said, 'Well I don't feel like it today.' I just had this attitude—these bastards at the SEC and the exchange had it in for me.'

"She said, 'You ought to shave.' And I said, 'I'm growing a beard until I'm cleared.' Then I said, 'Hey, that's a pretty good line. I'll have that in the New York *Times* tomorrow.'"

Dirks did get his line into the *Times* the next day. Eventually he shaved off the beard.

The searing question the government and the exchange regulators will ultimately have to ask themselves is not whether Dirks broke some highly technical and nebulous insider rules. The heart of the issue is whether Dirks did more good than evil. Without the Dirks disclosures, would anyone—the insurance departments of Illinois and California, the SEC or the stock exchanges—have been able to blow the whistle on Equity Funding? Certainly, it appears, not as quickly.

A portion of the following chapter concerning Equity Funding's hectic month of March is culled from Dirks' testimony before the SEC and the NYSE. It portrays an impressionable (his favorite word was "gee"), stubborn investigator who won't be turned back by the almost intimidating Equity Funding hierarchy. It describes Dirks calling his clients with his findings and being urged to check them out even more carefully. It shows his confusion and fear of the unknown. Dirks tended to overdramatize, which at times made him seem like a comical Sherlock Holmes.

Dirks best summed it up for a reporter by comparing the Equity Funding caper to a farce by Feydeau, a turn-of-the-century French playwright who was one of his favorites.

"Feydeau would create uproarious situations in which he had people showing up at unexpected times, saying ridiculous things, and being confronted with absolutely astonishing occurrences, one right after the other."

XIII
The Ides of March

TUESDAY

March 6

Secrist made two telephone calls. The first was to the New York Insurance Commission. The second was to Dirks.
"Hello. . . . Mr. Dirks?"
"Yes?"
"My name is Ron Secrist. I'm a former officer of Bankers National. I recently left the company. We have a mutual friend in Pat Hopper. I've something I've got to tell you."
"Yes?"
"One-third of the business on the books of Equity Funding Life is faked business. The irregularities go back at least to 1970."
Dirks was dumbfounded.
Secrist said the fake business had the code name "Y" and that at the same time the corporation had a cash problem. "A way to get cash for the parent company was to take cash out of the life insurance company and replace it with notes," Secrist told Dirks.
"Gee, what about the auditors?" asked Dirks.
The auditors were being taken in, too, Secrist added. "They have to make up insurance files to fool the auditors,"

declared Secrist. "Lately, though, they [the auditors] have been wising up and they think something is funny—or maybe they just think it's sloppy."

Dirks was scribbling notes on his office desk as fast as he could write.

After he hung up he turned to fellow Delafield, Childs analyst Allen Gorrelick and told him the story. Both felt it was totally incredible.

But, more importantly, Dirks didn't dismiss the story by any means. He had made a luncheon appointment with Secrist for the next day.

WEDNESDAY

March 7

Dirks, Secrist, and Gorrelick rendezvoused at P. J. Moriarty's, a New York bistro in which they were to spend three and one-half hours. Again, Dirks scribbled notes as fast as a bookmaker taking bets.

Dirks was impressed by Secrist's professed knowledge of what he was alleging to be a massive life insurance fraud.

"The key individual in the whole thing is Fred Levin," said Secrist.

To be sure, added Secrist, not everything being reinsured was phony. The coinsurers were getting some real insurance, too. He said that in 1969, when the scheme was thought to have its roots, the coinsurers were Connecticut General Life, Pennsylvania Life, and Congressional Life. In 1972, Ranger National of Dallas had the bulk of the reinsurance business.

"Levin is believed to have come up with the idea of starting a full-fledged 'Y' operation in 1970," Secrist told Dirks.

Secrist reiterated that in his opinion one-third of the approximately $2 billion of the life insurance that the life company had in force was phony—involving some 40,000 policies.

"Gee, that is six or seven hundred million," replied Dirks, taking another sip of his drink. Gorrelick just sat there listening incredulously.

"That's right," replied Secrist.

"Who in the company aided Levin?" asked Dirks.

"Jim Smith and Art Lewis were the architects, along with Fred," said Secrist, adding that some of Equity Funding's computer programmers also were involved.

Secrist said the "Y" business had almost become an "in" joke among the middle-management team of the life company that took part in the cabal. Once, he recalled, someone from Ranger, EFCA's biggest reinsurance customer, was in Los Angeles and had made an anti-Semitic crack over dinner. The next day, Secrist recalled, the conspirators decided to stick Ranger with a few million dollars more of the fake insurance business because some of the Jewish EFCA conspirators were affronted by the remarks. Dirks took this as an illustration to show that in many respects the phony plan was a haphazard operation.

Secrist said that Lewis had a particular way of rationalizing the sale of phony insurance to the coinsurers. Lewis, said Secrist, would look on the arrangement just as if Equity Life had borrowed money with no collateral. Then, said Secrist, Lewis would say that although the money could not be immediately paid back, it would be repaid at a future date.

But Secrist observed that in 1971 the company was still faced with the problem of needing more cash because although the life company would get 80 percent in cash in excess of a policy's first-year premium—which was all profit—it could only retain 10 percent the second year and would have to forward the 90 percent balance to the reinsurers. So it was a treadmill to oblivion, Secrist noted. The more phony policies that were created, the more cash would be needed to support the pyramid.

"Pat Hopper said you are the kind of guy that would do something about it," said Secrist.

"What do you expect me to do?" queried Dirks. "What

would you do if you were in my position?"

Secrist said he would give Dirks some names with which to check the story.

The former EFLIC executive spoke of wild stories going around the company in recent months. Some of the guys involved with the phony business, he said, were reported to be running around with lots of cash in their pockets. There was one story, he said, that Art Lewis always had a suitcase with $1,000 and a passbook in it.

"Aren't these guys nervous about what they're doing?" asked Dirks.

Secrist said that Lewis "has one of the worst twitches I ever saw" but that for the most part the conspirators were generally calm and loose about what they were doing. "They are all essentially in their thirties, with no extensive business experience and maturity but they are all brilliant, with IQs of 150," said Secrist.

"At the end of the year, however, they get a bad case of neuroses when the auditors come in," quipped Secrist. "They hope nothing will show up."

The luncheon meeting lasted late into the afternoon. Dirks was loaded for bear.

THURSDAY

March 8

The New York Insurance Commission, having talked to Secrist, telephoned Edward J. Germann, a California Insurance Commission official. The New York commission said it was concerned over the Secrist allegations.

The razzle-dazzle that is Los Angeles is a universe away from the prosaic Midwestern plains of Springfield, Illinois. But even so, thirty-one-year-old Sanford William Enslen could hardly be prepared for two eyebrow-raising events that occurred in March, 1973.

Enslen was hired by Jim Smith from the Horace Mann Educators Corporation, a group of Springfield-based insurance companies. Smith had suggested that Enslen, in his new post as vice-president of Equity Funding Life, was to use his management background to design better management control programs that would bring greater business order to the insurance subsidiary. So, in a sense, Enslen was prepared for the almost total lack of formal office procedures that he encountered in the Equity Funding Life subsidiary when he came aboard in November, 1972.

But what alarmed Enslen more was the discovery that at least one of the life insurance company's middle management personnel was committing embezzlement. What the employee was doing was altering the computer records so that a fictitious policy owner (at this point Enslen wasn't aware of the phony insurance scheme) would notify EFLIC that he or she wanted to cash in a policy. The phony policyholder would then receive a cash surrender check from the life company based on the policy's value.

But it was the embezzler who would cash the check instead, using common forgery methods. About $10,000 to $12,000 was involved in this minifraud.

Enslen reported the embezzlement racket to a supervisor, who took no immediate action.

Naturally, such shenanigans made the no-nonsense Enslen suspicious of the entire life-insurance operation and independently he began a quiet probe to see what made Equity Life tick.

Thirty-year-old Kiyofumi Sakaguchi, a native of Japan, came to the life subsidiary only a month before Enslen from the John Hancock Life Insurance Company. Sakaguchi worked under Lewis and was one examination away from a fellowship in the prestigious Actuarial Society. His primary responsibility was financial projections for the four subsidiaries of the EFCA insurance group. In March, 1973, Sakaguchi had no difficulty in projecting financials for

Bankers, Northern, and the New York life companies. But with Equity Funding Life, the figures always came out jumbled. Simply stated, as the life sub's business went up, its expenses remained relatively constant. Sakaguchi, a trained actuary, couldn't explain it.

"The discrepancy is due to the company's mass marketing activities," Lewis assured Sakaguchi.

Moreover, Sakaguchi uncovered more business on EFLIC's convention (financial) statement filed with the California Insurance Commission than he could actually account for in the internal insurance sales reports.

Independent of Enslen, Sakaguchi began his own investigation.

William F. Raff, thirty-nine, counsel for the life insurance group, had heard of a Secrist contact with the New York Insurance Department, which had relayed the report to the Equity Funding New York office. Moreover, Raff was friendly with Sakaguchi and had heard of his strange projection problems.

Independent of Enslen and Sakaguchi, Raff quietly began asking questions.

Goldblum had made a commitment to Equity Funding's three Eastern directors—Robert R. Bowie, Arkus-Duntov and Nelson Loud—that at least once a year the parent company's directors' meeting would be held in Manhattan. Such a meeting was held on Thursday, March 8, 1973.

The principal topic of the meeting was a public underwriting of $60 million worth of corporate bonds through Smith, Barney & Company. But unlike previous debt issues, there was no equity sweetener such as stock warrants (options to purchase stock at a future date) that had to be packaged with the bonds to make the issue more attractive. In short, the bond issue was a mark of maturity in the eyes of the financial community that Equity Funding Corporation of America had finally arrived.

With this bond offering, the parent company would have paid back its $50-million loan under the revolving credit arrangement with the First National City Bank consortium. Wiping out the $50-million loan would have released the collateral of Northern Life from Citibank so that the parent company would have been in an excellent position to negotiate a new loan. It thus appeared that Equity Funding was entering an era of even greater prosperity.*

At the same time, the directors decided to change the title of the parent company to Equity Funding Life Company since the firm's biggest product now was insurance, which the directors voted to have reflected in a new name.

FRIDAY

March 9

Germann, the California Insurance Commission official in Los Angeles, telephoned Leslie L. Ogg, a Los Angeles SEC official who had some background in the insurance and mutual fund industries. The two discussed the information relayed by the New York insurance agency. Ogg analyzed the information as the type of complaint that the SEC's Los Angeles office had had before on the company, stemming from back-office record-keeping problems. Moreover, Ogg felt the information was too sketchy for a full-blown probe.

"What about Equity Funding?" Gorrelick reminded Dirks during a work break. Dirks assured his colleague he would study his file on the company over the weekend.

MONDAY

March 12

Equity Funding Corporation of America reported record

---

*Goldblum told the authors he had no intention of going through with the Smith, Barney deal. He didn't elaborate.

earnings of $2.81 per share for the year ending December 31, 1972, up from $2.45 per share in 1971. In a news release on the company's earnings, Goldblum said consolidated net income rose to $22,617,000 in 1972, a 17 percent increase over the 1971 earnings of $19,332,000. Goldblum also announced that his board had declared its fourth consecutive annual cash dividend of 10 cents a share payable on May 7. At this point EFCA stock was trading in the high 20's.

Dirks was beginning his investigation of Equity Funding in earnest. At 12:30 P.M. New York time, the company's earnings report flashed across financial news tickers.

"This is a great excuse to call the company," thought Dirks to himself.

It was 9:30 A.M. in Los Angeles, and Goldblum's secretary, Ginny Sasse, told Dirks that her boss hadn't arrived yet.

"Ask him to call me back," Dirks replied.

At 2 P.M., New York time, 11 A.M. in Los Angeles, Goldblum returned the call, and a nervous Dirks, who hadn't talked to the chairman in more than a year, answered.

Dirks had rehearsed a brilliant opening.

"I see your earnings are out on the tape."

"Yes," replied Goldblum.

"Are you going to send out a press release on this?"

"Well," replied Goldblum with a tinge of sarcasm, "you know we always send out an annual report to our shareholders."

"What are the fully diluted earnings?" asked Dirks.

Goldblum called to his secretary and then answered, "Two dollars fifty-one a share."

Dirks apologized for not visiting Equity Funding in over a year and declared he'd like to come out to Los Angeles.

"Why don't you come out?" replied Goldblum.

"I think I am going to come out there on the week of the twenty-sixth."

"Fine. Call up my secretary whenever you get your schedule set."

Dirks purposely avoided tipping his hand about his conversation with Secrist.

Dirks then checked which of his firm's "clients" owned Equity Funding stock. Three who did were The Boston Company Institutional Investors, Inc. (a subsidiary of The Boston Company), Institutional Capital of Chicago, and Sears, Roebuck and Company pension fund.

The Boston group managed several billion dollars in pension, endowment, and trust funds and, like other big institutions, such as banks and insurance companies, was dependent not only on in-house stock market research in selecting securities for its clients' portfolios, but also relied on outside Wall Street analysts, such as Dirks.

Little wonder then that Dirks felt an obligation to Boston. Dirks talked to Thomas A. Courtney, a senior portfolio manager with the subsidiary. He also talked with Gerald S. Zukowski, one of its analysts. Courtney said he would see Dirks the next day in Dirks' New York office.

Jack Doyle and Jerry Fowler, two examiners from the Illinois Insurance Department, popped up suddenly at Equity Funding's Los Angeles headquarters. They also had heard disturbing reports and decided to make a spot audit of Equity Funding Life.

Doyle asked Edens where $25.3 million in bond assets were, and Edens quickly replied that they were in a Chicago bank—not saying whether it was the real American National Bank & Trust Company or the fake American National Trust Company, which Levin had set up the previous December.

In fact, Edens said, Seidman & Seidman, the life company's accountants, had received a confirmation that the bonds were in the Chicago bank. The confirmation was signed by "Joseph S. Phillips, second vice-president."

There was no such person at the real Chicago bank, but the Seidman firm didn't know that. Before Edens turned over the confirmation letter to Doyle, however, he made sure that the real bank's name and address appeared on the letter. It was a thoughtful move on Edens part because there is no branch banking in Illinois, and Doyle and Fowler surely would have become suspicious right away if they had seen an "American National" address in Highland Park, Illinois (not to mention the slightly altered name).

But before Doyle could send an examiner to the Chicago bank the next day to find the bonds, Edens told Doyle that they had been removed and used in other transactions.

Goldblum and Levin were clearly upset over the sudden arrival of the Illinois auditors.

Levin decided to throw a roadblock at the investigation by attempting to use his clout with the Illinois department, for which he had worked in the early 1960's. He called his old boss, John Bolton, the former Illinois deputy insurance commissioner. Levin complained that the Illinois examiners had walked in at a time when they were just completing their acquisition of First Executive Corporation of Los Angeles and at a point when their auditors, Seidman & Seidman, were in the final throes of completing an annual audit. Moreover, Levin said, the parent company was attempting to put together a major public offering (through Smith, Barney). In short, complained Levin, it was no time for insurance examiners to spring a surprise audit. Additionally, he was anxious to find out the reason for the sudden audit. At a minimum, Levin wanted a three-month delay in the Illinois examination.

Bolton listened attentively and then decided to call his old friend, Richards D. Barger, the former California insurance commissioner. Bolton asked Barger, then with the prominent Los Angeles law firm of Kalmbach, DeMarco, Knapp & Chillingworth, to make an inquiry to Gleeson Payne, the current California insurance commissioner. Barger instead called Christy P. Armstrong, California's chief insurance examiner. But Armstrong told Barger he was not at liberty to discuss the case.

"Who's assigned to the case from California?" Barger asked.

"Maury Rouble," replied Armstrong.

That was enough for Barger. Maurice D. Rouble, the veteran supervisor of insurance examinations under Armstrong, had the reputation of being one of the toughest and most knowledgeable insurance investigators in the country. When Barger heard Rouble was on the Equity Life case, a red light flashed in Barger's head and he stopped asking questions. He sensed that there might be a serious situation developing at Equity Funding. "I got the vibes that maybe I shouldn't pursue this further," Barger later recalled.

Levin, aware of the Bolton-Barger conversation, called Barger later that day and said he and Goldblum would like to meet in Barger's downtown Los Angeles office. Upon arrival, Levin came right to the point: He wanted to know the reason for the presence of Illinois auditors.

"I don't know whether it's ominous or not," replied Barger, staring across his desk straight at Goldblum and Levin sitting together on a couch. "I'm just going to tell you that something is bothering the California department. For all I know maybe somebody's putting money in a big black bag. For all I know, it could be you, Fred, or you, Stan."

Barger chuckled at his attempt to make humor.

Neither Goldblum nor Levin smiled.

"That's all I can tell you," Barger cut through the silence.

"I guess I'll have to make the most of it," replied Levin.

"I guess you will," said Barger.

The two then left as abruptly as they had arrived.

"Levin knew the jig was up," theorized one California insurance investigator, who believed Levin was attempting to apply muscle on the Illinois auditors to back off through pressure from Barger. At the least, authorities believed Levin wanted to gain a delay on the Illinois and ensuing California insurance audits (one week later Rouble was to begin his state's examination).

"I think Levin tried to use me," Barger remarked later on the incident.

Sol Block, the audit manager for Seidman & Seidman, let Vic Kramer, head of EFCA's public relations section, know that the accounting firm was issuing to the parent "cold comfort"—which meant that its annual audit was all but completed and that Kramer could expedite the company's annual report to the printer. Block, in effect, was telling Kramer that although the audit officially had about another week to run, he saw no reason to question EFCA's earnings statement for 1972.

Jerry Monkarsh found himself skiing down the same Vail, Colorado, slope with Herb Glaser. Monkarsh, thirty-seven, and his brother, Eugene, forty-one, were Los Angeles apartment house developers and had sold their real estate operation to Equity Funding in 1969. Like Herb, the Monkarsh brothers had a substantial stock position in Equity Funding.

Monkarsh asked Glaser about the recent decline in the value of the company's stock. Glaser said he felt the stock was tailing off due to depressed market conditions.

TUESDAY

March 13

Courtney appeared at Dirks' office at 10 A.M. He asked Dirks to go into detail and Dirks did for almost four hours. After describing the Secrist conversation, Dirks said: "What do you want me to do from here?"

Courtney said they should continue to check independently of each other to determine if Secrist's allegations had any truth to them.

WEDNESDAY

March 14

Dirks and Gorrelick attended a Wall Street luncheon and sat next to John M. Buszin, an insurance analyst with Bankers Trust. Gorrelick learned that Bankers Trust, a Delafield, Childs client, had Equity Funding stock. Dirks, later learning this, called Buszin and invited him to his office the next day to tell him about the events of recent days.

THURSDAY

March 15

"Well, I really don't want to hear any more. We are going to sell the stock."

That was Bankers Trust analyst Buszin talking after hearing the Dirks spiel on the Secrist conversation.

Meanwhile, the Boston subsidiary sold approximately 36,500 shares of its clients' Equity Funding holdings.

FRIDAY

March 16

Vic Kramer, the Equity Funding public relations man, was getting fidgety about getting the annual report to the printer. There were unexplainable delays. "Please get back to me on Monday with any suggested revisions as I am sure you realize the final figures came in very late this year and we are under the gun," Kramer wrote in a memo to Equity Funding's executive staff.

MONDAY

March 19

Bankers Trust unloaded 98,800 shares of Equity Funding common stock to open the week, and EFCA stock slid two points from 27 to 25 on the sale. Additionally, a total of 123,800 shares of Equity Funding changed hands, 109,300 in blocks spun off by big institutions. The heavy trading caused the New York Stock Exchange's computerized monitoring system to "kick out" Equity Funding and the Big Board began a routine investigation.

Dirks decided to call Herb Lawson, San Francisco bureau chief of *The Wall Street Journal*, whom he had once met at a West Coast cocktail party and who had impressed Dirks with his investigative reporting ability. Lawson listened to the Dirks story and said it appeared to fall into the Los Angeles jurisdiction of William Blundell, the bureau chief there.

Dirks called Institutional Capital of Chicago, another client.

Bill Maloney, the head of the firm, was naturally startled by the story. But Maloney also thought it was absurd for Dirks to bring up the allegations without first checking them out with Goldblum.

"Well, I did call about the earnings report, and apparently they don't feel they have any false policies on the books or they wouldn't have put out their earnings report," said Dirks.

"Well, you have to call up Goldblum right away and ask him whether he has any fake policies," Maloney shouted.

"Well, I think that's not the way I would want to go about it," replied Dirks quietly. Dirks then told Maloney he was scheduled to meet with Goldblum on the twenty-seventh, anyway. In the meantime, he said, he would continue to check the phony insurance reports.

But Maloney was adamant. "If you go out there right away

and look him straight in the eye and ask him whether he has any false policies, you will be able to tell just by the way he responds, or his face looks," Maloney declared.

Dirks thought to himself: "That's ridiculous."

Nevertheless, Dirks replied: "Well, gee, maybe you're right." After all, thought Dirks, Maloney *is* a client.

"In fact," quickly added Maloney, "you ought to get on the next plane. In fact, we'll pay your plane fare."

"Okay."

"If you don't go out right away, I'll call him myself and ask him," Maloney said.

That did it. Dirks made up his mind that he would catch a plane for Los Angeles that night.

But first, Dirks placed a call to his friend Pat Hopper in Los Angeles.

"Pat, I haven't talked to you for a long time. I got this call from a fellow named Ron Secrist. Do you know him?"

"Yes," replied Hopper.

"What do you think of him?"

"He is a very honest, reliable, credible individual," replied Hopper.

"Well," said Dirks, "he's told me a pretty incredible story. What do you think?"

"It's probably true," said Hopper.

That night, before leaving for Los Angeles, Dirks kept a dinner engagement at Le Steak, a Manhattan restaurant, with two block-traders from Goldman, Sachs & Company, which had bought Equity Funding earlier that day. Then without packing any bags, Dirks dashed for the airport.

"I am a bachelor, and I can get on the next plane, and I kind of like to do that," Dirks was later to recall. "I love to get on the next plane. When I took my girl, I was going to Jamaica, and the next plane was going to Bermuda, so I went to Bermuda. That's the kind of guy I am. If it had been going to London, I would have gone to London. I just don't care."

Dirks arrived in Los Angeles at 5:30 A.M., California time. Upon checking into the Beverly Wilshire Hotel he found a note waiting for him. It was from none other than Goldblum. A nervous feeling began to creep up on the little insurance analyst from Indiana. Maybe Goldblum suspected that Dirks knew too much.

California insurance investigator Rouble was ensconced on Equity Funding's executive floor, and began probing the books independently of the Illinois auditors. Rouble was in constant consultation with Lawrence Baker, the assistant California insurance commissioner, and Armstrong, the state's chief insurance inspector, both of whom were becoming extremely suspicious of various activities at Equity Funding. As a result, certain precautions were taken to make sure that their investigation activities were kept as quiet as a Pentagon file on a new secret weapon. Some of the security steps even took on the appearance of an old vaudeville comedy.

The pipe-smoking Rouble, for example, was instructed to make no telephone calls from Equity Funding's twenty-eighth floor. Instead, every time he had to contact Baker, his boss, Rouble took the elevator down to the building's basement lobby to use a pay phone. Each call to downtown Los Angeles from Century City was worth about 95 cents, but Baker figured it was worth it rather than take a chance on a telephone line being tapped. His suspicions were to be borne out.

Rouble was jumping into the elevator more and more to tell Baker that he couldn't comprehend how Equity Funding's business could keep increasing when at the same time its lapse rate—policies not renewed—went down. Normally, thought Rouble, the lapse rate would increase proportionately to new business. Rouble discussed the perplexing problem with chief actuary Art Lewis, but didn't get an answer that satisfied him.

TUESDAY

March 20

Lawrence Williams, forty-two, was called one of the toughest sons of a bitch in the Securities & Exchange Commission's enforcement section in Washington. Loeb helped convince Goldblum to hire the Harvard Law School graduate in September, 1969, to form a strict enforcement section within Equity Funding that would keep the company in good standing with the SEC. (In the wake of the scandal, some investigators reflected that the hiring of the innocent Williams was a smokescreen for the fraud.) Williams proceeded to develop enforcement standards that were envied by other corporations.

Williams had flown to New York to discuss with the New York State Insurance Commission how he would take on insurance as well as mutual fund compliance procedures and had stopped at the Equity Funding office on Forty-Second Street in Manhattan to chat with Arkus-Duntov.

Arkus-Duntov commented that one Jarvis Slade, the principal officer of New York Securities, the firm Equity Funding's outside director, Loud, helped found, had heard general statements of fraud in the insurance area at EFCA. Williams, an executive on the twenty-eighth floor, had heard nothing about the rumors. Arkus-Duntov said Slade had attended a luncheon with a portfolio manager from Bankers Trust. And, said Slade, the Bankers Trust source confided that a Ray Dirks, an insurance analyst, was the source of the report.

Williams called Equity Funding's chief counsel, Rodney Loeb, and strongly recommended that the company go to the New York Stock Exchange with the story. Loeb had been receiving almost daily inquiries from the Big Board about the heavy trading and drop in Equity Funding stock and had responded that he knew no reason for the activity or the nosedive.

Williams dictated a memo to Loeb on the remarks by Slade. Later that afternoon, Loeb took the memo to Goldblum, who assured Loeb there was nothing to the story. Goldblum urged that the memo be destroyed because it could be detrimental to the company if it fell into the wrong hands—advice which Loeb did not heed. Both Loeb and Slade reported to the NYSE the next day.

The second thing Dirks did when he got up on Tuesday morning was to place a long-distance call to his New York office to find out what was happening with Equity Funding. Dirks was told that Goldblum had tried to reach him the previous day. What Dirks suspected but didn't know for sure was that Institutional Capital's Maloney had already leaked the story to Goldblum. Dirks gazed at the door to his room, which he had barricaded with chairs the night before to protect himself against an invasion of—what? An Equity Funding army spearheaded by General Goldblum? Dirks wasn't sure himself.

Dirks then called Hopper to let him know he was in town. Hopper told Dirks he could put him in contact with Frank Majerus, EFLIC's comptroller in 1970, who had since resigned, but who knew a lot about the phony insurance scheme.

That night Hopper picked up Dirks and they went over to Beneficial Standard Life Insurance Company, where Majerus was working, and took him back to Dirks' room at the Beverly Wilshire. Majerus appeared apprehensive, so Dirks tried to handle him gently.

At first, Majerus didn't acknowledge the phony "Y" business by that name, but then said he became aware of it in 1971, couldn't stand it anymore, and then resigned. Majerus said the point of the exercise was to create earnings. He then confirmed various parts of Secrist's story.

WEDNESDAY

March 21

Dirks was awakened by the phone jangling in his hotel room. He looked at the clock and saw it was 8 A.M. It was Goldblum, and Dirks was nervous again.

Goldblum said he had heard rumors that Dirks was making certain allegations about Equity Funding.

Dirks confirmed he had talked to three institutions about certain information he had.

"Why don't you come over for breakfast?" said Dirks, working up some courage. "I'm at the Beverly Wilshire, as you know."

"Okay," replied the chairman.

Dirks met Goldblum at the hotel's Hideaway Bar at about 8:45 A.M. Fred Levin accompanied Goldblum. By the time the two arrived, Dirks had assembled about twenty-five pages of hand-scrawled notes he had collected from his interviews with Secrist, Hopper, and Majerus and laid them on the breakfast table.

Again, Dirks couldn't think of a clever opening, so he nervously fell back on "How are you?"

"Not too good," replied Goldblum. "The stock just traded at nineteen, down four points."

"My God," said Dirks, "it was twenty-three and a quarter a half-hour ago when I was upstairs."

"Yes," replied Goldblum, "but a block of three hundred sixty-eight thousand shares went at nineteen and a quarter."

Dirks recalled that just before he left his room he called Boston and heard they were considering unloading a big chunk of Equity Funding.

"I guess that's The Boston Company," Dirks told Goldblum and Levin.

Dirks disclosed he had talked with three of Goldblum's former employees and he displayed the notes containing the allegations.

Goldblum and Levin said the whole thing was preposterous.

Dirks was getting more uncomfortable, if not downright scared, while swallowing his favorite breakfast of bananas and cream. He asked Goldblum and Levin if they wanted anything to eat and they said no. They were too engrossed in Dirks to think about eating.

Goldblum and Levin began looking over Dirks' notes and the names of some thirty individuals who allegedly knew of the fraud. Fred's name was on the list, but Stan's wasn't because no one Dirks had talked to had connected Goldblum with the phony insurance.

Dirks learned that the insurance examiners were in the Equity Funding offices, and suddenly Dirks began to feel uncertain again. If the auditors were combing through Equity Funding's books, why hadn't they discovered the fraud yet?

The forty-five-minute breakfast conference ended with Goldblum asking Dirks to ride with them over to their Century City headquarters. Goldblum took Dirks for the five-minute ride in his Rolls-Royce while Levin trailed in his Bentley.

Upon arrival at the executive suite, Levin quipped: "Well, you can see this is the twenty-eighth floor, but you don't have to worry because the windows are locked."

Dirks wasn't amused and declared that most of his suspicions were contained in his notes, which alleged that there was phony insurance on the life company's books under the code name "Y."

"How do you spell that—W-H-Y?" asked Goldblum.

"No, just the capital Y," said Dirks.

The meeting went on for three hours in Levin's office and over lunch with Goldblum, Levin, and certain EFLIC officers. Art Lewis, the chief actuary, brought in charts and lectured Dirks on how it simply couldn't happen. Jim Smith, the head of insurance operations, supported Lewis' view.

Then Goldblum handed Dirks a news release that he was

sending out in a few minutes. It was headlined: EFCA PRESIDENT COMMENTS ON MARKET ACTIVITY IN COMPANY STOCK. It read:

"Stanley Goldblum, president and chairman of Equity Funding Corporation, said today that there have been no adverse developments in the company's operations which would account for the market activity in EFCA stock during the past three days.

"Mr. Goldblum said that the company is 'in the strongest financial and sales condition in its history.' He added that revenues, earnings, and sales reached record highs in 1972, and that the upward trend has been continuing during the first quarter of 1973.

"EFCA's chief executive stated that the company's annual report, to be released by the end of March, will indicate, as did the earnings announcement on March 12, 17 percent gains in both revenues and earnings, and life insurance sales increase of 22 percent for total sales, and 33 percent for individual sales.

"Mr. Goldblum said that life insurance sales and operations are the company's primary business and account for approximately two-thirds of corporate earnings. EFCA owns four life insurance companies, and is currently negotiating for further insurance acquisitions, Mr. Goldblum said."

It had been a long day. Goldblum wanted to know if Dirks was finally convinced.

"Well," said Dirks, "it certainly appears that everything you say could well be true, and on the other hand these three individuals [I talked to] sounded plausible."

"You are not going to talk to any more people about this?" asked Goldblum as Dirks prepared to leave. "I mean we have neutralized you, I hope."

"I don't know," replied Dirks. "I'm in a muddle. I think I'm going back to my room and think about it."

Dirks went back to his hotel after lunch in midafternoon.

Loeb couldn't understand. He had walked over to Levin's

office and had found the door locked. Levin's office door was never locked.

Mary Lonn, Levin's personal secretary, said her boss was meeting with Ray Dirks.

"Ray who?" asked Loeb.

WEDNESDAY

March 21

William Edward Blundell never studied journalism as a college undergraduate and still doesn't have a journalism degree. But the thirty-eight-year-old, reddish-bearded Los Angeles bureau chief for *The Wall Street Journal* came close to winning journalism's most coveted award, the Pulitzer Prize, for almost single-handedly scooping the newspaper fraternity with the Equity Funding story.

After graduating from Syracuse University, Blundell spent two years in the Army. Upon being discharged, he asked his wife what he should do to feed her and the children. Since he had done a lot of writing in college, Blundell decided to enroll at the William Allen White Graduate School of Journalism at the University of Kansas, where he did well enough but didn't quite finish his master's thesis for his graduate degree.

The *Journal* recruited Blundell off the Kansas campus and he joined the paper in its Dallas bureau, where he worked for two and a half years. After a transfer to the *WSJ* home office in New York City, where for five years he worked as a reporter, rewrite man, and one of five page-one editors, Blundell was transferred to Los Angeles in 1968.

Following Dirks' call to Lawson in San Francisco, Lawson called Blundell and filled him in on the Dirks story.

Blundell met Dirks that Wednesday afternoon in the same Hideaway Bar where Dirks had confronted Goldblum and Levin.

For three hours, Dirks unloaded names, places, whom to

contact, and the whole bizarre story of what he had heard about Equity Funding Life Insurance Company.

Blundell concluded it was a fascinating story but that all of Dirks' information was secondhand.

"Dirks is a stock analyst and I'm not going to take one word of what Dirks tells me as the truth," Blundell thought to himself. He then set out on a painstaking road to prove the allegations.

Dirks got a phone message from Walter Delafield, his boss, who said he had just heard from Jarvis Slade of New York Securities. Delafield said Slade heard reports that an analyst at Bankers Trust had a few drinks with another analyst and discussed Dirks' fraud allegations. Delafield suggested that his firm was laying itself open for a possible libel suit.

Dirks told Delafield he was alleging no such thing. He remembered, however, that he had told Goldblum of his Bankers Trust contact and that Slade worked for a house that had an Equity Funding relationship. Could Goldblum be indirectly threatening him? the insurance analyst asked himself.

THURSDAY

March 22

Dirks' telephone jangled, again at 8 A.M. It was Goldblum, who said he was flying to New York the next day to attend the Institutional Investors' conference. "While I am in New York," said Goldblum, "would you mind if I go down to the New York Stock Exchange and tell them that you are not alleging fraud at Equity Funding?"

"No, Stanley, you are welcome to go back to the NYSE and say that I am not alleging fraud at Equity Funding, and I think that's terrific," declared Dirks.

Vic Kramer had flown to New York ahead of Goldblum to

set up the Equity Funding booth in a conference hall at the New York Hilton. As he was fussing about the booth, two individuals walked by and declared, "Ray Dirks is really giving it to you guys." Kramer was puzzled. Kramer knew Dirks and was aware that the insurance analyst had just visited Equity Funding's home office. But that's all he knew.

Kramer called Levin to relate the story about the two Wall Street types who had made the comment. Levin said he didn't want to discuss the matter on the telephone. Levin said he would try to talk it over with Kramer when he saw him at the Equity Funding International Tennis Tournament that Sunday at Georgetown University in Washington, D.C.

FRIDAY

March 23

Goldblum, in New York for the Institutional Investors' Conference, and Arkus-Duntov had breakfast with Laurence A. Tisch, the chief executive of Loews Corporation, a diversified company in tobacco, hotels, and theaters, which had a portfolio of more than $400 million in securities. On March 21, Loews had bought a block of 220,000 shares of Equity Funding at $19.25. Goldblum was delighted to hear about someone still interested in buying EFCA stock amid all the rumors. Naturally, Tisch wanted to know what sort of condition the company was in.

"Everything is fine at the company," Goldblum told Tisch over coffee at Manhattan's Regency Hotel. And both Tisch and Goldblum agreed that it was smart strategy to buy low and sell high. Tisch would later find out that he'd only have a chance to fulfill half of that success formula.

Tisch was concerned that although he had picked up a big block of Equity Funding, the stock was still dropping.

But Goldblum told Tisch during the twenty-minute meeting that business was excellent, earnings would be up, and the outlook was generally bright.

Obviously, Tisch was impressed with Goldblum's presentation, because right after breakfast he went out and bought another 53,100 shares at $19 to $19.75 each.

Thus, Loews had bought, since March 21, some 273,100 shares of Equity Funding through the investment banking house of Goldman, Sachs & Company.

On March 26 even stranger things were to happen involving Tisch's company. John W. Bristol & Company, an affiliate of The Boston Company, sold the investment banking firm of Salomon Brothers a 445,400-share block of Equity Funding plus a subsequent block of 11,800 shares, also of Equity Funding—an $8 million package. On the same day, Salomon acted as an agent for the sale to a third party of 298,100 shares of Equity Funding at $17.50. Salomon didn't identify the buyer. But Loews officials indicated that on that same day the company bought 216,900 shares of Equity Funding from Salomon.

Loews subsequently instructed Salomon to refuse delivery of the stock and also tried to undo the March 21 and 23 purchases from Goldman, Sachs.

Salomon, in litigation filed in the United States Court for the Southern District in New York City, filed suit against Bristol. Salomon said it was refusing to take delivery of the Bristol stock because Bristol hadn't informed Salomon of its conversations with Dirks.

And Dirks got in the last word on March 26 when he returned a telephone call to Wallace Bowman, the portfolio manager at Loews.

"I just heard that you know something about Equity Funding," Bowman said.

Dirks had already learned that the 445,400-share block had been unloaded that day by Bristol, the Boston affiliate, and that Salomon had bought the package and then sold off a big chunk of it to Loews.

"Eight million dollars down the drain," thought Dirks to himself. It would turn out to be one of the most colossal losses ever in one day.

"Wally, sit back in your chair and relax," Dirks told the

flustered Loews portfolio manager. "I am going to tell you the same story I have told every other institution I talked to."

Dirks then related the tale he had told to a couple of dozen institutions by that time. And Pat Hopper, who was with Dirks in his hotel room at the time, even got on the phone for half an hour to give Bowman his side of the allegations.

Finally, Dirks said, "Wally, what else do you want to know?"

"Well," replied Bowman, "Larry Tisch bought this stock, not me."

Loews was finally able to unload 102,000 of their 490,000 Equity Funding shares at $17, on March 27, just before trading in Equity Funding was suspended by the Big Board. By that time, however, the proverbial horse had long galloped out of the subsequently locked barn.

But back to Friday, March 23. Goldblum was getting ready for the Institutional Investors' Conference and at the same time was denying the fraud reports to anyone who would bring up the subject. The chairman also made an appearance before the New York Stock Exchange. Goldblum told them there was nothing amiss at Equity Funding.

At the same time, at First National City Bank's midtown Manhattan headquarters, a strange luncheon meeting was taking place between Fred Levin and Jerry Brewer, Citibank's chief account man, concerning a four-bank consortium loan to EFCA; a meeting which was to turn out as bizarre as the other EFCA events of that month.

When Gerald E. Boltz, the forty-one-year-old chief of the SEC's Los Angeles office, gets his teeth into a case, he doesn't let go until it's resolved. So it wasn't any wonder that on that day he was still at home recovering from the flu after working around the clock to bring to a conclusion the Goldstein, Samuelson swindle in which the owner of a once-booming Los Angeles-based commodity house pleaded guilty to fifteen counts of mail fraud.

That's why when *The Wall Street Journal* reporter Blundell

called the SEC to check out the Dirks yarn, he got Ralph H. Erickson, the SEC's regional counsel, instead. Erickson refused to comment on Equity Funding but told Blundell to call Stan Sporkin, the SEC's deputy director of enforcement in Washington.

Later that day, Boltz received a call at his sickbed from Sporkin that Blundell had heard reports of fraud at Equity Funding. Boltz got back to Erickson and the two discussed setting up a meeting with Blundell. Additionally, the SEC's New York office called the Los Angeles office to inform Boltz' staff of the fraud and phony insurance rumors that were sweeping Wall Street.

Meanwhile, Dirks made another contact at Equity Funding, this time with Donald Goff, who worked under Gootnick in the computer section. The two had lunch and Goff said there might be some truth to the phony insurance reports.

Dirks then called Michael Balint, a partner at Haskins & Sells, the company auditors before Seidman & Seidman took over in 1971, and discussed the story with his friend.

"Where are you staying?" asked Balint.

"The Beverly Wilshire."

"How many people know you are staying there?"

"Quite a few."

"Ray, if I were you I'd leave immediately and get a room in another hotel for your own personal safety."

Dirks thought to himself: "Here is a partner in one of the biggest accounting firms in the country telling me to move out for my own safety."

Dirks hurriedly left the Beverly Wilshire without officially checking out and checked into the nearby Beverly Rodeo Hotel under the name of his associate, Allen Gorrelick. In retrospect, Dirks did not show much imagination in choosing Gorrelick's name. Anyone intent on "getting" Dirks surely would have recognized the name of his associate.

SATURDAY

March 24

Dirks, a basketball nut, was watching the UCLA-Indiana game of the NCAA national basketball finals on TV when he got a call from Robert Spencer, a senior partner in the Seidman firm. He had wanted to talk to Seidman officials for some time.

Spencer told Dirks that his firm had decided to hold up their EFCA audit, scheduled to be completed within two days, and that they wanted to see Dirks' notes.

"I asked him for the notes so that we would know more about what we were doing," Spencer later recalled. Spencer then photocopied the by now more than fifty pages of hand-scribbled material and returned the originals to Dirks.

To his horror, Dirks was later to learn that Spencer turned the notes over to Goldblum the following Monday. Dirks claimed it was an overt breach of confidentiality. But Spencer claimed, "I had a fiduciary responsibility to my client."

That Saturday night, Dirks met with Balint, the Haskins & Sells partner, and disclosed his conversation with Majerus.

"Why, I've known Frank for years," Balint said. "I just talked to him a couple of weeks ago. You're telling me he knew about the fraud?"

"Yes. And he went to his minister about it, who concluded that he could do nothing about it but resign and get another job, which he did," Dirks said.

"But," replied Balint, "you're telling me that forty or fifty people knew about it. That I find impossible to believe. I can understand how a management can conspire to rig the books and fool the auditors, but I don't understand how all those people would fail to come to me and tell me about it."

Dirks agreed that, indeed, it did sound incredible.

SUNDAY

March 25

Blundell got his big break on the story. Majerus and Hopper accepted Blundell's invitation to drop over to his suburban La Canada home. Majerus said he couldn't stand it any longer and told Blundell everything he knew about the EFCA forgery operations. Hopper filled the reporter in on what he had seen from his vantage point at Bankers Life.

By Sunday, Raff, Enslen, and Sakaguchi had connected up their separate probes. They had finally concluded over lunch at a restaurant in a shopping center across from Equity Funding's Century City headquarters that there was something very wrong with their company.

Sakaguchi got hold of Al Green, the computer programmer who had left the company the preceding month, and said that he, Green, was in trouble stemming from their findings. The three then arranged to meet with Green in Westwood, not far from Century City.

Raff told Green he was facing legal problems and that Green's only recourse would be to tell all to Gleeson Payne, the California insurance commissioner. Green later did, but felt he was bluffed into the confession. Raff denied this and reflected that he was simply advising Green to do the proper thing based on the facts of the investigation.

On Sunday night, Stephanie Bland, a secretary in Loeb's office, was working late. As she pushed the elevator button to leave the twenty-eighth floor at 7:30 P.M., Jim Banks, Larry Collins, and two other men carrying electronics equipment stepped out from the elevator. The secretary knew that Banks and Collins had no business on the executive floor. But they told her they were "installing some stereo equipment."

"It doesn't look like stereo equipment," she thought to herself.

It was a correct assumption, as investigators were later to find out. With Banks and Collins were a couple of individuals who knew how to install sophisticated electronic bugs. They were to return in a few days to complete the installation.

And even later that Sunday night, Dirks treated himself to a bottle of champagne and congratulated himself for blowing the lid off what he felt was the biggest stock fraud in the nation's history.

MONDAY

March 26

Dirks received hair-raising news from Goff, the Equity Funding computer man. The notes Dirks gave to Spencer of the Seidman firm, said Goff, were turned over to Goldblum —names, contacts, and all.

"Holy Jesus Christ!" exclaimed Dirks in a state of panic.

He had heard rumors of Mafia connections with Equity Funding. He recalled the conversation he had had with Balint about moving out of the hotel room for his own personal safety.

Dirks dashed from the Beverly Rodeo, notes under his arm, and looked desperately for a taxi. It was Los Angeles, not Manhattan, and none was to be found.

Finally, Dirks ran into a nearby Bank of America building and into a phone booth.

First, Dirks called Hopper, who could provide little consolation.

The Wall Street Journal's Blundell was the next to hear from the frightened Dirks. Blundell admonished Dirks for turning his notes over to Spencer, and Dirks urged Blundell to print something quickly about the fraud.

Dirks then called Lawson of the *Journal*'s San Francisco office with the same story on the notes.

At 11:40 A.M., Erickson, of the SEC's Los Angeles office, got a call from Lawson, who said "the biggest insurance fraud in history" was brewing at Equity Funding. Erickson relayed this conversation to Sporkin in the SEC's Washington office. At that point, Sporkin decided to formally advise his bosses—the SEC commissioners—that there were big problems at Equity Funding Corporation of America.

At 6 P.M., the SEC's Boltz, Erickson, and Ogg met with Blundell in the *Journal*'s Wilshire District office. Blundell told everything he knew and was asked by the SEC officials to contact Majerus and Hopper and to convince them to go to the SEC with their information.

Blundell told Boltz that at least one of his informants was scared that he might lose his job. But Boltz insisted on talking to the contacts.

The intense Boltz, every inch the loyal SEC investigator, left the meeting with his antennae up high because, he told himself, nothing as wild as the story he had just heard could be made up.

That night Boltz received separate telephone calls from Hopper and Majerus. They said they would come in the next day to talk to the SEC.

Jerry Monkarsh encountered Art Lewis and Jim Banks about to catch an elevator in the Equity Funding building. Monkarsh, noting the rumors and the battered stock, asked them: "What the hell's going on around here?"

"I don't know, but I just got a margin call from my broker," replied Lewis. "I've got to go and make the margin call good."

"You shouldn't be playing games like that, Art," Monkarsh said in jest.

Kramer, the public relations man, noticed several executives scurrying about the twenty-eighth floor in a state of anxiety. There were closed-door meetings all over the place.

Gootnick, who hadn't been involved in the fraud, was called into a meeting with Smith, Edens, Banks, and Lewis. They told Gootnick it appeared things were ready to blow up and they needed his help to cover the tracks.

"Lewis and Edens asked me to destroy all the [computer] tapes that had any information pertaining to the policies," recalled the chief of Equity Funding's data-processing facility. "They asked me to mix up the numbers in such a way that no one could really identify what were the good policies and what were the bad policies."

Smith, remembered Gootnick, proposed writing some letters to real people unknowingly holding bogus policies, declaring they were selected as the lucky persons to participate in a special marketing plan of Equity Funding and would get a special price on a company policy—in case auditors double-checked on whether policies were actually held by the individuals named as policyholders in the company's records.

"It was a very hectic time and I was kind of swept up in the thing," Gootnick explained. "I indicated I would go along with their request."

Gootnick ordered that the computer tape index be jumbled, but couldn't go along with destroying certain tapes. He later found he couldn't go through with any of the plan and unscrambled the index.

Gootnick later analyzed why he even listened to the last-minute plan in the first place: "I was bothered for a long time because I never really felt that I was part of the management team. I had the title and had a nice office but I was never in on any real decision-making meetings. It bothered me a lot. I tried very hard to become part of the management clique. I guess I saw this [the cover-up] as just another opportunity to become a little closer to the clique."

Later that week Gootnick was to see Goldblum.

"How are things going?" asked Goldblum.

"Terrible," said Gootnick.

"What do you mean?"

"I don't like what's going on and I really don't want any part of it. I would really like to resign."

"Don't resign," urged Goldblum. "I understand what you're going through, but things are going to get better. It's all going to come out clean."

Loeb got a call from Ginny Sasse, Goldblum's secretary. Goldblum wanted to see Loeb at 2 P.M. so that they could meet with Seidman & Seidman, the current accountants for the life company, and Haskins & Sells, the former accountants. Both firms had requested that Loeb be at the meeting. Loeb had a feeling it was an important meeting and asked associate counsel Williams to accompany him.

At 2 P.M. Loeb and Williams walked into Goldblum's office. Goldblum was seated in front of his desk, and Bob Spencer, the senior Seidman partner, and three Seidman associates were gathered around him. Spencer related the meeting with Dirks the previous Saturday. Then, Spencer, on Goldblum's request, handed the chairman photocopies of the Dirks notes and the discussion turned to Dirks' allegations. At the same time, Goldblum buzzed his secretary and asked her to make him three or four copies.

Loeb proposed that a massive audit investigation be started on the basis of Dirks' charges.

Loeb later that day told *The Wall Street Journal* that he still could not substantiate any of the rumors. "If this expanded audit shows something, we would be the most surprised guys in the world," said Loeb.

Some in the room noticed that Goldblum subtly shifted gears and didn't seem to be the take-charge chairman he usually was—that he sat almost passively, listening to the allegations being reviewed.

The next audit team that paraded into Goldblum's office was led by Mike Balint, the senior partner in Haskins & Sells. Balint also described his weekend meetings with Dirks.

"Mike," asked Loeb, "you audited this insurance subsidiary for four years. Was there anything which Dirks said which rang a bell with your former experience so that you could say you thought there was something funny there?"

"No," replied Balint.

Loeb and Williams then called Milton Kroll, EFCA's Washington, D.C., counsel with the law firm of Freedman, Levy, Kroll & Simonds,* and told Kroll to go to the SEC the next day to explain what Dirks was saying about their company and to tell the SEC that Equity Funding had organized its own probe of the charges.

Late in the afternoon, Goldblum, Levin, Lowell, Lewis, Banks, Smith, Collins, and Edens met in Levin's office to review the Dirks notes.

That night one of the most bizarre tales of the entire Equity Funding saga was to surface. The story reflected the fact that the investigative net was drawing tighter around the small group within the company that had been merrily coasting along with the audacious conspiracy without fear of detection. But now major cracks were appearing in the scheme. People were talking. Investigators were uncovering shreds of evidence.

And, as a direct result, the conspirators were becoming desperate—driven to engaging in plots that sophisticated men of their intelligence wouldn't dream of considering under different circumstances. The criminal mind was taking gradual control of the corporate intellect.

Gardis Holmes, who for three years had been the twenty-eighth-floor cleaning woman, related the strange story for the writers of this book. The forty-year-old Miss Holmes recalled that she had noticed four men, whom she didn't recognize, working late that Monday night in both Goldblum's and Levin's offices. One of the men, apparently

---

*Kroll's firm had represented EFCA in Washington, primarily on SEC matters, since 1962.

not expecting the cleaning woman, gave Miss Holmes a strange look. Miss Holmes remembered hearing activity in both offices but couldn't see anything because the doors were kept shut.

Two men returned the next (Tuesday) night and Miss Holmes became scared. One of the men—"the short one"—was carrying a ladder and wore a tool-equipment belt. Upon seeing Miss Holmes, he exchanged greetings with her.

Miss Holmes pretended to work in the executive kitchen while the men worked next door in the executive conference room, again keeping the door closed. After a few minutes, she called the building security guard, who went into the board room but soon returned to tell the confused Miss Holmes that he didn't see anyone.

"They're in there," replied Miss Holmes, and so the guard and the cleaning woman decided to take a second look. They walked over to a ladder in the middle of the room. The security guard climbed the ladder and near the top looked into the open ceiling-paneling and saw the short man working.

"Hi, what are you doing?" asked the guard. The short man called his associate, who said he had an order from Goldblum to work there. The security guard accepted this and the men went on working.

Later that week, Gardis discovered two reel-to-reel tape recorders, one in Goldblum's washroom, behind the toilet, with a wire running to the washroom ceiling; and a second recorder under Levin's desk. She reported to Loeb what she had seen and heard—showing Loeb the tape machines.

Levin, in changing his plea to guilty, admitted before Federal Judge Curtis that he had approved a plan to place a tap on a telephone about the time the Illinois and California insurance examiners arrived at EFCA's headquarters. He told the judge "a group of defendant employees" had come to him as their immediate supervisor asking for approval of the wiretap plan.

Count 71 of the Federal Grand Jury indictment alleged

that the group Levin referred to consisted of Collins, a vice-president of the insurance subsidiary, and Banks, a lawyer for the life company. Additionally, federal investigators said that in the installation of the electronic surveillance equipment they sought the help of one Steven Michael Goodman, who said he was a private detective (but the FBI couldn't find a record of Goodman's license to practice) and Lorn Aiken, who worked in the electronics business.

"I was advised of the plan and I approved it," said Levin.*

Actually, the insurance examiners had been suspicious of why Equity Funding officials had practically insisted that they set up their examination command post on the twenty-eighth executive floor rather than on the sixth floor, where the insurance subsidiary was located. The EFLIC executives had argued that the examiners would have more space and better access to the company's officials on the top floor. In retrospect, it became evident the conspirators simply wanted to keep a closer eye on the insurance inspectors.

TUESDAY

March 27

Dirks, Majerus, Hopper, and Blundell filed into Boltz' SEC office. They were introduced by Blundell. Former comptroller Majerus was still nervous and his initial statement was taken off the record, but then on the record later. Dirks and Hopper also testified about reports of massive fraud at the company.

SEC investigator Boltz then called his agency's top investigators in Washington—Sporkin and Irv Pollack—and discussed whether they were witnessing "a bear raid" whereby certain individuals might want to shatter Equity Funding's stock and then buy into the company and make a

---

*Banks, in his subsequent guilty plea, also admitted participating in the electric surveillance scheme.

killing. It was decided that in any case, based on the Majerus and Hopper testimony in combination with the heavy selling of the stock, trading should be halted. Therefore, at 12:45 P.M., the New York Stock Exchange stopped trading in Equity Funding and the SEC moved to suspend trading the next day on all other exchanges.

Boltz called Equity Funding's compliance chief, Williams, and asked for affidavits from the company's principal executives denying the fraud rumors. Boltz' staff then sat down with the staff of the California Insurance Commission to sort out what was happening at Equity Funding.

Kramer, at the direction of Goldblum, issued another news release.

"Rumors have been circulating recently in the financial community regarding the accuracy . . . of life insurance sold and in force as reported in previous years. The company knows of no basis for such allegations."

The release noted that in response to the rumors, the company was conducting an expanded audit of the life company and had thus requested extra time in publishing its 1972 annual report.

The statement continued that EFCA would purchase "up to one million shares of its common stock in the open market to take advantage of the currently depressed price of the company's stock."

Goldblum called Kramer into his office and said that because of the expanded audit he wasn't sure when Kramer could give the green light to the printers to run off the annual report. Kramer noticed during the conversation that people were calling Goldblum to ask what was amiss. "In this world anything is possible," Goldblum replied to one caller.

Herb Glaser was concerned, and called a meeting of the executive planning committee for 2 P.M.

Glaser looked down the long conference-room table where

his colleagues had gathered for so many meetings over the years, and declared he had called the meeting because of the insurance rumors. Glaser said he wanted to get on the record from Goldblum, Levin, and Lowell whether there was any truth to the rumors.

"I know nothing about it," replied Lowell.

"The stories are bizarre," asserted Levin. "There's no credence, no believability, no truth whatsoever to these bizarre accusations."

But Goldblum was more philosophical in his answer. "I don't know, it could be true," he said. "It could not be true." Then he added: "I don't believe there's any truth to it."

Loeb told the gathering that the Seidman accounting firm was conducting an expanded probe on the basis of the rumors.

But Glaser said that wasn't enough and requested that the legal division, including Williams, make an independent probe.

Loeb then called Washington counsel Kroll and his associate, Peter E. Panarites, again and urged them to take a plane to Los Angeles on Wednesday to aid the legal department in the investigation. Goldblum didn't appear happy over the prospect of more investigators joining in the hunt (no one was quite sure what they were hunting for), but the Washington lawyers flew to Los Angeles anyway.

Williams, the former SEC investigator, was clearly shocked by the reports. Moreover, his shock was compounded by a conversation in Goldblum's office. The chairman had said: "Larry, anything could happen, I don't know . . . maybe it happened . . . I don't know anything about it."

Williams, working on the assumption that Goldblum wasn't involved, told his chairman that if the reports were true, those responsible in the insurance company would have to be kicked out even if it meant a top-to-bottom housecleaning.

"But Larry," said Goldblum, "who is going to run the insurance company?"

WEDNESDAY

March 28

The investigation by the Securities and Exchange Commission was in full swing atop the already started probes by the California and Illinois insurance agencies.

Williams complained to the SEC that its suspension of trading imposed on Equity Funding was unjustified and damaging to the company. Williams had been under the impression that such a decision wouldn't be made until the SEC met with Equity Funding officials, a meeting set for that Friday. Afterward, he concluded the SEC had found something suspicious.

It was also the day Williams formally opened the legal office's investigation that had been requested by Glaser. Perhaps it was a throwback to his bureaucratic days at the SEC, but in any case, Williams showed up that morning dressed in a dark suit reminiscent of his attire when he was a Washington bureaucrat. The "tough son-of-a-bitch" of the SEC had been revived, but this time Williams didn't have the leverage of subpoena power and he found that various EFCA management people he wanted to interview were putting him off with appointments and other excuses.

Williams couldn't find Banks, but finally located, questioned, and got denials of any wrongdoing from Smith and Lewis. Both emphasized to Williams that given their positions as chief administrator and chief actuary for the insurance subsidiary, they would *have* to know if there were problems.

What probably set Williams back on his heels more than anything was another conversation he had with Goldblum that day. Williams informed Goldblum that the SEC had requested that he—Goldblum—sign an affadavit disavowing any knowledge of fraud within his company.

But Goldblum replied that he had retained an attorney,

Frank Rothman, of the Los Angeles law firm of Wyman, Bautzer, Rothman and Kuchel, and didn't know whether Rothman would allow him to sign an affadavit.

Williams then urged Goldblum to go to the SEC and at least give a deposition to the same effect.

Goldblum said he wasn't sure he could do that, either.

"Why?" asked Williams.

Because, said Goldblum, people tended to arrive at hurried conclusions out of such testimony and while the allegations might have some truth to them, he—Goldblum —wasn't involved and he didn't want anyone to conclude otherwise.

Williams reminded the chairman that the SEC could subpoena him. Would Goldblum hide behind the Fifth Amendment?

No, answered the chairman, he would never do that.

Williams wanted to believe his boss. But his faith had been shaken.

Boltz called Williams and learned that Williams was having difficulty in getting affadavits from anyone; no one in the executive hierarchy wanted to talk to the SEC. Boltz also discovered that some of the executives were retaining their own counsel. What could have been a wild-goose chase had suddenly become a lot more serious.

THURSDAY

March 29

The SEC opened talks with First National City Bank, the lead bank in the $75-million revolving credit arrangement with Equity Funding, as the agency shifted gears and moved into an all-out probe of EFCA. The SEC wanted to learn as much as possible about Equity Funding's financial activities.

Levin talked to a sales meeting in Los Angeles, which

included some newly hired regional sales reps from New York, in addition to regional marketing vice-presidents. The new sales executives were bewildered by the chaos around them. As the meeting began on the twenty-eighth floor, Levin introduced Sy Miller and Marv Goldberg, the new salesmen, to the staff. Then Levin, just as coolly, suggested there could be some truth to the rumors that there was fraud in the company and abruptly left the meeting. Kramer, the public relations man who also was at the meeting, suddenly understood why everyone had been putting him off on printing the company's 1972 annual report.*

Later that day, Levin met Kramer in a corridor. "I'm finished, I'm wiped out," declared Levin.

It was 9:15 A.M. Washington counsel Kroll had arrived from the nation's capital and was sitting in Loeb's office. Loeb had located Goldblum in Levin's nearby office and asked the chairman if they could join him for a few minutes.

*The report, which was never published, contained a bright company outlook from Goldblum. Some excerpts:
"Over the past five years, the company has successfully evolved from a mutual funds-insurance sales organization to a major national corporation whose revenues and earnings are solidly based on life insurance marketing and operations. As a result of internal growth and acquisitions, we have become a major factor in the U.S. life insurance industry and we expect to further strengthen our position in the future. . . .
"We estimate that Equity Funding's life insurance subsidiaries, taken as a group, would now rank in the top one per cent of the [insurance] industry in terms of U.S. sales of individual insurance, and well within the top two per cent in terms of total sales, including group life insurance. . . .
"Our strongest asset remains our highly effective sales organization, whose technical and sales skills, dedication, and loyalty have made it possible for Equity Funding to be singled out by *Fortune* magazine in its May, 1972, 'Top 500' issue as the company with the highest 10-year earnings growth rate of the top 50 diversified financial companies in the U.S.
"During 1973 we expect to continue and extend our past record of achievement."

"You know," said Goldblum, almost casually, "I've hired a lawyer."

Loeb and Kroll replied that if their chairman had nothing to hide there was no reason to seek counsel.

Goldblum then said he had to return to his meeting with Levin.

At 11 A.M., Ginny Sasse, Goldblum's secretary, called Loeb and said he was meeting with Frank Rothman, the lawyer, and Rothman wanted to next meet with Loeb.

At 11:50, Goldblum buzzed Loeb and said Rothman was on his way to Loeb's office.

Less than five minutes later, Rothman, an old friend of Loeb's, walked into the office of Equity Funding's chief counsel, and Loeb asked him to sit in front of his desk next to the sixty-two-year-old Kroll.

"Rodney," said Rothman, "I've just spent two hours with Stanley and he's engaged me as his attorney. I've heard a story which is incredible and which has very frightening consequences."

Rothman added that he couldn't allow Goldblum to voluntarily testify under oath before the SEC, which had requested Goldblum's appearance the next day, Friday, or to sign any affidavits.

"Frank," replied Loeb, "if you don't let Stanley go down tomorrow morning and testify under oath in front of the SEC at eight thirty, when he's scheduled to appear, they'll just get a subpoena out at nine o'clock and he'll be testifying under subpoena at nine thirty. That's senseless."

"If they tell my client to testify under subpoena, I'll advise him to take the Fifth Amendment," Rothman said in a steady voice.

Loeb's office fell silent. If anyone cared to look, it was 12:02 P.M.

A *whoosh* of air escaped audibly from Loeb's mouth as he and Kroll exchanged glances. Kroll muttered something inaudible.

Loeb's mouth remained open and another minute of excruciating silence passed as the implication of Rothman's remark began to sink in. The hurtling events of the past few days began to take shape. A giant financial conglomerate in which so many talented individuals had staked their careers, charmed by the charisma of Goldblum and an empire that couldn't stop growing, was suddenly crumbling. Goldblum would take the Fifth. Could he know that something was seriously wrong? Loeb and Kroll were shaken by the ominousness of the situation.

"Do you know what that means?" Loeb asked Rothman.

"Yes."

"Look," declared Loeb, "if a man who is the president of a company takes the Fifth Amendment, the SEC will go in and get a receiver immediately and won't permit him to manage the company."

"I've explained this to my client," Rothman said.

(Rothman added that he also had advised Levin and Lowell to seek counsel, suggesting Joseph Ball, the well-known criminal lawyer.)

At that point, Goldblum, who had been absent during the Loeb-Rothman exchange, walked into Loeb's office. The chairman sat down on the couch in front of Loeb.

Neither Loeb nor Kroll knew quite what to say to Goldblum. Then Kroll swung around, and, facing Goldblum, said that Rothman had just informed them Goldblum did not intend to testify before the SEC and, if subpoenaed, would hide behind the Fifth Amendment.

"Look, Milton," said Goldblum to Kroll, "I've known you for ten years. If there's one thing I've learned in associating with you, it's to follow the advice of my counsel. I've hired Frank Rothman here as my counsel. I'll take his advice."

"Do you understand the serious consequences?" asked Loeb, edging forward in his chair and staring squarely at his boss. "Receivership is a real possibility."

"I realize it," replied Goldblum.

Loeb could go no farther. It was clear what he had to do.

With Goldblum at his elbow, Loeb buzzed his secretary and told her that he—Loeb—as secretary of the company, was calling a special meeting of the company's board of directors. She must contact all the directors—wherever they were—and determine how soon they could gather in Los Angeles. Of the firm's nine directors, four were in the Los Angeles headquarters. Five, however, were out-of-town directors. Loeb therefore instructed her to begin with the outside directors by contacting those farthest East, and to begin with Professor Robert R. Bowie of Harvard.

Goldblum, strangely enough, was not challenging Loeb's move.

Loeb's intercom buzzed back in a few minutes. Bowie had been located. He was in Brussels, Belgium, to give a lecture. Loeb told his secretary to get to Bowie immediately as he began to establish in his mind a possible board meeting for Saturday, March 31.

Three minutes later, Bowie was on the line from Brussels.

Loeb rose to take the Bowie call in his outer office. Goldblum was still sitting on the couch smoking his usual Winstons.

The second call was to Judson Sayre in Chicago. Again, Loeb excused himself and went to the outer office to explain the situation to Sayre.

As Loeb got off the phone, Herb Glaser appeared in the outer office of the legal department. Loeb walked over and gently took Glaser by the arm the way a man would escort a woman. Loeb was well aware that Glaser had been a business sidekick of Goldblum's for a decade and was about to receive a severe emotional shock.

"Can you step into my office for a minute, Herb?"

"Sure."

As Glaser entered, he saw Rothman, whom he, too, had known for years.

"Hi, Frank. What are you doing here?" asked Glaser.

"I'm representing Stanley," said Rothman softly.

With Goldblum still sitting on the couch, Loeb and Kroll

filled Glaser in on the events that had occurred only minutes earlier.

Then Rothman said he felt he had to repeat to Glaser that he had advised Goldblum not to talk about the fraud rumors or give an affidavit to the SEC.

Goldblum got up, walked over to the bookcase behind the couch, and leaned almost casually against it, watching Glaser's reaction.

Glaser was clearly stunned. It was one of the big shocks of his life and he couldn't immediately respond.

"Why can't you make an affidavit?" Glaser finally asked, glaring at Goldblum. "I can make an affidavit."

"I can make an affidavit that you can make an affidavit," replied Goldblum, to make his point that he—Goldblum—well knew that Glaser knew nothing about the scope of the charges.

A torrent of words to the effect that the situation was terrible came from Glaser. Goldblum, asserted Glaser, would hurt thousands of Equity Funding investors by remaining silent. The stock would plummet. Shareholders and employees alike would be ruined, warned Glaser, because Goldblum by his silence was implying that the charges were true.

"You've always told me to follow my lawyer's advice and that's what I'm doing," said Goldblum. Before Glaser could respond, Goldblum added:

"You must think I'm a prick."

"Yes," responded the usually sophisticated Glaser, "you are a prick."

Glaser, himself a well-structured six-footer, was standing but a few feet from the powerfully built Goldblum, and the heated exchange triggered apprehension lest words should turn into something worse.

Loeb, Kroll, and Rothman remained frozen in their chairs.

"Herb," said Goldblum, "you have the right to call me anything you want or think anything you want to. It doesn't hurt me at all."

Loeb's intercom buzzer broke the tension. It was his secretary with his call to Nelson Loud. Again, Loeb went into the outer office to talk to Loud, the third outside director, who was in New York, and who, as a founder of New York Securities, had a hand in Equity going public in 1964. As he was talking to Loud, Loeb saw Goldblum leave his office, followed by Glaser.

Kroll, fearing he didn't know what, followed the two.

It was indeed a macabre scene being played out. The world was tumbling down rapidly on Equity Funding and there was little time for perspective and appraisal of words and actions. So Kroll followed Glaser, who was following Goldblum.

Goldblum disappeared into his office at the other end of the twenty-eighth floor and Glaser went inside, too. Kroll looked on from an outer office.

Goldblum folded his massive frame into the chair behind his equally massive desk. Glaser completely lost his cool and exploded.

"How could you do such a thing?" yelled Glaser, bending over and slamming his right fist on Goldblum's desk. "I have to believe you're guilty."

Goldblum said that some day Glaser would believe in his innocence but that for the moment he just couldn't talk about the case. Those looking in on the scene could see tears welling up in Goldblum's eyes as he confronted one of his closest business associates.

"There are too many public investors, there's too much at stake," declared Glaser. "Why don't you talk about it?"

"You should be glad you don't know anything about it," said Goldblum, looking straight up into Glaser's eyes.

Goldblum's secretary brought lunch to his desk. The tears were still in his eyes.

Glaser left Goldblum to his lunch. As far as Glaser was concerned, his business and personal relationship with Goldblum was finished. But a little of Glaser also was smeared and destroyed. Any higher professional or, indeed, political ambitions he might have harbored were damaged until the company's name could be cleared. As Glaser abruptly left, he knew that Goldblum would have to be deposed.

Later that day, Arkus-Duntov, in New York, reached Glaser to ask again what was happening. Glaser related some of the details of his shoot-out with Goldblum. "I felt like jumping out of the window," Arkus-Duntov later was to recall.

At about 4:30 P.M., Lowell wandered into Loeb's office and sat on the same couch where only a few hours before Goldblum had held court.

"I heard Fred Levin tell a story today in a lawyer's office and I just couldn't believe it," Lowell said. "You know, I'm going to be tarred with the same brush as those other guys. What do you advise me to do?"

"Sam," said Loeb, "if you're not involved in whatever took place I advise you to do two things: Get separate counsel and don't volunteer anything to me because as far as I'm concerned I'm representing the company and anything you tell me I'm going to tell the authorities."

Lowell defended himself, declaring that like accountants in other aggressive business situations, he had "played games with numbers" but that he knew nothing about the allegations involving phony insurance on the books of the life company. Lowell then left.

EFLIC counsel Bill Raff had pieced together some of the puzzle in concert with his two colleagues, Sakaguchi and Enslen. That afternoon they had done a computer check of some life policies and several phonies had turned up. Raff decided to turn ten random computer pages of policies over to the Seidman accounting firm.

At 4:30 P.M. Raff called Loeb to set up a meeting with EFCA officials so that Sakaguchi and Enslen could explain what they had found. Kroll said it wouldn't be proper for Loeb and himself to sit in on the meeting and that instead a session with the Seidman firm should take place at Kroll's room at the Hilton.

At 6:30 P.M., Raff, Enslen, and Sakaguchi appeared at Kroll's hotel room, where Loeb and two members of the Seidman staff were waiting.

After Loeb left, the three provided the Seidman staff with bits and pieces of information about the fraud. The group ended up taking a ride over to 341 Maple Drive in West Los Angeles in the predawn hours to take a look at the office where the phony policies were being manufactured.

Loeb, meanwhile, advised Glaser and Kroll of the information he had on the tape-recording equipment that Gardis Holmes, the cleaning lady, had discovered. Glaser, in turn, called Goldblum, who declared that Loeb was "full of crap." Goldblum invited Glaser to go back to the office with him that night to check out the story, but Glaser declined.

The United States Attorney's office and the Federal Bureau of Investigation were later to report that the bugging equipment had been hurriedly pulled out of the twenty-eighth-floor office where the Illinois insurance examiners had been working, but that wires and microphones had been left in the walls. A sloppy undercover job, indeed.

FRIDAY

March 30

Loeb decided to retain the Los Angeles law firm of Buchalter, ·Nemer, Fields and Savitch following a breakfast meeting at Glaser's house (attended by Loeb, Williams, and Kroll). The company had reached a point where it definitely needed hard-nosed corporate counsel to represent it.

Meanwhile, the SEC began looking into whether Goldblum and other Equity Funding insiders were selling off their stock, and an attempt to freeze funds and securities was begun. Goldblum was thought to be working through the New York brokerage house of Dishy, Easton & Company, his longtime Wall Street contact.

It was learned by the SEC that on March 26, Goldblum had filed a sell order with Dishy, Easton to sell 50,000 shares of Equity Funding stock with a market value of about $900,000, the day before the New York Stock Exchange halted trading at $14.37½ per share. The transaction never went through.

Goldblum later said that he was motivated by the fact that "I was more than one million in debt and I felt I had to sell some stock for personal and financial reasons . . . the rumors didn't bother me . . . there was no hanky-panky in the stock sale. . . ." In any case, said Goldblum, his accountant had set up a tax program for him that involved selling stock four times a year—and that was the time to sell.

As the SEC was to later find out, Goldblum had been an active seller of Equity Funding stock in recent years.

Other Equity Funding officers also were selling toward the end.

Lowell unloaded 4,000 shares on March 26, 1973, for around $65,000.

Arkus-Duntov peeled off 1,000 shares on March 21. Duntov's bank tried to unload 44,245 shares on March 26, but a broker in the transaction sued and the sale was frozen in litigation.

And on March 26, Michael Sultan, the corporate comptroller who reported to Lowell, almost eliminated his holdings by selling 2,200 shares.

For three years, Gleeson Payne served as the president of the Founders Life Insurance Company, next door to Equity Funding. Founders, in 1970, was rated as the second-fastest-growing insurance company in the United States, just ahead of Equity Funding Life—but EFLIC was making a lot more money than Founders. Payne's staff therefore made a conscious effort to get to know the EFLIC people to figure out how they turned a tidy profit. Finally, recalled Payne, "we determined that they were just brighter business people than we were."

On November 1, 1972, the fifty-four-year-old Payne was appointed by Governor Ronald Reagan to be California insurance commissioner. On Friday, March 30, 1973, Payne, only a few months on the job, faced one of the toughest decisions of his life: whether there was enough evidence to use the commissioner's rarely used powers to seize an insurance company facing a financial crisis.

Payne and his number-one assistant, Larry Baker, thirty-seven, felt they were taking a calculated risk in triggering the seizure action.

In the first place, like the SEC, they didn't know if there was a plot afoot to drive the price of Equity Funding's stock down in preparation for a quick takeover. Secondly, no one had yet conclusively proven that there was large-scale manufacturing of phony life insurance policies going on. Thirdly, seizing the company—rightly or wrongly—could have a devastating impact on the confidence of both the company's policyholders and its shareholders.

If Payne and Baker were wrong, there would be another obvious consequence of which both also were aware: In all probability it would cost them their jobs.

"I would say that on the whole we approached this decision to seize the company with some trepidation and I would say that we didn't have a hundred-percent case that we could make in court," said Baker. "It was a calculated risk."

Declared Payne: "I simply said to myself I would rather be at fault being aggressive than being fearful and timid."

Motivating the seizure decision were the following events:

There was the discovery that week that the $25 million in corporate bonds counted as EFLIC assets were not in a Chicago bank as the company had originally declared.

Christy Armstrong, the California chief insurance examiner, had learned that computer tapes were being erased that week and instructed California and Illinois examiners on the Equity Funding premises to try to stop it.

And perhaps most importantly, Equity Funding Life had

$5.5 million in bearer certificates of deposit in what the commission considered a loose custodial account at the Century City branch of the Wells Fargo Bank (actually, the CD's were in a safety deposit box at the bank and put into the custodial account only a few days before the seizure). The CD's could easily be cashed, prompting Payne to reflect "that was the real thing that gave me the chills" for that was the difference in paying or not paying insurance claims.

The commission had solid information of recent activity in the Wells Fargo account. That Wednesday, March 28, Levin and Smith, the top executive of the Life company, had opened the safe deposit box and removed the CD's (which EFLIC never listed as assets). On March 30 Levin returned the CD's to the bank.

Assistant Insurance Commissioner Baker first called Douglas Luna, the manager of the Century City branch of Wells Fargo, and ordered him not to let anything out of the Equity Funding accounts. But Luna told Baker that he didn't think he could cooperate simply on the basis of a telephone call. This disturbed the tough-minded Baker, who then replied: "If you let anything go I'll come out and hang you up by your thumbs."

Luna then called the Wells Fargo counsel in San Francisco, who conceded that the commission did have the authority to freeze the accounts.

Later that day, Baker and a deputy went to EFLIC and served everyone in sight with seizure orders. They left little doubt as to who was in charge, asking personnel to leave, changing locks on the office doors, and posting security guards.

Baker notified the Illinois Insurance Department of the seizure and noted that he and Payne would be on the premises the next day, Saturday, to assess the situation.

By this time, Glaser and Loeb were manning the ship, running around attempting to keep the company from crumbling, fending off hundreds of Wall Street and shareholder calls, and making stabs at maintaining some order out of the ensuing pandemonium.

Loeb had said he would meet Glaser at a Century City restaurant Friday afternoon so they could bring each other up to date on the fast-breaking events. As Loeb walked toward the restaurant, he met Levin.

"I hope you don't hate me, Rodney," declared Levin.

"Freddie," replied Loeb, "I don't hate you. This is not a time to express hate. What you need is sympathy and understanding."

"Well," said Levin, "I've been a naughty boy. I've done some bad things, but I've told Jerry Brewer [of Citibank] and Harold Richards [the largest single stockholder from Fidelity Corporation of Richmond, Virginia] about it. Please don't think ill of me."

"Freddie, you and I have been close friends for a long time and I have no hard feelings against you."

As Loeb and Glaser talked over lunch at the nearby Hamburger Hamlet, Bill Gootnick, the head of the company's computer operations, came to their table.

"Should I hire a lawyer?" Gootnick asked Loeb.

"I don't know whether you should hire a lawyer or not," replied Loeb. "It depends on whether you have anything to hide."

Sometime Friday afternoon, the diminutive Williams looked up from his desk to find the 6-foot-2-inch Goldblum hovering over him. Goldblum wanted to see the notes Williams had taken during the course of his investigation.

It was an interesting situation for two reasons: Williams had a nerve problem which made his handwriting almost unreadable; and, secondly, since few had cooperated with Williams, there was little to report. Goldblum went away empty-handed.

On Friday night, following a seventeen-hour journey from Brussels, the sixty-three-year-old Professor Bowie of Harvard, one of the outside directors, arrived in Los Angeles and, accompanied by Loeb, went to the home of attorney Stuart Buchalter, whose firm was now helping Equity Funding attempt to piece together a story which was growing more strange by the moment. Loeb told Bowie and Buchalter all that he knew to that moment. They parted about 2 A.M. after setting up a meeting for 1 P.M. Saturday.

Jim Steen, one of the Illinois insurance investigators, called Bill Blundell at home to tell the *Jounal* reporter that the $25 million in bonds claimed by Equity Funding on its books wasn't in Illinois. "That rips it," said Blundell, who then grabbed a sleeping bag and decided to spend the weekend in his office in order to write the story of his life.

William Good, the executive vice-president for marketing at Bankers National Life, and Michael Capurso, the manager of EFLIC's New York office, were in Los Angeles for a staff meeting. Levin had ducked questions earlier that day about the fraud rumors, and Good and Capurso had been attempting to analyze the situation over dinner at the Yamada Steak House in the Century Plaza Hotel.
After dinner, while walking through the lobby, they bumped into Levin and Harold Richards, the head of Fidelity of Richmond.
"Look at this son-of-a-bitch," said Richards to the startled Good and Capurso. "It's a big joke to him. He just fucked me out of twenty-three million."
Levin left. Richards then recounted what Levin had told him about the phony insurance on the books of EFLIC. Good and Capurso were thunderstruck.

SATURDAY

March 31

Larry Baker is the kind of person you show your identification to without waiting for him to ask. The slim, almost slightly built California assistant insurance commissioner is every inch the investigator. He exudes authority and integrity and falls into the perfect mold of a government untouchable. Baker's handsome features belie a toughness that tells you at once that you had better be telling him the truth. A University of Michigan graduate, Baker came to the commission from The Travelers Insurance Company of Hartford. His dedication to breaking the Equity Funding case, which became practically an around-the-clock obsession during the last week of March, played a key part in wrapping it up.

Baker, who had worked until 2 o'clock that morning, showed up at the Equity Funding headquarters at 6 A.M. He had calls to make and last-minute details to attend to—and a meeting with his boss, Commissioner Payne, at 9 A.M.

As 9 A.M. approached, Baker took the elevator to the subterranean parking garage to meet Payne. Apparently, the two crossed elevator paths and Baker couldn't find Payne when he got to the parking area. Just then, a Bentley pulled beside Baker's 1966 Mustang and out stepped Fred Levin and (Baker was later to learn) an attorney friend. Baker hadn't met Levin before, but he noticed that the Bentley pulled into a space marked F. LEVIN.

Baker introduced himself.

"Are you aware that we've seized the company?" asked Baker.

"I am," said Levin.

Baker invited Levin to see a copy of the seizure order on the twenty-eighth floor.

Payne had parked in the garage of his old insurance company. He thought as he walked to the 1900 Avenue of the Stars building about how Founders had once been puzzled over the way Equity Funding could make piles of money in those go-go years of the late 1960's. Gazing back at his former ground-floor office in the 1800 building, Payne thought: "Maybe we weren't so dumb after all."

Payne had been up all night conferring with Illinois

Insurance Comissioner Fred Mauck and other officials on the seizure action. The decision still weighed heavily on his weary mind.

Payne went up to the twenty-eighth floor, where the California and Illinois insurance inspectors had the command post. He started trying all of the executive office doors to see if anyone was left aboard.

One door was open. A single glance told Payne he was entering the office of Stanley Goldblum. The splendid—almost regal—office could belong to no one else. Goldblum, on the phone, motioned Payne into the room. Neither knew the other and they stared at each other for a moment.

Goldblum: tall, muscular, 200 pounds. Payne: 6-feet 4-inches, a not-so-muscular 210 pounds.

"May I help you?" said Goldblum.

"Yes, I'm looking for the Insurance Department."

"Are you with the Insurance Department?" asked Goldblum.

"I am the insurance commissioner. What's your position?"

"I am Stanley Goldblum, chairman of the board," said Goldblum, walking out from behind his desk.

"Did you get our seizure notice?" Payne asked.

"I did and I would like to tell you what a horrible mistake you've made." Goldblum proceeded to point out that in his opinion the order was substantially damaging the company.

Payne said he wasn't there to discuss the merits of the decision, but simply to find his colleague, Baker. Goldblum then took Payne into the corridor and directed him to where the insurance investigators had been working.

At that point, Levin and Baker arrived. Baker said they should all go to the insurance command post and he would give Goldblum and Levin copies of the seizure order. At that point Goldblum became verbally aggressive.

"Well, now that you have this company," said Goldblum, "I would like to ask a favor. I would like to ask you to give my men permission to sell insurance. You know the value of an insurance sales force. If they can't sell insurance the sales organization will be destroyed. I'm sure you would not take the food from the mouths of these men's children."

Goldblum was quickly cut off by Baker. From memory, he read Goldblum and Levin their rights under the Fifth Amendment. Baker asked if both understood. In subdued voices they both replied, "Yes."

Baker then asked the whereabouts of the company's assets. Before they could answer, Levin's attorney friend stepped forward and said that both should talk to a lawyer and that they couldn't answer that question.

Baker contended that he had the right to ask the whereabouts of the assets. "Are you refusing to answer this question at this time?" asked Baker. Both men said yes, but that they would be back shortly after talking to their attorneys.

It was at that point that Payne and Baker uttered a mental sign of relief—for the first time they were convinced they were on firm ground regarding the seizure. The failure of the company's top officers to reveal the location of the assets, Payne and Baker knew, constituted all the legal grounds they needed to seize the company.

Goldblum and Levin didn't bother to return to the twenty-eighth floor that day.

At 1 P.M., Loeb, Williams, former insurance commissioner Barger (called in as an adviser), Arkus-Duntov, Bowie, the SEC's Boltz, and three staffers from Seidman and Seidman met in the Nemer law firm's tenth-floor office at the 1900 Avenue of the Stars building to review the situation. The meeting lasted until 9:15 P.M. The pieces of a massive fraud began to fit into place.

The story was told by the Seidman firm of the Maple Drive office, where the phony policies were manufactured; of how the auditors were fooled; and of millions of dollars in phony assets—no one dreamed how much—that were on the books, stemming from the fictitious loan programs.

Boltz demanded that Goldblum, Levin, Lowell, and others

be forced to resign. He said their dismissals should be made known in no uncertain terms the next day at the directors' meeting. Boltz also disclosed that the company's distorted financial picture went back much farther than the start of the phony insurance scheme in 1969 or 1970. Boltz had talked to former Equity Funding comptroller Majerus and former Bankers Life vice-president Hopper and had heard quite enough about the financial sleight of hand. It was time, he had decided, to take a get-tough stance.

It was late Saturday night. *Journal* reporter Blundell had begun typing his Equity Funding story for the Monday edition. As he finished the lead page, the telephone rang. It was his wife.

"You'll never forgive me," she cried into the telephone, "but I've burned down the kitchen."

"Are you all right?" asked Blundell.

"Yes."

"Did the firemen come?"

"No, but it's out."

"Don't worry about it."

A grease fire on the stove was to cost the Blundells $900 in damage to their La Canada home. But at that point in time nothing short of a catastrophe would have stopped Bill from completing the story. He hung up and continued typing.

SUNDAY

April 1

At 9 A.M., Blundell had his story ready but decided he would make one last attempt to contact Goldblum. The maid answered and said her employer was taking a nap.

Blundell tried again at 10 A.M.

"Mr. Goldblum?"

"Yes."

"This is Bill Blundell of *The Wall Street Journal*. Ordinarily, I'd give you more time to reply to this but considering the events of the last week—"

"What events?" broke in Goldblum.

"Well," replied the still calm Blundell, "they [the California Insurance Department] came and took your company." Blundell then queried Goldblum about the phony policy allegations.

Goldblum said he couldn't comment.

That was enough, Blundell thought. They'd had their chance to comment. He forwarded his story to the *Journal*'s editorial desk in New York. Blundell, who hadn't been to bed for sixty hours, staggered into his car to drive home. He had to stop two or three times during the forty-five-minute trip to stay awake.

XIV
The Banker and Mr. Levin

MIKE Riordan and H. C. "Jerry" Brewer, Jr., grew up as schoolboy chums in New Rochelle, New York, less than an hour's commuting time from Manhattan. Riordan went on to Cornell and later became a leading Wall Street securities wholesaler, finally heading the Equity Funding organization. The athletic-looking Brewer went to Harvard, and after a three-year stint in the Army, joined First National City Bank, where he was to cap a twenty-seven-year career by taking over the bank's insurance accounts outside of New York City and, in particular, the loan agreement with Equity Funding.

In March, 1973, the legacy of Riordan—Equity Funding Corporation of America—was to all but destroy the career of Brewer in an embarrassing sequence of events involving the old master of the hard sell, Fred Levin.

Brewer's first contact with Equity Funding actually came after Riordan's death, in 1970, when Brewer was invited to a lunch at the company's Los Angeles headquarters. By June, 1972, he had become the chief account man on a $75-million line of credit to Equity Funding in which Citibank led a consortium of underwriters. The other banks were Wells Fargo, National Bank of North America, and Franklin National Bank. Approximately $35 million had been taken down from the agreement by Equity Funding to acquire the Northern Life Insurance Company of Seattle. Equity

Funding pledged 100 percent of the stock of Northern, 100 percent of Bankers National Life of New Jersey, and 60 percent of Equity Funding Life to the bank as collateral—the stock certificates held in Citibank's New York vault. Another $15 million was subsequently borrowed by Equity Funding, making the loan outstanding approximately $50 million.

Through frequent telephone conversations and visits when Levin was in New York, Brewer and Levin had become good business acquaintances and social friends when a chain of events which Brewer will never forget began to break in the last few weeks of March.

Our tale actually begins on March 22, when Jack Doyle, the Illinois insurance examiner, suddenly appeared at Equity Funding's Century City office and demanded to see the $25 million in bonds Equity Funding Life claimed was being held in a Chicago bank. Before Doyle could call the company's bluff, Lloyd Edens declared that the $25 million had been used up in three different transactions, the bulk of which—$15.7 million—was paid to EFLIC's parent, EFCA, in exchange for 80 percent of Northern. The Northern certificate was in a safety deposit box at the Century City branch of the Wells Fargo Bank, said Edens.

Doyle checked and, sure enough, the 80 percent of Northern was indeed at Wells Fargo. What Doyle didn't know was that the certificate had only just been prepared and then backdated to the original Northern transaction of February, 1973. The reason Levin had to have the new 80 percent certificate created was that the real certificate—all 100 percent of it—was still in the Citibank New York vault, as the original collateral for the $35 million loaned to Equity Funding by the consortium to purchase Northern.

Jerry Brewer's woes really began at that point.

Levin told Brewer that EFCA had been advised by its tax staff that if it was able to consolidate its accounts with Northern it could save $700,000 in federal taxes. "That's very interesting," replied Brewer.

Levin then jumped on a plane and arrived in Brewer's

office at Citibank on Friday, March 23. Levin explained that he would need 80 percent of Northern Life's stock to effect the tax saving for EFCA and if Brewer would hand over the 100 percent certificate that was being held for loan collateral, he would in turn give Brewer a certificate representing 20 percent of Northern.

Although Brewer had discussed the curious transaction with his colleagues, he recalled in an interview: "I made the decision myself."

"It was no great sacrifice," said Brewer, emphasizing that Citibank would still have 60 percent of the stock of EFLIC, plus 20 percent of Northern.

Looking back on the deal, the ruddy-faced Brewer said, "I was just faked right out of my socks."

Brewer also believed that Levin may have been softening him up for the kill by calling him a few times in February with the news that the company's new tax man believed a great tax saving could be effected if there was a consolidation of EFCA and Northern assets. (What Levin failed to tell Brewer was that there was a serious question as to whether the consolidation could go through with the Northern stock sitting in Citibank's vault.)

"I thought this guy and everything about him was legitimate," declared Brewer, in explaining why he did what a banker is never supposed to do: return collateral on a loan outstanding. Brewer even had Levin and his wife, Carol, over to his Wilton, Connecticut, home the night after the Citibank vice-president handed over the Northern stock.

Brewer had almost forgotten about returning the collateral to Levin when Thursday, March 29, came around.

It was midafternoon as Brewer looked out of his office, daydreaming about the hunting trip he would soon take in the Adirondacks. The telephone brought him back to his senses. On the other end was L. E. Holloway, vice-president of Wells Fargo Bank.

"He told me of a horrible rumor that he had heard from a source," said Brewer. "The rumor indicated a massive, monstrous, unbelievable fraud at Equity Funding Life, which was big enough to spill over and bankrupt the parent company."

"At this point I fainted," he said. "That's an exaggeration, of course. But I did feel as if I had been stripped naked."

Brewer, after a brief strategy session with colleagues, was determined to get the Northern stock certificate back at any cost. Here is Brewer's description of the scenario:

"I called Levin and his secretary said, 'He's out of the office.' I said I must talk to him immediately. She said, 'I'll get in touch with him and have him call you back.' "

Within minutes Brewer got a call from Levin.

"Fred, I've got to have that stock certificate back."

"I'm out of the office," replied Levin. "I can't get it now."

"Get the hell back to the office and get it right now and put it in the mail to me."

Levin said he would see if he could get someone to do it.

"No," declared Brewer, "you do it. I don't want anyone else to do it."

Brewer hung up. He then had second thoughts about Levin mailing the collateral. It would be safer to have a banker—in this case someone from Wells Fargo, a member of the loan consortium—pick up the certificate.

He called Levin about the new arrangement, but Levin said he couldn't be back at his office to hand over the certificate and that Jim Smith would have to do it.

Brewer tracked down Smith in Goldblum's office.

The last time he'd seen the certificate was in the hands of an EFLIC lawyer, said Smith.

"I don't care who the hell's got it, get it!" answered the now flustered Brewer. "No shilly-shallying."

Brewer huddled with Citibank officials to review EFCA's figures and to determine if the fraud reports could have any validity.

That evening, Brewer had a dinner he'll never forget. Among those attending the gathering at Jimmy Weston's, a midtown Manhattan restaurant, was Harold Richards, president of Fidelity Corporation of Richmond, Virginia, the insurance and savings and loan holding company, which, with $23 million invested in EFCA, was it's largest stockholder.

Richards also had been trying to get in touch with Levin on March 29 because he had heard the same rumors. He had left a message with Levin's office that he would be at Weston's after 7 P.M.

In the middle of dinner, the waiter told Richards that Levin was returning his call. Brewer remembered that everyone stopped eating. Trading in Equity Funding stock already had been stopped by the New York Stock Exchange and the Securities and Exchange Commission the day before and the fraud reports were getting louder.

"It was eight thirty, nine o'clock," recalled Brewer. "Richards was away from the table for about three or four minutes. He came back from the phone and repeated the essence of his conversation. He said that Levin acknowledged that it [the fraud allegations] was true. There were four of us at dinner. I think we were all in a state of shock. Harold Richards had been fooled by this guy the same way that I had.

"Harold said Fred asked to speak to me. But Harold said, 'No, I'll have him call you later.' I guess Harold wanted to spare me going splat on the floor of the restaurant."

At about 10 P.M. Brewer went back to the bank and called Levin, using the Los Angeles number Fred had given to Richards.

"I talked to Fred Levin for about three or four minutes," said Brewer. "He knew I had been with Harold Richards. My first question to him was: 'Fred, why did you do it?'"

Brewer was mentally knocked out by the answer:

"Jollies," was Levin's reply. Brewer later said he took this as meaning something like "for kicks."

Admitting that he still had no idea of what kind of fraud had actually taken place, Brewer asked Levin, "How long has it been going on?"

"It was going on when I got here," answered Levin. "I fine-tuned it. It was brilliant."

"Freddie, what is it? Tell me about it. What happened?" implored Brewer.

"The phones aren't entirely reliable," answered Levin. "When I see you I'll tell you about it."

Brewer was still in the dark.

"In the meantime I had gotten a call back from the Wells Fargo banker on the West Coast. He had picked up the certificate supposedly representing the hundred percent of Northern Life and he said he was dispatching it immediately," said Brewer.

Brewer stayed up most of the night at the bank continuing to go over all of the Equity Funding material available to him, and then caught an hour's sleep at Harold Richards' New York City apartment.

He got back to the bank at seven the next morning and, after consultation with lawyers and colleagues, it was decided that a delegation from Citibank would go to Washington to tell the Securities and Exchange Commission what they knew.

After all, it seemed as if Brewer had what appeared to be the first real admission that frauds had taken place at Equity Funding, and he apparently had it from one of the key participants.

The SEC meeting took place late in the afternoon of Friday, March 30.

Brewer said he told Stanley Sporkin, associate director of the SEC's enforcement department, that he wanted to go to the West Coast the following day to protect the bank's position, but sought SEC permission.

"They assured us that it would be perfectly OK if we went out there," said Brewer, "because, after all, we weren't representing the SEC."

Brewer went home to Connecticut, getting to bed about 11 P.M. It had been a tough couple of days and there was more to come.

Upon arriving Saturday afternoon at the Century Plaza Hotel, a short walk from EFCA's headquarters, who was the first person Brewer ran into? Why, Levin of course. Levin, who was there with Richards, put his arm around Brewer's shoulders and walked away from Richards with his Citibank friend. Richards had arrived the preceding night and had already had a hair-raising session with Fred. Levin had confirmed the phony reinsurance scheme.

"I'm really sorry that this whole thing happened," Levin told Brewer. "I don't want to see you hurt by it."

Brewer recalled he was still in a state of shock.

That afternoon, Richards, Brewer, and a bank associate of Brewer's went to Goldblum's house in Beverly Hills. Brewer observed that the usually robust Goldblum looked ashen, "like he had lost twenty pounds."

Goldblum was largely evasive on questions of whether insurance fraud existed at his company. The EFCA chairman prefaced his answers with phrases like, "If anything like this does exist. . . ."

After about twenty minutes, Brewer recounts, he realized the visit was just a waste of time. As the group was getting ready to leave, someone commented that Goldblum's house was lovely.

"Yeah, it will make someone a nice home," Goldblum quipped. Goldblum added he was strapped for funds and didn't have enough money even to pay his lawyer.

The group left.

That night Levin sat down with Richards and Brewer in the Citibanker's hotel room and—mainly for Brewer's benefit—fully explained the phony insurance scheme. Levin didn't mention Equity Funding's shareholders, but said that some of the reinsurers might be hurt.

"Levin, as far as I know, was completely candid," recalled Brewer.

"Gee," declared Levin toward the end of the two-hour session, "you look awful." He then slapped Brewer's knee and said, "I haven't felt this good in years."

The confused Brewer escorted Levin to the elevator. Brewer remembered thinking that "even though this guy has damn near ruined me, I am more disappointed than angry at Levin."

Levin again put his arm around Brewer. "Well, I hope that buys back ten percent of our friendship," said Levin, disappearing behind the closing elevator door.

That was the last time Brewer saw Levin.

Brewer was later to learn that Levin had prepared yet another 100 percent Northern stock certificate on Friday, March 31, apparently to try to expedite the return of the certificate (the first one hadn't been signed correctly anyway) to Citibank. That made 300 percent worth of Northern certificates outstanding! In all the confusion and double-dealing, Citibank held 220 percent and EFLIC had 80 percent of Northern. Whether the real stock certificates could be sorted out was another problem.

Reflecting on the chain of events which led up to the release of the Northern Life collateral, Brewer said in the interview:

"I felt that I had had a relationship with Fred Levin that I thought was a close one of mutual trust, sharing of ideas, of various business attitudes . . . basically, it was a most unusual relationship because Levin and I as two people are as different as black and white . . . I feel sick about it now. . . ."

Citibank subsequently transferred Brewer into a new marketing job where he retained his rank as vice-president.

Larry Baker, the chief deputy to the California insurance commissioner, later commented that Citibank's action in returning the collateral "shows a very friendly relationship with the principal perpetrators of this fraud." Baker said it was a "cock-and-bull story" that Citibank simply returned the collateral because of fraudulent misrepresentations on the part of Equity Funding, which claimed it needed the Northern stock certificate for tax reasons.

XV
The Last Supper

SUNDAY

April 1

IT was a lovely, warm, spring day. Jerry Nemer was playing tennis when his wife rushed to the court and declared that Stuart Buchalter, one of his law partners, had just telephoned and that there was great urgency in his voice. Jerry should telephone Stuart right away.

Just two days earlier, Loeb had asked Nemer's firm to become special counsel to Equity Funding's board of directors. The alarmed Loeb had contacted Stuart, a personal friend and the son of Irwin Buchalter, a partner in the firm. Glaser, equally apprehensive, had contacted Irwin.

Nemer hadn't been aware of the chain of events, but the telephone call breaking up his morning tennis game changed all that. The personable sixty-two-year-old Nemer immediately returned Stuart's call from his Brentwood home. His associate declared that the Equity Funding case demanded their immediate attention. Jerry picked up Stuart and they drove to their law firm's Century City office on the tenth floor of 1900 Avenue of the Stars.

All hell was breaking loose eighteen floors above their small office, Stuart told Jerry. In a torrent of words, he tried to describe some of the events as he had heard them described by Loeb. Nemer still didn't have the slightest idea what Buchalter was talking about, but he sensed that something horrendous was happening.

He was told that an emergency board of directors meeting was being called for that afternoon and that Equity Funding's directors wanted to use the law firm's broom-closet-size quarters instead of their own offices, so as to be on neutral ground. More importantly, Loeb feared that all the Equity Funding executive offices were bugged. Stuart quickly explained that a cleaning woman had discovered and informed Loeb of electronic equipment in Goldblum's office and there was no telling how extensive the bugging operation had become.

Nemer, a shrewd veteran attorney, was stunned by what he heard. He agreed that the 10 × 12 foot conference room should be the setting.

Loeb showed up at his twenty-eighth-floor office before noon. He was nervous. As general counsel for the past three and a half years, he had primarily played a background role. Moveover, the scholarly Harvard lawyer was on the opposite end of the personality spectrum from the dynamic Goldblum. Loeb was a good lieutenant but no general. He was miscast for the role he had to play. He wasn't used to the nasty infighting of corporate wars. But more importantly, he was going to have to challenge Stan, Fred, and Sam all at once.

They were men of strong personalities. They had built a financial empire, had commanded the respect of the insurance industry, and had Wall Street in awe. They could intimidate an employee by their very presence.

Loeb had to assume the role of prosecutor, He had to seek the board's concurrence on their resignation. As secretary of the meeting he would have to draw up the agenda and present the charges. It was one of the longest days of his life. John Schneider, Loeb's young assistant, and his secretary were waiting for him.

Schneider began combing through EFCA's eighty-one

subsidiaries to find out who were corporate officers or directors of what companies. Stanley was an officer of all the subsidiaries but Fred and Sam were not. They finally agreed to draw up one resignation document for each principal.

"I, Stanley Goldblum, resign from the following corporations," the document read. Thus, Goldblum would have to sign just one nine-page document instead of eighty-one separate ones. Fred's and Sam's resignation documents were also nine pages long. That would take care of the "Big Three." Only one page long were the resignation papers for Lewis, Smith, Banks, Edens, Collins, and Symonds, the so-called "Little Six."

Would they resign, as the Securities and Exchange Commission was demanding? Loeb couldn't be sure. The alternative was a self-destructive battle with federal and state regulatory authorities.

A preliminary meeting to prepare for the showdown began in the Buchalter office at 1 P.M. The SEC's Boltz showed up, as did Glaser, Bowie, Arkus-Duntov, Williams, and Washington counsel Kroll. Nemer and Buchalter were there, too. So were Gleeson Payne and Larry Baker from the California Insurance Commission, who did some talking. And so did some representatives from First National City Bank, while wondering if they would ever see their loan money again.

And as the cast of characters wandered in and out of that small, besieged Buchalter office, there was Richards, president of Fidelity, pondering how much would be in the bag he would be left holding. That bag contained 579,096 shares, or 8.7 percent, of EFCA's outstanding stock. Moreover, not only had First National City Bank led a consortium that had lent $50.5 million to EFCA, but the New York bank also was into Richards for $25 million. No wonder Brewer had quickly left his Connecticut home to show up on Saturday in Los Angeles. Richards had collateralized his Citibank loan with Equity Funding stock!

Richards had a plan. He offered to take over EFCA after

its principal officers were fired. He noted that Fidelity also sold insurance and mutual funds, had a savings and loan association, and wasn't too unlike EFLIC. Moreover, he said that as an insurance holding company, Fidelity even resembled EFCA to a degree.

Richards made sure Boltz was aware he was the largest single stockholder and suggested that at a minimum he should have a seat on the shuffled-up board. Was Richards making a move to take over a company five times the size of Fidelity?

Boltz and Baker would have none of it and Richards was rebuffed.

At 3:30 P.M., Loeb excused himself from the preliminary session and returned to the twenty-eighth floor to tape a big handwritten sign on the door of Equity Funding's boardroom stating that the directors' meeting was on the tenth floor in Room 1030.

The showdown board meeting convened at 4:15 P.M.

The small room was suffocatingly warm. It was Sunday and the building's air conditioning was turned off.

The seating around the square conference table put Goldblum at the head, the proper place for EFCA's chairman. Directly across from him at the other end sat Loeb.

To Goldblum's right sat Judson Sayre, an outside director from Chicago, who as a top official of the board of the old Bendix Home Appliances company helped pioneer the automatic home washing machine. To Goldblum's left sat Lowell. Clockwise from Lowell were Levin, inside director Arkus-Duntov, former California insurance commissioner Richards Barger, called in as a consultant, Nemer, Loeb, Buchalter, outside director Professor Bowie of Harvard, Glaser and two more outside directors, Loud and Gale Livingston, a former commercial airline pilot, then an executive with Litton Industries of Beverly Hills.

Seated for lack of space against the wall were Kroll, Peter Panarites, Kroll's Washington law firm associate, Larry

Williams, and attorney Schneider, who was appointed to take minutes.

Loeb, sitting behind a pile of papers including the resignation documents, handed out the agenda. Goldblum glanced at it and knew immediately he was in for a fight. Item 1 was a discussion of the problems. Item 2 was the resignation of Goldblum and his management team. Item 3 was the appointment of a special management team to replace them. There was nothing to hide. The hairs must have stood up on Goldblum's massive neck.

Livingston, still loyal to Goldblum, whom he had known since 1962, joined with his friend in challenging the reason for the meeting. Both wanted to know at the outset why the Buchalter and Kroll law firms, and Barger, were allowed into the board meeting.

Loeb countered that he had discussed this with Glaser and that they had decided they could bring in whatever legal counsel was necessary to represent the company.

"We need the expertise," declared Loeb.

"Isn't Kroll enough?" asked Livingston.

Everyone edged forward in their chairs. The opening shots were being fired. The battle had commenced.

Goldblum challenged the right of the Buchalter firm to represent EFCA. He declared they had represented both EFCA and himself in past matters and that there was a conflict of interest. But Loeb said that as general counsel he had the authority to hire attorneys for the corporation.

Then Livingston directly addressed Loeb.

"Why are you doing all the talking?" asked Livingston. "We still have a chairman."

Loeb, attempting to prevent the meeting from turning into a waterfront brawl, told Livingston in a low voice that as secretary he was empowered to call the meeting. Loeb said he had discussed calling the meeting with the SEC, the insurance commissions, and First National City Bank. His voice contained a note of annoyance.

Goldblum asked Loeb whether any other meetings had taken place that day.

Loeb described the earlier meeting and then began a chronology of events leading up to the board meeting. As Loeb began to relate the material Seidman & Seidman had gathered, Livingston, Sayre, and Loud said the dimension of the events was still unclear and requested that Loeb go back yet another week so that they could get a better handle on the events.

Loeb then touched on the Illinois Insurance Commission's audit of EFLIC; the meeting with Seidman & Seidman and Mike Balint of the Haskins & Sells auditing firm; and the Dirks notes that the Seidman auditing firm turned over to Goldblum.

Step by step, Loeb took the meeting through the false-policy allegations, the halt in trading by the New York Stock Exchange, Williams' inability to get statements from those who might have been involved, and the dramatic meeting in Loeb's office when Rothman revealed that Goldblum would take the Fifth Amendment rather than answer questions about the charges.

Williams then related his difficulties in getting Goldblum to sign anything or testify before the SEC.

Loeb came back with the Raff meeting with Seidman and Seidman and described the discovery of bugging equipment on the twenty-eighth floor and the tape recorder in Goldblum's washroom.

Goldblum was becoming more heated and would ask questions with greater frequency. Levin and Lowell said little.

Finally, Loeb, sensing that Goldblum was on the edge of a blowup, stopped the presentation and said he didn't want to discuss the charges any further because the responses of the accused could be used against them later in a courtroom.

A court reporter to record the meeting verbatim was

requested by Goldblum, but the request was interpreted by some present as a ploy to delay the proceedings, since it would have taken hours to find one on a Sunday.

"It would be disruptive to go out and get a court reporter unless Stanley has one in the hallway," replied Loeb.

The meeting moved on.

Buchalter summarized his talks with the SEC—that there might be up to $1 billion in false insurance on EFLIC's books ($2 billion would have been a closer estimate); and that there might be approximately $25 million in missing securities in Chicago.

Then Buchalter dropped the bomb. The SEC would go into federal court and seek to put the company into receivership and take the company away from current management unless Goldblum, Levin, Lowell, and the "little six" resigned. He noted that the SEC also was seeking EFCA consent to an immediate injunction and consent order that it would abstain from committing certain false financial practices in the future.

Buchalter noted that the SEC was looking for an independent auditor to replace the Seidman firm and also suggested that Loeb, Glaser, and a bank representative might form a three-man interim management committee.

Loeb disclosed to the meeting the details of the California Insurance Commission seizing the company that previous Friday night. He said the Illinois commission also had been there and that Illinois was holding a meeting the next day, April 2, on the case.

Goldblum cut in again. He demanded to know why Levin, Lowell, and himself were being singled out for persecution.

That brought Williams to his feet. Looking squarely at Goldblum, Williams said the SEC's Boltz had informed "us attorneys" that "you three" either had knowledge of or had directed the illegal activities that were being alleged. Moreover, declared Williams, the SEC indicated it had information to substantiate the allegations.

Goldblum, becoming more argumentative, declared he didn't believe that a management committee could run the company without the services of Levin, Lowell, and himself. Even if they had to resign because of an SEC order, he said, the three would still be needed to keep the firm out of bankruptcy and to keep the sales force from disintegrating. Irrespective of what position he retained, Goldblum said it would not be in the best interests of creditors and shareholders for them to be kicked out. Goldblum said that at a minimum they should be retained on a consulting basis.

If the allegations were true, there wouldn't be much to sell, suggested Loeb. Kroll agreed.

Under any circumstances, shot back Goldblum, receivership should be avoided.

Loeb advised Goldblum that the EFCA chairman's continued refusal to tell anything to the SEC precluded his further participation in the company in any capacity.

At that point, Lowell warned that if he were forced out, the banks would call their loans and the company's operations would cease anyway.

Goldblum shot in that the SEC should slow down its investigation.

Bowie, a contemplative soul by nature, was getting more irritated as the statement and counterstatement match became more heated. He declared forcefully that Goldblum had no choice but to leave, as the SEC had requested. Bowie said there could be no negotiation with the SEC over keeping anyone on as a consultant.

Loeb and Williams agreed. Of course, they added, if Goldblum was willing to testify before the SEC, that might be another matter and Boltz might then consider what help Goldblum could be to the company.

"What the hell is the SEC interested in—putting people behind bars or preserving the company for its stockholders and creditors?" yelled Goldblum.

Kroll interjected that the SEC did want to preserve EFCA

but that Boltz also had to get at the facts. If, noted Kroll, Goldblum would testify under oath before the SEC there might be a way for him to remain with the company.

The tide of the meeting was beginning to turn against Goldblum, Levin, and Lowell. Livingston was asking Goldblum simply to refute the charges and he, Livingston, would walk out of the meeting. But Goldblum insisted he could not make any statements except on advice of counsel.

Rising tempers fueled the already steamy room.

Buchalter said the information available was perhaps only the tip of the iceberg and that the SEC knew a lot more than had been described at the meeting by Loeb. Buchalter exclaimed that if there were any missing securities he could understand why the SEC didn't want current management around.

Glaser then took some of the wind out of Goldblum's argument by declaring that he, Glaser, had already talked with the sales managers, who assured him the salesmen would stay with the company because they could still sell the products of Bankers and Northern.

Sayre had been simmering up to this point. Then he exploded.

"I'm no sophisticated lawyer," Sayre told the meeting, "but if you guys refuse to testify there must be something to this. You owe it to the other directors to lay it on the table and tell us what it's all about."

Goldblum reiterated, however, that he wanted to help the company but he wasn't prepared to make a decision on testifying.

Once again Goldblum leaned forward and emphasized that the company still had great value and that "nothing but more damage would result" if they were thrown out.

Questions shot back and forth like Ping-Pong balls as the meeting went on without a break. Practically everyone was sweating profusely by late afternoon. No one had eaten yet. Washroom excursions were all that forced anyone to leave for a fleeting moment.

A discussion then centered on the missing bonds, and Buchalter said the authorities weren't sure who was involved and that everyone—all the directors—were under suspicion.

Bowie was getting more impatient. "It's impossible for current management to remain," he said. And Goldblum, for the first time, appeared to agree that it looked hopeless for him to remain in light of the adamant stand being taken by the SEC and the insurance authorities.

Levin broke the impasse. He said he would resign as an officer and director of the parent company and all the subsidiaries on which he served. Furthermore, he said, he would offer whatever services he could to set things right again. Levin explained that he had met with Citibank and with Richards, his friend from Virginia, and other interests in an effort to raise money to help the firm. He said he talked to his staff, the "little six," and that he had received assurances they would also be available for help if requested by the company. But Levin also declared that he agreed with Goldblum that the company needed their services as consultants to survive.

Lowell wasn't as agreeable. He said he would try to help straighten things out but had no intention of resigning.

Bowie reiterated the SEC's position that if they didn't resign the SEC would appoint a receiver. Lowell finally was convinced he had little choice.

Loeb underscored that the SEC was demanding their resignation and that they had to be off the premises.

Goldblum got madder. He accused Loeb and the SEC of acting in a "high-handed manner" without the authority to do so and of treating the accused officers as if they had already been convicted.

Livingston, apparently still unsure of his allegiance, then inquired if the SEC was acting properly.

The calm and organized voice of Bowie cut through the air. "Let me understand this," Bowie said. "Stanley, we're your board of directors. You're the chief operating officer. Are you telling us that you're not going to tell us what you know with regard to the affairs of this corporation or its subsidiaries?"

Goldblum said he would have to talk to his lawyer.

The magnitude of the situation was just beginning to sink into attorney Nemer's head. Until that time, through hours of discussion, he had remained quiet. Now he chose to speak.

"Well, gentlemen," Nemer said, "I've been quiet for a lot of hours here which is unlike me because I'm trying to sort out the problems of this corporation. Now I'd like to ask you, Mr. Goldblum, a couple of questions."

Drawing on decades of trial experience, Nemer queried:

"Would it be a fair statement that public confidence in Equity Funding is likely to be at a very low ebb tomorrow [Monday]?"

"I think that's a fair statement," said Goldblum.

"Isn't it also a fair statement," continued Nemer, "that public confidence is going to be further diminished if there is not some statement from the chief executive officer?"

"I guess that's a fair statement," replied Goldblum again.

"Well," said Nemer, "if I understand your position correctly, you're not going to give your board of directors or anybody else any statement other than, 'Don't worry, I'll pull you out.'"

Suddenly the room fell silent.

"Under the circumstances," said Nemer, "don't you think that you ought to resign for the good of your corporation?"

"I'll have to talk to my attorney," came the familiar Goldblum reply.

Bowie had had it. Casting aside his Harvard panache, he riveted his eyes on Goldblum. He warned Goldblum that if he didn't make a full revelation to the board that instant about what he knew, the board should remove him then and there.

The world stood still. The directors looked at each other and at their counsel.

Nemer later recalled that the silence was reminiscent of

that instant just before two gunslingers draw. The air became electric between Goldblum and Bowie.

Lowell cut in to make his own defense. Lowell said he wasn't involved whatsoever in the insurance operations. He said he assumed he was being condemned because he had the financial responsibility for the parent company.

But Goldblum wasn't through—although it appeared to several that he had hardly picked an appropriate time to discuss the next topic on his mind: severance pay.

Even the lowest Equity Funding clerk who had been with the firm only a few months was entitled to severance pay, Goldblum observed. The chairman pointed out that he had been with the company for twelve years and that when you terminate an executive you get a month's salary for every year you've been with the firm. Plus, added Goldblum, he hadn't taken his vacation that year and was therefore entitled to vacation pay.

Additionally, he said, if the directors did decide to keep him on as a consultant, his fee would be in the neighborhood of $250 to $500 a day.

(Levin and Lowell agreed. Yes, that would be a fair consulting fee if they were kept on in that capacity. What the board didn't know was that Lowell had drawn $9,000 that Friday from Mike Sultan, representing his $1,000-a-month entertainment allowance for the rest of the year.)

Goldblum was standing now and leaning over the table. He was talking some more about severance pay.

For the first time, Bowie raised his voice in anger. He said he could not stand to listen anymore to talk about severance pay. It simply was not a negotiable subject at that time, asserted Bowie, who had never before served on the board of a major corporation.

First, reemphasized Bowie in a louder voice, there must be resignations.

Loeb took the cue, rose, and walked over to Goldblum, Levin, and Lowell. He handed them the prepared written resignation forms. Only one signature was required from each of the three.

Stanley signed his at the table. But Sam and Fred said they would discuss it with their lawyers. Sam's ultimately came in six weeks later; Fred's, eight weeks afterward.

Stan and Fred left the room. But Sam stayed on to say a little more to the group.

"I'm being tarred with their brush," said Lowell. "I haven't done anything wrong." Lowell said he may have "played some games in the financial area" but that he was not involved in an insurance fraud.

"Just because I was in charge of financials, I'm being crucified," Lowell exclaimed. He then left.

At that point, Goldblum poked his head back into the room and said he was resigning for the good of the company and, secondly, because the SEC demanded it. Goldblum had just finished talking on the telephone to his attorney, Frank Rothman.

Loeb inquired of the board of directors after Goldblum left whether it was their understanding that Levin and Lowell had submitted their oral resignations. There was agreement that they had and that the directors could proceed on this assumption and appoint replacements.

As the meeting continued, Loeb heard voices in the outer office and went to investigate. Stan, Fred, and Sam were talking right outside the door. Loeb said it might seem petty but that the offices were owned by Buchalter, Nemer, Field, and Savitch and they had been asked to leave the premises because of the board meeting. (This also prevented any eavesdropping, noted one participant.)

Goldblum was somewhat offended, inquiring why he couldn't talk with Levin and Lowell in the outer office.

Loeb responded by saying it wasn't Equity Funding's office.

Goldblum and his two lieutenants weren't used to being told to do anything, much less leave the premises. But they left.

Shortly thereafter, the Monkarsh brothers showed up. Jerry and Eugene Monkarsh were executives with Equity Funding's real estate operations and had been trying to reach their friend Glaser all day. They had heard about the meeting and, of course, with a substantial amount of stock in the company, they were concerned about the reports of the past few weeks.

By that time, the conference office smelled like a high school locker room after a football game. Moreover, no one had eaten for hours. By the time the Monkarsh brothers arrived, dinner had become something to consider.

Since the makeup of the room was about 75 percent Jewish and 25 percent Gentile, there was strong support that the Monkarshes go to Junior's, a popular Westwood delicatessen, and buy the place out.

Bowie, however, said he wanted a ham sandwich.

Monkarsh, the product of an orthodox Jewish upbringing, had never bought ham in his life. "Okay," he told Bowie.

At Junior's, the Monkarshes ordered $26 worth of corned beef, pastrami, rolls, pickles, soft drinks—and Bowie's ham sandwich.

Who devoured the ham sandwich isn't known. Bowie had corned beef and pastrami on rye.

As Loeb was munching away on his sandwich, Livingston called him aside and said he had heard a story of phony insurance at Equity Funding before. It seems that Livingston and Goldblum had teamed up, independently of the EFCA operations, in an Indonesian oil venture in 1971. A former Litton employee, Jack Warshauer, headed the oil venture, called Indonesian Development Corporation, and for a time was allowed free office space on Equity Funding's twenty-eighth floor.

Livingston said that in December, 1971, Warshauer heard a false insurance story from Bill Mercado, the EFCA comptroller. Warshauer relayed the report to Livingston, who queried Goldblum. But the chairman said it wasn't true, that it was sour grapes from a disgruntled employee.

After the meeting resumed, Glaser sensed that many of his colleagues were uneasy with him in the room as they began to discuss some of the more sensitive areas of the case. Glaser had been professionally close to Goldblum for over a decade and understood their apprehension. He said he wanted everyone to feel more comfortable so that they could speak freely. He then left the meeting, along with Arkus-Duntov, another director closely associated with the company's growth.

Loeb did much of the narrating. The bearded Equity Funding counsel related as best he could the story that he had pieced together during the last four days, including the Maple Drive operations where the phony policies were created by Mark Lewis and his all-female team. (The office had first been rented in May, 1971, was empty between January and April, 1972, and then was reactivated until April 2, 1973, when, like everything else, it was closed down.)

Loeb said that at least three auditing firms had missed the fraud. Seidman & Seidman audited the parent company. Haskins & Sells had the responsibility of auditing EFLIC. And Ranger National, which had purchased the most reinsurance from EFLIC, had requested that Peat, Marwick, Mitchell and Company review EFLIC's records before it bought the insurance—which it did, and found nothing. Bowie and Arkus-Duntov had been particularly critical of the auditors for not uncovering the phony insurance.

The outside directors and Loeb were still confused as to the scope of the fraud. The lawyers kept asking how many were involved. No one knew how widespread the conspiracy was or how deep into middle and lower management it extended. Some of the directors feared that as many as forty individuals were in on the scheme. It was clearly startling that so many could keep such an outrageous plan quiet for so long.

"I want to know whether or not Stanley is involved," declared Nelson Loud.

Loud was told that the entire scheme was known to Fred Levin and that Levin apparently encouraged it. He was also told that at a very minimum Goldblum and Lowell knew about the phony insurance and had taken no action to stop the practice.

Livingston asked for an explanation of the motives behind the scheme.

The lawyers said it appeared those involved were clearly motivated by personal profit. They were receiving major stock bonuses and the stock was obviously reacting positively to all of the new insurance business.

Was there any embezzlement? The directors and counsel knew of at least one case of embezzlement involving death claims by lower-level personnel—but not on the part of senior management.

It was then made clear that the SEC had requested assurance from the outside directors that they would agree to resign if asked to do so by the SEC.

Loud objected. He said he didn't want to resign if it raised an inference of guilt.

It was plain that the outside directors were stunned by the scope of the fraud and could not be sure how deep it went. More importantly, even among themselves, they could not be sure who was guilty through involvement or through inside knowledge of fraud. (In any case, warned Buchalter, there would be a substantial number of lawsuits against the outside directors even though they might be ignorant of the allegations. He was right.)

Glaser and Arkus-Duntov returned to the meeting at 7:30 P.M. along with Bob Spencer, the head of the Seidman Los Angeles office, and two other Seidman officials—Neil Freeman and John Abernathy. They told the group they were preparing for an audit and had twenty to thirty men on the job going over Equity Funding's books. Spencer said it was costing the firm $8,000 a day to perform the massive audit.

Spencer then made a report—requested by Bowie*—that his firm had selected three computer runs for analysis; runs that included business reinsured by Ranger National, Kentucky Central, and Great Southern insurance companies. He said Seidman checked eighty-two reinsurance policies and in twenty-eight instances there were no telephone numbers on the individual applications. On eight, he said, there were wrong numbers. Of eleven calls, there were no answers. On thirty-five telephone conversations, ten people said they did not have EFLIC policies but did have Bankers policies; ten had Northern policies; two said they had no policies at all; and seven said they were unsure as to whose policy they had. Only six individuals said they had EFLIC insurance policies.

If nothing else, the Seidman survey confirmed suspicions that the fraud had used names and data contained in the policies of Bankers and Northern.

Seidman officials said they had tried to run the sample based on insurance in place on the last working day of 1972, but that it may have been fouled up and that they were having a terrible time going through the company's microfilm files.

Barger wanted to know how long it would take Seidman to determine the number of phony policies. The answer was that there were 92,000 policies and it would be a time-consuming project to check out each one.

Barger said it seemed to him inevitable that Equity Funding faced receivership.

Seidman was then asked to give their estimate of how many individuals were involved. The Seidman officials couldn't give an exact count.

Was it conceivable, queried Bowie, that the scheme could

---

*Bowie had been flabbergasted by the fraud story he had heard from Loeb and others. Therefore, to make absolutely sure there was substance to the report, he demanded that the auditors take a random sample of policyholders that EFLIC had on its books.

have existed without Goldblum, Levin, or Lowell knowing about it?

Yes, replied the Seidman representatives.

But Loeb and the other counsel for the company disagreed and felt if the charges were true, then the "Big Three" had to know.

At 8:45 P.M., it dawned on those left that they had just wiped out a big chunk of their management. Who was going to run the company? "Don't worry," replied Barger, "the Insurance Department will take care of that."

Bowie and Sayre declared they were willing to resign as outside directors but felt an obligation to the shareholders and creditors to stay on.

The SEC also had demanded that a new auditing firm replace Seidman. The firms of Touche Ross & Company and Price Waterhouse and Company were suggested. Touche Ross was finally selected to perform a complete audit of EFCA, which could take several months.

"I'm sure there will be criminal action brought against the people who were terminated today," commented Loeb. He then recommended against paying any severance pay. "I think it would look terrible," Loeb declared.

Glaser and Loud said, however, it was their opinion that the management committee would need the help of those fired a few hours earlier to help run the company. Therefore, they said, it might be necessary to pay them for their help.

Barger replied that the courts probably wouldn't permit such action until the criminal matters had been cleared up.

Bowie added that since Goldblum, Levin, and Lowell might have had their hands in the EFCA cookie jar, it would be improper to pay them for anything at that time.

The issue of requesting help from those just fired then came to a vote. Bowie, Sayre, Livingston, and Loud voted not to request their assistance or discuss such a move with the SEC until they had a clearer picture of what was happening. Glaser and Arkus-Duntov abstained.

Williams and Loeb reported that Lewis, Banks, Edens, Smith, Symonds, and Collins had refused to cooperate with their internal investigation and were on the SEC's list of prime suspects. The board authorized their immediate termination without severance pay or benefits and instructed Loeb to fire them.

The lawyers were authorized to prepare a press release on Monday noting the nine terminations stemming from the serious fraud allegations.

The meeting adjourned at 10:30 P.M. Equity Funding was in a state of siege. The Goldblum era was over.

XVI
April

MONDAY

April 2

"BEVERLY Hills—One of the biggest scandals in the history of the insurance industry is beginning to break around Equity Funding Corporation of America, a financial services concern with a go-go growth record in insurance sales. The scandal centers in Equity Funding Life Insurance Company, a key subsidiary."

So began the lead story in *The Wall Street Journal* of April 2—an amazingly accurate piece considering its complexity and the speed with which it broke. Blundell had scored a clear news beat. He didn't get a pay raise. But his managing editor did send him flowers, which were actually for Blundell's wife, who had had a tough weekend in her own right.

The SEC's Boltz was figuring out various ways that the company might be saved. It was decided that the SEC would bring a formal injunctive action in court alleging a scheme to defraud; that a completely new board of directors would have to be formed; that a special investigator would have to be named; and that a special blue ribbon group would have to be brought in—including a trustee—to hold things together until the company could be put on its feet again.

EFCA officials entered into a consent decree as a result of a civil action brought by the SEC before Federal Court Judge Harry Pregerson.* The civil suit charged massive fraud within EFCA and various violations of securities laws. Judge Pregerson then issued an injunction, stemming from the consent decree, which restrained the company from further violations of the securities laws (somewhat akin to telling a rapist he can't rape anymore! said one company official) and appointed a special investigator to begin a Federal Grand Jury investigation into the case.

John Marshall Newman, Jr., a young member of the federal prosecutor's staff, was appointed to head the investigation. Newman, a 1966 graduate of Georgetown University, was out of Harvard's law school just a few years when he received the Gargantuan assignment.

Boltz finally telephoned his Washington supervisors to tell them he had enough evidence to draw up several counts of fraud against certain company officials.

It was chaotic that Monday, recalled attorney Nemer. "The SEC was making a tremendous effort to try to keep this thing from just exploding." It was hoped, Nemer explained, that the injunctive order restraining the company from any further violations of the securities laws would somehow restore public confidence.

Meanwhile, the banking consortium, led by Citibank, to whom Equity Funding still owed $50.5 million, met with the SEC and EFCA representative. The banks were urged not to seize what was believed to be approximately $12.5 million in a compensating balance that Equity Funding was required to keep on deposit with the consortium under the loan

---

*The consent order was thrashed out Monday night between EFCA's remaining directors and Boltz. Every EFCA board member who hadn't been terminated initialed the decree and it was filed with the court the next morning.

agreement, since, without it, the company couldn't pay its bills.

The banks said they might consider holding off if they could also have the stock of the Liberty Savings & Loan subsidiary as further collateral. This was viewed as blatant blackmail by some of the EFCA directors.

On Tuesday, April 3, the banks went ahead without notice and seized the compensating balance which, for a reason explained by no one, turned out to be approximately $8 million, not the $12.5 million required under the loan agreement. Whether the banks or a reorganized EFCA would keep the money may be finally decided by the courts. In addition, the loan agreement was secured by 100 percent of the stock of Bankers National Life; Equity Funding's 100 percent stock interest in Northern Life; 60 percent of the stock of Equity Funding Life.*

The chaos became worse after the banks moved in. Since Sunday, April 1, EFCA had been without its three top operating officers. Several other members of its management staff were under criminal investigation. But now, everyone suddenly stopped doing business with the company. Telephone companies terminated services in EFCA offices across the country or threatened to do so unless substantial cash deposits were posted. Landlords attempted to force the payment of rent in advance and, in some cases, actually locked out EFCA salesmen and seized furniture and office equipment. And the sales force found itself with nothing to sell.

*The agreement was entered into on June 29, 1972, between EFCA and First National City Bank of New York, Franklin National Bank of New York, The Wells Fargo Bank of California, and National Bank of North America. Under the agreement, EFCA could borrow up to $75 million at any one time until June 30, 1975, and was to pay back any monies borrowed in installment payments by June 30, 1980, at a fluctuating interest rate of not more than 1 percent above the prime rate. As of March 30, 1973, EFCA's total indebtedness under the agreement was $50,535,688, of which Citibank had loaned $23,583,321; Wells Fargo, $10,107,137; Franklin, $10,107,138; and NBNA, $6,738,092.

On top of all of this, Glaser, who had been appointed EFCA's temporary chief operating officer, and Loeb, his top lieutenant, were faced with the prospect of figuring out how to meet the company's April 13 payroll with no money in the bank.

Thus, EFCA's remaining officers and legal counsel tried to operate, but had practically no choice but to seek protection under Chapter 10 of the Federal Bankruptcy Act—and they did so on Thursday of that week.* Using hindsight, if Chapter 10 had been sought immediately it would have precluded the banks' offset maneuver.

Equity Funding employees had been paid the previous Friday but not everyone went to the bank with their biweekly paycheck that day. Some, like Rosemary Day, a secretary, waited until Monday, April 2, to take their checks to the bank. Miss Day went downstairs to the Union Bank, where she usually cashed her paycheck. By then, *The Wall Street Journal* had been as well circulated around Century City as a Bible at a revival meeting. The Union Bank teller took one look at the check—and at Sam Lowell's signature on it—and refused to cash it. Miss Day, like many of her colleagues that day, had to scramble to find a bank that would take a chance and cash an EFCA paycheck.

*Chapter 10 is designed to rehabilitate and reorganize a corporation in financial trouble. The rationale is that this procedure, rather than liquidation, is of greater value to the creditors and shareholders. A company continues to operate under Chapter 10, but is protected by the court from litigation and claims on its assets. Under this proceeding, a trustee is appointed by the court to supervise the company. Declared Trustee Robert M. Loeffler in his February report to Federal Judge Harry Pregerson:

"EFCA was a classic case for relief under Chapter 10. Virtually all its operations were imperiled by the revelations of the fraud and the ensuing attempts by creditors, especially secured creditors, to coerce payment of their claims. EFCA's top management had resigned in the face of charges of fraud and its financial condition was precarious. Only the broad protections afforded by Chapter 10 have preserved EFCA to date. The power to adjust the rights of creditors and shareholders will undoubtedly be needed to accomplish a successful reorganization."

The lawsuits were pouring in against the company and its officers. The class action claims—so named because one law firm handles and consolidates hundreds of claims on behalf of shareholders—may take years to sort out. The litigation was later consolidated within a single court jurisdiction in Los Angeles.

Among those sued by shareholders were the five inside and four outside directors.

The outside directors—Loud, Bowie, Livingston and Sayre—naturally felt unfairly put upon since they claimed they were not as privy to the company's internal business as those who spent their working lives at Equity Funding. At least one of the outside directors noted that countries such as West Germany protect outside directors from corporate liability by insulating them from lawsuits arising from charges of company misconduct, fraud, and the like. The theory in these countries, this director noted, is that an outside director can't possibly know enough to be held liable for the way his company conducts its business.

No doubt, thousands of outside directors of United States corporations slept uneasily the night of April 2.

Also named in the class action suits were the accountants; investment banking firms which acted as underwriters for the parent company; a host of so-called tippee defendants who purportedly were tipped off to the fraud allegations through the institution handling their stock portfolio (these ranged from Amherst College to the Sears, Roebuck Pension Fund); big New York banks; and brokerage houses that may have had access to the original rumor reports. And in a consolidated complaint filed on October 29, 1973, in the Central District of California, the New York and American stock exchanges and the Illinois and California insurance departments were named as defendants for failure to properly regulate the securities and insurance business of Equity Funding.

That Monday, Goldblum received two checks for a total of $531,487.50.

In the chaos that enveloped the company on April 2, someone in the company's securities department released the checks to Goldblum, which the chairman claimed constituted his investment in the company's three mutual funds.

Loeb, on learning that the two checks had been handed over to Goldblum against Loeb's orders, hit the ceiling, but by then it was done. Boltz became furious at Loeb for allowing Goldblum to get his hands on the checks, one in the amount of $458,849.70, payable to Goldblum, and the other for $72,637.80, payable to his wife, Marlene. In the Monday pandemonium of phone calls, auditors, and investigators combing through the company, however, the President of the United States could have walked through the executive offices without being noticed.

The following day, an associate of the Beverly Hills law firm of Wyman, Bautzer, Rothman & Kuchel, which originally represented Goldblum after he was ousted as chairman, flew to the United Missouri Bank and negotiated both checks. Goldblum had a loan at the bank in the amount of $355,753.57 which was paid off. The balance, $175,733.93, was held by the Wyman, Bautzer firm despite attempts by Goldblum to get it back after he had changed attorneys. Additionally, litigation initiated by EFCA's trustee kept the money tied up.

The suit filed by court-appointed trustee Robert M. Loeffler, also tried to establish claim to $375,000 held by Bank of America, money given to the bank by the Goldblums in return for a cashier's check made out to Dishy, Easton & Company, the New York brokerage house with which Goldblum had a personal account. Bank of America and Dishy, Easton subsequently agreed that the check should be stopped until the Equity Funding case could be sorted out.

Trustee Loeffler's moves were part of an overall $1-million suit he filed against Goldblum in May, charging the chairman with perpetrating the phony insurance scheme. The $1 million included Goldblum's compensation as an employee of Equity Funding.

THURSDAY

April 5

Loeb felt an immense despair. Like Glaser, his distant relation, Loeb feared he would forever be professionally doomed by the Equity Funding debacle. Arriving home in a stupor in the early morning hours of Thursday, Loeb sat half undressed next to his rolltop desk in the upstairs bedroom of his Westwood home. He had just signed a nine-inch-high stack of bankruptcy petitions in the Buchalter law offices. For the first time his wife saw her husband cry.

"I'll never get another job again as a lawyer," sobbed Loeb. "That's not like starting from scratch—that's worse. I'm starting behind the eight ball now. I'm lost. I don't know what I'll do to support you."

In the half-light of the bedroom, Loeb's wife, Magda, a former concert pianist, replied: "Don't worry about it. I'll give piano lessons."

Forty-nine-year-old Bob Loeffler had been in tougher spots. As a lieutenant JG in the Navy, he had participated in the D-Day landing and had been wounded when his destroyer was hit by a kamikaze attack off Okinawa. In a sense, being asked to take over as Equity Funding's trustee was like going into battle again.

Loeffler had flown to Los Angeles on Sunday, April 8, from Minnetonka, a suburb of Minneapolis. Accompanying Loeffler was Pat O'Connor, a longtime friend and attorney. Judge Pregerson had selected Loeffler from a blue ribbon list of candidates to take over the remnants of Equity Funding and, as trustee, remold the company into a living and breathing entity again.

Loeffler was making a comfortable $150,000 a year in salary and fringe benefits as senior vice-president—law of Investors Diversified Services, Inc., the giant Minneapolis-based mutual fund concern. Rather than give Pregerson an answer that night, he told the judge after a lengthy meeting that he would sleep on the offer to, in effect, become Equity Funding's chief operating officer.

Loeffler went back to his hotel room at the Century Plaza, where O'Connor was waiting for him. After a few drinks, O'Connor fell asleep.

"What in the world do I need with this," thought Loeffler. But Loeffler began to also think about turning fifty that summer and he lectured himself: "I don't want to stop at fifty. When the day comes," he thought, "when a man is so comfortable that he would turn down a challenge, then he's dead." So Loeffler, a veteran of some of the biggest corporate wars, took the job on April 10. "I haven't had any second thoughts about the decision," he was later to remark. "It's been fascinating."

XVII
The Insider Issue:
A Study in Obfuscation

SCENE: The board of directors meeting of the Popoff Button Company. Business has been bad and the directors vote to omit the quarterly dividend. The meeting ends and the directors race for the telephone to place sell orders with their brokers before the public gets wind of the news. Word finally gets out and the Popoff stock plummets. But at least the directors didn't lose their shirts. They were able to unload Popoff stock on the basis of their inside information.

Of course, this common occurrence of a bygone Wall Street era can no longer happen. The Securities and Exchange Commission and the stock exchanges have seen to that. But in the early days of this century there were few insider trading restrictions of which to speak. However, even today, under the SEC Act of 1934, the SEC has found it extremely difficult to prove that an individual had inside information on a company that would materially affect its stock—and then used it to advantage over other investors.

Insider trading generally takes two forms: trading in stock on the basis of factual information that simply wasn't available to everyone; or once being aware of inside information, falsifying it to fool the public.

Securities lawyers and veteran Wall Streeters see the Equity Funding case as one which will sharpen or change insider laws, which many legal scholars don't really view as insider laws at all, but rather loose language telling an individual employed in the securities industry that he or she cannot engage in deceptive or manipulative practices.

The particular section of the Securities Exchange Act of 1934 in question is 10(b) and Rule 10(b)-5 which was applied by the SEC in 1961 in the case of the New York brokerage house of Cady, Roberts & Company and the Curtiss-Wright Company.

A Cady, Roberts official was a member of the Curtiss-Wright board of directors. He sat in on a closed board meeting called to discuss Curtiss-Wright's profits outlook. After the meeting, the official tipped off his brokerage firm to what was discussed. The SEC ruled this action improper. This established the so-called tippee rule which declared the SEC's intent to prevent an insider from passing corporate information to an outsider.

Another major case involved Merrill, Lynch, Pierce, Fenner & Smith, Incorporated, the world's largest securities house, and Douglas Aircraft Company of Santa Monica, prior to Douglas' merger into St. Louis-based McDonnell Douglas Corporation. The SEC charged in 1966 that several Merrill, Lynch officials had received information from Douglas—in connection with an underwriting—that Douglas' financial outlook was not as bright as Wall Street thought. The SEC said the Merrill, Lynch representatives passed this word to fifteen large institutional investors without warning the public. In August, 1970, the civil case was settled through a consent decree under which the defendant promises not to violate the law in the future while not admitting to any guilt. Several Merrill, Lynch officials were censured and, in effect, suspended.

The Texas Gulf Sulphur Company litigation of the 1960's is considered the landmark case in spelling out the current definition of insider trading. The Texas Gulf rule declares, in effect, that if an employee of a public company has information affecting the price of that firm's stock, this information cannot be used for personal profit without first making it public for the benefit of shareholders and the investment community at large.

THE INSIDER ISSUE: *A Study in Obfuscation* 267

The Texas Gulf case began in April, 1964, when a company news release threw cold water on reports that it had discovered a rich ore vein in Timmins, Ontario. Then, four days later, the company issued another news release describing the vein as a major strike of zinc, copper, and silver.

The SEC charged that during a four-day period, thirteen Texas Gulf officials bought their firm's stock, told their friends to buy it, and accepted stock options on the basis of their insider information about the big mining strike. The case ended in 1971 when the U.S. Supreme Court refused to review—and thus let stand—a lower court order directing Texas Gulf to pay $2.7 million in damages to former shareholders.

But Texas Gulf; Merrill, Lynch; and Cady, Roberts notwithstanding, the securities and corporate communities are still uncertain over their liability under insider doctrines. The Equity Funding case could clear up a great deal of this uncertainty and crystallize at least two of the central issues: what obligation do corporate employees and securities industry personnel have to make news available to the public? And what news constitutes *material* information?

Other issues that have resulted from the Equity Funding scandal involve a more precise definition of what is an insider? Can an "outsider" spread "inside information"?

Complicating the case is the fact that Ron Secrist, the former EFLIC executive who helped blow the whistle on the scandal, revealed to insurance-stock analyst Ray Dirks what he knew about the fraud while he was working for Equity Funding Life Insurance Company, the EFCA subsidiary. But Secrist was no longer an employee of the subsidiary when he decided to tell all to Dirks. Accordingly, under the law, Secrist could no longer be considered an insider—or could he?

The Wall Street Journal, which broke the Equity Funding scandal, called the case "murky" in the context of what constitutes insider trading. Generally, said the financial daily, inside information is considered to be facts that travel from someone within a company to an analyst or underwriter, who then passes it on to investors who act on these facts. "But," the paper added, "Dirks' information came from an outsider [Secrist], not an insider. And when he [Dirks] got it, it was a rumor not a fact."

Dirks was the subject of SEC and New York Stock Exchange inquiries into his role in the spreading of the initial Equity Funding information to some of his clients. Dirks maintained that the *real* insider violators were Equity Funding officers like Goldblum and Levin, who were denying all along—until the day the Big Board stopped trading—that anything was wrong.

These denials, argued Dirks, must be considered inside information. After all, he said, these were the people who were on the inside. If they didn't know what was going on within their company, who did? And, indeed, in those final chaotic days before trading was halted, these same officers were attempting to dump most of their own stock holdings. Why were they so anxious to sell out? Was it on the basis of inside information? The courts will have to answer that question.

In fact, this very issue was the subject of complex litigation involving millions of dollars in class action suits on behalf of thousands of shareholders. It could take years to resolve.

The Equity Funding story didn't break publicly until April, 1973. But as far back as 1971 and 1972, key executives of Equity Funding were selling their stock, and making substantial profits. Investigators have a theory about this activity. Some believe that a substantial portion of the loans to EFCA, particularly the millions in foreign loans, was used by EFCA officers to buy their own company's stock and bonds for EFCA's treasury.* This is a common practice used

---

*In 1969, EFCA had inventoried 64,000 of its own shares, considered a high amount to be stashed away in a corporate treasury. After 1969, this practice stopped and by 1972 there was a little over 5,000 EFCA shares in the EFCA treasury.

by companies to strengthen their firm's stock and, hopefully, drive it upward.

In Equity Funding's case, corroborating the theory, the stock indeed roared upward, and was then sold off at a fat profit, from which the loans were at least partly paid off with a tidy sum left over. "Outsiders," of course, had no way of observing this activity (although outside shareholders also saw their EFCA stock increase in value) nor could public shareholders perceive that much of the vitality of EFCA stemmed from the amazing growth of its insurance subsidiary which was built upon a foundation of phony insurance.

To be sure, if the public had even perceived the tip of this iceberg, the company would have collapsed a lot sooner under an avalanche of sell orders, and a lot of shareholders who were hurt would not have been.

The man who did most of the EFCA selling in the early days was EFCA chairman Stanley Goldblum. Records show that in January, 1971, Goldblum owned 277,520 shares of Equity Funding, more than 3 percent of the company's 7.8 million shares then outstanding. During that year, according to records on file with the SEC, Goldblum sold 18,875 shares and gave away another 2,000 shares. Also during 1971, the EFCA chairman acquired 5,000 shares through a company benefits plan begun that year.

But by the time 1972 rolled around, the chairman was in more of a selling than an acquiring mood as far as his firm's stock was concerned. By the end of 1972, Goldblum had sold 21,000 shares, most of them in January, October, and November, for almost $800,000.

Ten thousand of those shares brought in $390,000 for Goldblum, significantly more than he paid for them. The other 11,000-share block was sold for $385,000.

Goldblum's final sell order—for 50,000 shares—was placed on March 26, 1973, two days before the Big Board halted trading with the final sale of EFCA common at $14.37½.

Goldblum attorney Thomas Sheridan said that the sale was made through Goldblum's broker—Dishy, Easton. He said that Goldblum received a confirmation order from the brokerage house but never received the cash. At a later date, according to Sheridan, Goldblum received another order unraveling the sale.

Sheridan noted that the case of the 50,000 Goldblum shares appeared to resemble a similar situation in which EFCA director Arkus-Duntov found himself when he sold 44,245 shares on March 26. But the broker in the transaction sued and a federal judge halted payment on part of the trade. Arkus-Duntov also sold 1,000 shares on March 21, 1973, and did some minor selling in the two previous years.

Among others selling stock at various times in 1971, 1972, and 1973 were EFCA directors Lowell and Loud.

Those who would talk about their decisions to sell denied their actions were based on inside information that the company was about to crumble. Their thesis was that they generally needed the money, the stock's price was declining, and the security no longer seemed the good investment it had been a few years earlier. Also, some of EFCA's officers were getting margin calls from their brokers after the crisis began to surface—brokers were demanding that they put up more cash on Equity Funding stock they had purchased with a down payment.

In sorting out the complexities of the insider issue, the courts and the securities industry will no doubt have to focus upon the two principal characters around which the issues swirl: Secrist and Dirks.

How must Secrist, who had left Equity Funding, be defined: as an insider or an outsider?

To whom should Dirks, a securities analyst, have been responsible—the public (in which case he should have reported his findings to the SEC) or his institutional clients?

"Does the [insider] rule mean that securities analysts whose professional obligation is to their clients must instead become unpaid SEC informants whenever they pick up important unpublicized information?" asked *The Wall Street Journal.* "Does the rule apply to everyone who gets information from an analyst? And who is liable for damages and how much?"

The SEC said that for the purposes of its investigation of the Equity Funding case, it planned to consider both present and former employees as insiders. The agency also declared that the proper conduct by both Secrist and Dirks would have been to immediately inform the commission of their findings or suspicions before telling anyone else, letting the SEC decide if or when trading in the stock should be suspended. The courts might conclude differently.

Wall Street securities lawyers view the Equity Funding case as a classic test of insider issues. The reason is that so few insider cases have reached a final judgment in the courts. For one thing, the illegalities usually are difficult to define and prove. Secondly, many of the cases are settled out of court, thus leaving the issues up in the air.

But the Equity Funding case may lead to a landmark decision. "This one may be in the courts for years, perhaps even a decade," said one securities lawyer.

Professor Edward S. Herman of the University of Pennsylvania's Wharton School of Finance, writing in the *UCLA Law Review** on Equity Funding, commented on why the insider issue may not be considered seriously enough by the public:

"Perhaps this form of fraud is not regarded seriously because the market is so full of arbitrary advantage, privilege and insider-outsider relationships; it is such a combination of casino and jungle, and the legal and regulatory efforts to enforce equal information opportunity are so puny, that lambs foolish enough to enter such a den of wolves are asking to be eaten."

Continued Professor Herman on the role of the stock analyst:

---

*Edward S. Herman, "Equity Funding, Inside Information and the Regulators," *UCLA Law Review*, Volume 21, No. 1 (October, 1973), p. 1.

"There is enormous pressure on analysts and advisers to pass on [company] information, perhaps with a warning as to its source and legal status, and to let the client decide whether it can and should be used. . . .

"In the Equity case, the information provided by Secrist to Dirks and then outward . . . was definitely not authoritative, and was potentially libelous if publicized and not true. If Dirks had not used the information, there is a real possibility that the scandal would still not have surfaced. . . . [Dirks] claims to have been moved by a sense of moral obligation to bring to light a major fraud if the Secrist allegations could be confirmed. . . . The New York Stock Exchange charges against Dirks state that he should have disclosed his 'rumor' of 'material adverse information' to the exchange itself or to the SEC. But it was neither a rumor nor confirmed adverse information that Dirks received, merely an allegation with mainly hearsay support that needed further corroboration before it would be worth passing on as credible. Dirks went about collecting more information, which in the context seems sensible even if risky."

Professor Herman concluded that if Dirks indeed had gone to the authorities first before doing his own legwork, Equity Funding's officers involved in the fraud scheme might have had sufficient time to cover it up given the time it takes for bureaucratic machinery to shift into high gear.

"The SEC can move quickly on occasion," said Professor Herman, "but it often moves slowly . . . the SEC moved rapidly in the end, but as Secrist had forecast, in response to price and market events brought about by the activities of Ray Dirks."

One major case to surface from the Equity Funding quagmire involved a collision of two Wall Street titans: Salomon Brothers of New York, the big investment banking house, and The Boston Company, the substantial financial services management firm of the city of that name. Securities industry lawyers felt it could take the courts years to untangle this case and come up with a decision—unless it is ultimately settled out of court.

Salomon filed suit on April 11, 1973, within a few days after the Equity Funding case broke. The targets of the litigation were The Boston Company, two of Boston's subsidiaries, and dozens of the subsidiaries' clients.* This was done in an effort to rescind a sale of $8.3 million in Equity Funding common stock and $255,000 in EFCA bonds sold to the New York investment banking house by Boston and John W. Bristol & Company, Incorporated, an affiliate.

Salomon charged in United States Court for the Southern District (of New York) that the defendants possessed material information about the problems at Equity Funding—which it had acquired from Dirks but did not disclose to Salomon—when it sold 457,200 EFCA shares and the subordinated bonds to Salomon on March 26, 1973, the day before the Big Board stopped trading in EFCA stock.

A month after Salomon filed the lawsuit, a counterclaim was filed by the defendants denying Salomon's allegations that it unloaded Equity Funding securities based upon inside information about the fraud.

William W. Wolbach, president of The Boston Company, maintained that his firm "did not have inside information" and that the Salomon deal was "a bona fide trade." (This raised another interesting aspect of the litigation—the time-honored Wall Street tradition that "a trade is a trade," under which the trading principals are bound).

Salomon has paid for the EFCA bonds but not the stock.

"We've got the money," said Donald Feuerstein, a Salomon lawyer and general partner, who came to the firm from the Securities and Exchange Commission, where he had helped prosecute the landmark Texas Gulf insider case. "We had heard absolutely nothing [about the troubles at Equity

---

*Included are such prominent clients as Princeton University, Sarah Lawrence College, and Allied Chemical Corporation.

Funding] or I can assure you we would not have been bidding on the stock. We had not heard of the rumors when we bought the stock."

Feuerstein asked a series of rhetorical questions about the litigation, questions which he obviously expected the courts to meet head-on: "Was the information Bristol had inside information? Was it material [to the sale]? Did Bristol act on that basis? Is Salomon somehow disqualified from complaining because they [Salomon] had certain [material] information? Our position is we didn't. They [Boston] are going to try to prove that we did."

Bristol doesn't disclaim having talked with Dirks about Equity Funding *before* it made the sale to Salomon. How then does it argue that it made its decision to sell the big EFCA securities package independent of the reports it gathered from Dirks?

Boston refused to elaborate on its position. A spokesman simply reiterated Wolbach's statement denying that "it or its affiliates acted on the basis of inside information."

XVIII
The Real Losers

"I DON'T know of any financial fraud as massive as this and so dramatically fraudulent. I can't think of anything even remotely comparable."

So declared Robert Loeffler, the court-appointed EFCA trustee, in summing up the Equity Funding affair.

But the real tragedy, said Loeffler in an interview, didn't involve Wall Street or the reinsurers. Feeling most of the burden of grief, he said, was the public shareholder, not to mention big employee pension funds such as the State of Ohio Teachers' Retirement Fund, which lost over $10 million. (Unlike EFCA, however, no pension fund collapsed.)

EFCA had almost 10,000 shareholders, who had bought $500 million worth of interest in the corporation in the form of $300 million in stock and $200 million in bonds. Much of this was in the hands of the institutions, Wall Street's sophisticated moneymen who work for the banks, insurance companies, and mutual funds. But much of it also was in the hands of individual investors.

Loeffler recalled receiving a letter from a couple who said their son was a college student in desperate need of an operation. The parents declared they had begged, borrowed and scraped together enough money to invest in the hope that the security they selected would show near-term growth to finance the medical costs. The stock they selected was

Equity Funding. They purchased 500 shares just a few days before trading in the security was suspended. The letter said that all the family's savings went down the drain with Equity Funding and so did their son's chances of getting the operation.

An elderly suburban Los Angeles couple filed a shareholders' claim against the company for $987.03, representing their purchase of twenty-five shares of EFCA common. The wife said that outside of the couple's monthly social security check, their few stocks were "what we live on." She recalled her broker had called a short time before trading was suspended and urged the couple to unload because "he didn't think it was right. I said, 'I think it will straighten out.'"

Loeffler estimated that at least half the EFCA stock was held by individuals, as opposed to institutions. Who knows how many of these stockholders used their EFCA security as collateral on bank loans and how many individuals were faced with foreclosure on their homes, or personal bankruptcy? Several file cabinets in the office of the Los Angeles bankruptcy referee were stuffed with thousands of shareholder claims.

There were, of course, striking similarities between the EFCA case and the Watergate affair. Loeffler drew one of the obvious parallels.

"You cannot have a fraud of this nature without it being conducted from the top," Loeffler observed. "I don't know if Nixon knew of Watergate or not. But you had to have the moral climate that reflects the top . . . people don't do things that they know isn't all right with their boss . . . otherwise they'd be scared to death they'd be caught doing them."

There is also a vast *difference* between the Equity Funding case and Watergate, wrote Page Smith, the historian and biographer, in the Los Angeles *Times*—"a difference which may ultimately make Equity Funding loom the larger."

"The Watergate scandal is attributable to leaders of a political party which may be reformed or replaced (albeit only after several shaky years). Since a lack of confidence in politicians is nothing new, we have every reason to believe that its economic consequences will be limited both in effect and in time. The Equity Funding affair could have much more irremediable ramifications."

As far as investor confidence in the marketplace was concerned, the Equity Funding case's timing couldn't have been worse, coming as it did almost back to back with Watergate and following the financial collapse of the Penn Central Railroad. It came at a time when Wall Street was attempting to woo the public back into the market to provide badly needed liquidity, especially for middle-sized and smaller businesses which depend on the individual shareholder to provide them with operating cash. It came at a time when the public was questioning the values—political, business, moral—of our society. Loeffler's objective as trustee was to put the EFCA pieces back together again through a reorganization of the corporation (which was not completed at this writing) so that, he said, "we can at least restore some confidence in the ability of the system to step in and right things that had gone wrong."

Could it happen again? It appears inconceivable that fraud on the scale of Equity Funding could happen again in the business world, given the role of the regulators and the auditors, who have supposedly become more aware and enlightened in the wake of the disaster. But no investigator or regulator who worked on the case was prepared to say there couldn't be another Equity Funding lurking inside some outwardly respectable company that we recognize and do business with every day.

The corporate world must continually be resourceful and on guard to prevent further Equity Fundings, or the foundation upon which the capitalistic system rests—trust in dealing fairly and honestly with your competitor, the general public, the consumer, and the stockholder—will be severely damaged.

To be sure, corporate crime is nothing new. Collusion and market rigging have a long history. However, it is doubtful that one would find any precedent for the massive corporate fraud perpetrated in the Equity Funding case, involving millions of dollars in losses for the investing public and an orgy of corporate deceit built atop $2 billion in phony life insurance. The blow to the business community was incalculable, and it may take years to restore confidence in the integrity of an economy that can allow an Equity Funding to happen.

XIX
Goldblum Speaks Out

You have been forewarned that he was a big man. Well, he is even bigger in person. Dressed in a comfortable blue Paisley shirt, brown slacks, and loafers, Goldblum welcomed the authors into his comfortable $450,000 home at 909 North Whittier Drive, near Sunset Boulevard in Beverly Hills, and invited us to watch the last two minutes of the Minnesota Vikings-Washington Redskins football game in his den while a maid brought coffee and cookies on a silver tray and matching service.

Goldblum relaxed in a big, stuffed easy chair in a corner of the den and appeared in an expansive mood throughout a four-hour interview. (It was nine months after his termination from Equity Funding.) From time to time, Marlene, his wife, an attractive blonde, and his children wandered in and out. Bo, the family's golden retriever, played on the patio.

The former chairman was relaxed despite the tension of recent months, and freely discussed his early history and business experiences, frequently smiling and occasionally drifting into a philosophical discussion of life and people.

For example, in describing the aggressive tactics of his sales force in selling the insurance-mutual fund package in the early days of Equity Funding, Goldblum quoted Schopenhauer:

> To the establishment, every idea is first considered

ridiculous, then violently opposed and then is accepted as being self-evident.

But, he added, "I'm not a philosopher, I'm just a guy."

Throughout the interview, Goldblum maintained his complete innocence of the forty-five counts brought against him in the criminal indictment returned by the Federal Grand Jury.

"When I pleaded not guilty, I meant it," said Goldblum emphatically.

Moreover, he appeared astonished when questioned about the petty fraud being perpetrated under his nose by EFCA's upper and middle management. He showed surprise when he heard from the authors that money was being siphoned off to pay for the furniture of a New York woman, or that other executives were pocketing phony death claims and were involved in other deceptions.

Goldblum said that the case had greatly complicated his life. For one thing, he claimed he was financially wiped out. Much of his money was tied up in now worthless EFCA stock. He referred with bitterness to the litigation initiated by Robert Loeffler, the trustee, and asserted that Loeffler had no right to tie up "my money that I had acquired over the years."

Goldblum didn't mention a real estate asset he was believed to have sold that summer in order to raise badly needed cash. The sale was reported to have brought him approximately $750,000 in cash.

Goldblum exhibited rare anger during the interview when it was suggested he might have a secret Swiss bank account.

"I don't have any Swiss bank account," he emphasized. "I have no accounts outside the United States."

Moreover, he vigorously denied reports he was seen in Geneva in 1972 when he was supposed to be at an investors' conference in London and that he ducked into a doorway to avoid having to answer embarrassing questions.

"Sure, I've been to Switzerland," said Goldblum. In fact,

he said, he went there on vacation the first year he was married to Marlene. But Goldblum added that stories like that one about him being somewhere he wasn't really got him mad. "Tell the guy who told you that that he's full of shit," said the former Equity Funding chairman.

Goldblum reflected on some of the events that took place in those hectic few days before the company collapsed. As the rumors began mounting, Goldblum claimed he turned to his top lieutenant, Fred Levin, to ask if there was anything to the reports, and that Levin replied they were all "bullshit."

Finally, Goldblum said, the rumors began to mount and when he "saw what was happening" he realized that he was carrying more than $1 million in personal debt. That's why, Goldblum said, he wanted to sell off 50,000 shares through the brokerage house of Dishy, Easton. Furthermore, he said, the sale of stock each year "was in the context of my tax program." He added that the cash received from the stock sale would have been invested in municipal bonds. But the sale was blocked by the SEC as the company began crumbling.

Goldblum tossed aside the charge by some investigators that part of the motivation behind the phony insurance was to raise money to meet the company's dividend commitments. This was foolish, he said, when one considered that the dividend payout was only about $800,000, against some $15 million the company had in various banks.

He had made mistakes, though, no doubt about that, said Goldblum. Too late, he said, he became aware of some of the shortcomings of his personnel. "I was a fool," he declared.

His recollection of the showdown directors meeting of Sunday, April 1, 1973, also was one of bitterness. Goldblum contended that all of a sudden he was thrown into a situation where "I found my loyalty stretched between the company I'd built and my own responsibility to protect myself and my family. Do I become a Joan of Arc on the Cross?" he asked rhetorically. "I had to turn against the company I founded . . . I had to follow the advice of my counsel."

On the latter point, Goldblum, looking back, disagreed with his counsel at that time, Frank Rothman, about remaining silent at the meeting. "The advice I got from my lawyer gave me no room to move. It was a bad error of judgment. It foreclosed dialogue."* Goldblum said he had wanted "to test the water and find out who was the ringleader" behind the coup but his lawyer had advised him otherwise.

Nevertheless, Goldblum said he was still surprised at the outcome of the meeting during which he, Levin, and Lowell were ousted. "It was a big mistake" to throw out the officers, he declared. "It was like taking an army in the field and wiping out a whole echelon of officers—who would tell the foot soldiers what to do?"

"If they had left the company alone, it would have come out of it," he asserted. "They [the directors who fired Goldblum, Levin, and Lowell on April 1] acted on the strength of their emotions and not on the facts." He said the auditors should first have been allowed to finish their audit, which—when the rumors mounted—he claimed he had asked them "to do over again."

"There were things I didn't know about," said Goldblum without elaborating.

Goldblum continued:

"I have confidence that all the facts will be brought out . . . I have confidence in the trial system . . . I don't believe that I'm guilty . . . I have confidence that the system of justice will help me . . . I will not go to jail."

When asked about the case being built against him,

---

*In yet another irony in the Equity Funding case, Rothman, the lawyer with whom Goldblum obviously had had differences of opinion over how to handle his case, was a partner in the same Beverly Hills law firm as Eugene Wyman, another partner who was Goldblum's late good friend. Rothman told one of the authors that because of his previous client relationship he couldn't comment on the Goldblum statement.

reportedly by several former EFCA management employees, including Levin, in cooperation with the United States Attorney's Office, Goldblum responded: "If people tell lies, they will be disclosed as lies . . . facts are facts, lies are lies." He said that massive guilty pleas wouldn't necessarily mean that he, Goldblum, would throw in the towel, too. (At this writing, of the top three officers—Goldblum, Lowell, and Levin—only Levin had pleaded guilty to any of the fraud counts brought by the Federal Grand Jury.)

Goldblum was particularly critical of media accounts of the case which called it the biggest business fraud of the century. "Bullshit," he said. "It's the bubble of the century, not the fraud of the century. The implication that it is the biggest fraud of the century *is* the biggest fraud of the century."

In response to other questions about the case, Goldblum said he couldn't speak specifically about them on advice of his new attorney, Thomas Sheridan, one of the country's leading criminal trial lawyers. (Sheridan's background includes working for the United States Attorney's Office in Los Angeles, being prosecutor in the Sinatra kidnapping case, and a close association with Robert Kennedy when Kennedy was United States Attorney General.)

Quite obviously unless Goldblum decides to talk publicly regarding all that he knows about the charges, the full story of the EFCA scandal may never be known. And, at this writing, there were no signs that he would in any way change his mind or enter a guilty plea.

Goldblum repeatedly underscored his innocence and attempted to leave the impression that he had been put upon by those who do not understand what really happened at his company.

When asked to select a passage out of Shakespeare that, in his opinion, best characterized the Equity Funding affair, Goldblum smiled and recited from memory from Act V, Scene V of *Macbeth* when Macbeth declared:

To-morrow, and to-morrow, and to-morrow
Creeps in this petty pace from day to day
To the last syllable of recorded time;
And all our yesterdays have lighted fools
The way to dusty death. Out, out, brief candle!
Life's but a walking shadow, a poor player,
That struts and frets his hour upon the stage
And then is heard no more: it is a tale
Told by an idiot, full of sound and fury.
Signifying nothing.

On October 8, 1974, in a dramatic and unexpected turnabout, Stanley Goldblum stopped his trial in Los Angeles federal court to plead guilty to five criminal charges in connection with the massive fraud. He pleaded guilty to one count each of conspiracy, securities fraud, the interstate transportation of fraudulently obtained property, and the filing of false documents with the Securities and Exchange Commission.

Epilogue

IN the end, the plan of the trustee was to transform what was once the Goldblum-Riordan financial empire into a small holding company which could fit snugly into a few offices at Century City.

The other subsidiaries were to be spun off, with the exception of Bankers National Life Insurance Company of Parsipanny, New Jersey, and Northern Life Insurance Company of Seattle, Washington. Equity Funding Life was dismantled; its policies earmarked for Northern. Some 70 percent of EFLIC's policyholders stayed aboard, a tribute to trustee Loeffler and to J. Carl Osborne, who took over as conservator of EFLIC. Loeffler and Osborne established an "instant" communications system between EFLIC and its policyholders in an effort to assure EFLIC's customers that their policies were still good with the reorganized company.

Additionally, Loeffler retained some of EFCA's key executive personnel to aid in the reorganization, including Rodney Loeb, the corporation's general counsel.

In his report to United States District Judge Harry Pregerson under Chapter 10 of The Bankruptcy Act,* Loeffler reflected upon the fraudulent acts:

"[They were] basically of three types: the creation and

---

*Report of the Trustee of Equity Funding Corporation of America, February 22, 1974, p. 32.

inflation of assets in the balance sheet, the failure to record liabilities for borrowed cash, and the creation of bogus insurance which was co-insured with other insurance companies. The effect of all three practices was to inflate earnings and assets, and create the appearance of sustained growth at a substantial but measured rate. The insurance fraud also provided funds for EFCA's critical cash needs."

Loeffler noted that the major fraud technique involved "significant distortions" in the EFCA loans to customers in the insurance-mutual fund program and the corresponding fictitious commission earnings from the sales of mutual funds and life insurance.

Fraudulent accounting entries may have gone back to 1964, the trustee's report said. They had been injected into EFCA's annual report at the end of each financial year. "But by 1972," said the report, "increases of $2 million a month were booked monthly and adjusted quarterly."

In his general conclusions, Loeffler declared:*

"The company presented to the public and financial community as Equity Funding Corporation of America prior to April 1973 was virtually a fiction concocted by certain members of EFCA's management. The fiction had been enlarged upon, year by year, until EFCA had been proclaimed the fastest growing diversified financial company in *Fortune*'s list.

"When the bubble burst and the true company emerged, the company could be seen as a relatively small and totally unprofitable one despite all its acquisitions. Contrary to what had been represented: it did not have the assets; it did not have the revenues; it did not have the sales; it did not have the net worth; and it had not made the profits.

"EFCA's senior management continually asserted to the financial community, indeed as late as March 1973, that EFCA had developed at its home office the most sophisticated of management techniques and had achieved remarkable

Ibid., p. 81.

efficiency in all operations. That was perhaps the greatest fiction of all.

"Certain operations and particular departments did indeed function reasonably efficiently and well. Others could only be termed a shambles, and it was in these where the fraud occurred. Generally speaking, there were two areas of operations, each under a specific direct line of authority, where no controls existed. One was the home office insurance and marketing operation under the direction of the Executive Vice President—Insurance and Marketing [Fred Levin]. The other was the accounting and fiscal area under the direction of the Executive Vice President—Corporate Operations and Finance [Sam Lowell]. Both executives reported directly to the President [Goldblum]."

Loeffler pointed out that EFCA's debt structure "was impossible to carry" with a balance sheet showing $160 million in outstanding debt when it entered into bankruptcy proceedings. Thus, said Loeffler, reorganization was imperative.

The trustee's report declared that EFCA's fundamental business of marketing insurance would remain, but that the combination of selling insurance and mutual funds—the Equity Funding Program—would be eliminated.

How would all the class action claims be settled? Loeffler wasn't completely sure as this book went to press. Perhaps an out-of-court settlement could be reached. Perhaps a pool of stock could be set aside and carved up by the litigants. Certainly, when the stock of the new holding company once again resumed trading it would be expected to sell for but a few dollars a share over the counter—a far cry from its glory days of 1969 when the stock traded at over $80 a share on the prestigious New York Stock Exchange.

The end came on a humiliating note: a public auction of EFCA's plush furnishings that symbolized an era of fraudulent growth and unreal financial power. The three-day auction began on Saturday, February 16, 1974, on the sixth floor of the 1900 building where EFLIC was once ensconced. The trappings of splendor that were once EFCA were there to be plucked by the curious public: expensive furniture, oil paintings, art objects, grandfather clocks, antiques, and all the accoutrements of the successful corporate life.

The auctioneer opened the bidding and the vultures began picking at the cadaver. It was almost surrealistic. But then, so was Equity Funding Corporation of America.

Appendix*

I. EFCA IN EARLY 1973

A. General Organization

In March 1973 EFCA was essentially a holding company which itself did little more than provide financing and administrative support for the funding programs and for certain of its subsidiaries. Its subsidiaries were engaged in a diverse array of businesses. The insurance agency and broker-dealer subsidiaries marketed a broad range of financial products and services, not all of which were issued or managed by other EFCA subsidiaries. EFCA's other major subsidiaries included four life insurance companies, an investment advisory company managing three mutual funds, a savings and loan association, an international merchant bank, and companies involved in cattle breeding, real estate, and oil and gas. The latter three groups of companies were managing limited partnerships providing tax shelter investments. In terms of their financial value, EFCA's life insurance subsidiaries constituted its major holdings.

Six of EFCA's subsidiaries had separate principal offices—Bankers in Parsippany, New Jersey; EFNY in New York, New York; Northern in Seattle, Washington; Liberty in Los Angeles, California; Ankony in Grand Junction, Colorado; and Bishop's in Nassau, Bahamas.

The following chart shows EFCA's structure at March 31, 1973:

*The following documents were taken from the *Report of the Trustee of Equity Funding Corporation of America*, February 22, 1974.

```
                EQUITY FUNDING
             CORPORATION OF AMERICA
              LOS ANGELES, CALIFORNIA
```

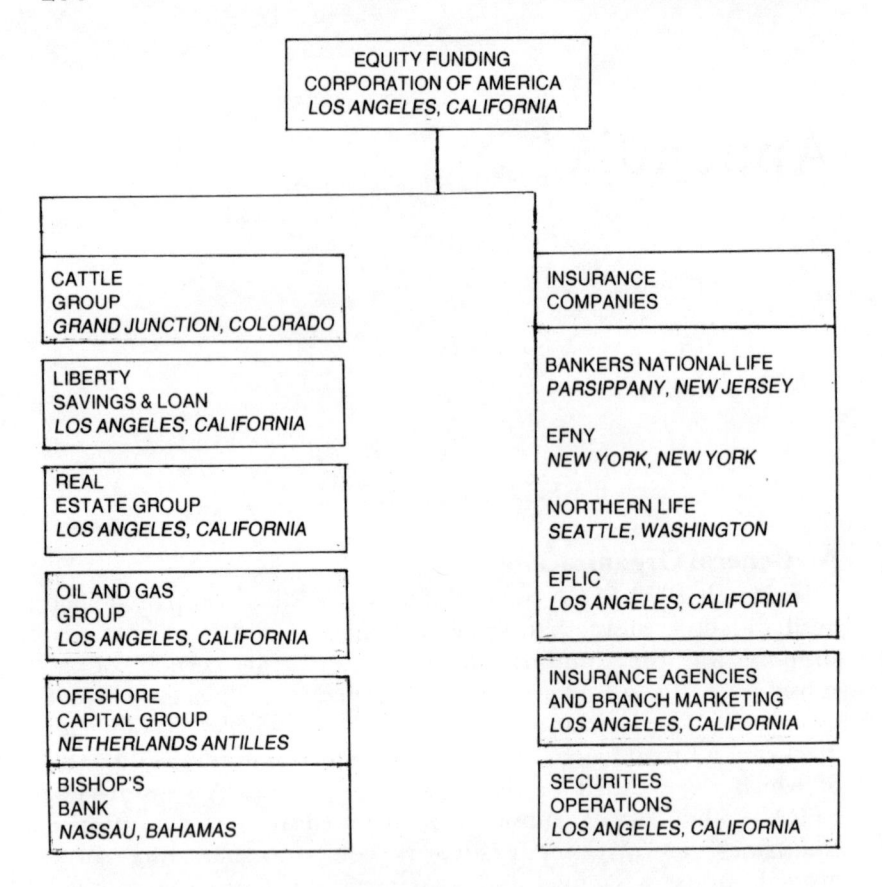

CATTLE GROUP GRAND JUNCTION, COLORADO	INSURANCE COMPANIES
LIBERTY SAVINGS & LOAN LOS ANGELES, CALIFORNIA	BANKERS NATIONAL LIFE PARSIPPANY, NEW JERSEY
	EFNY NEW YORK, NEW YORK
REAL ESTATE GROUP LOS ANGELES, CALIFORNIA	NORTHERN LIFE SEATTLE, WASHINGTON
OIL AND GAS GROUP LOS ANGELES, CALIFORNIA	EFLIC LOS ANGELES, CALIFORNIA
OFFSHORE CAPITAL GROUP NETHERLANDS ANTILLES	INSURANCE AGENCIES AND BRANCH MARKETING LOS ANGELES, CALIFORNIA
BISHOP'S BANK NASSAU, BAHAMAS	SECURITIES OPERATIONS LOS ANGELES, CALIFORNIA

The rest of EFCA's operations were conducted by approximately 650 employees out of EFCA's main offices at 1900 Avenue of the Stars in the Century City area of Los Angeles, California. Since operations were conducted along functional lines, rather than along lines dictated by corporate form, these employees performed services for a number of subsidiaries and were paid from a single payroll regardless of their ostensible positions with various subsidiaries. There were also approximately 100 salaried employees located in the marketing organization's branch offices.

At EFCA's headquarters there were seven executive vice presidents responsible for specific areas of the operations of EFCA and its subsidiaries, all of whom in turn reported to Stanley Goldblum, President and Chairman of the Board. The following table shows the areas of responsibility of the key executives:

Appendix

Name	Position
Stanley Goldblum	President and Chairman of the Board of Directors
Dov Amir*	Executive Vice President—Natural Resources Operations (directed the oil and gas operations)
Yura Arkus-Duntov	Executive Vice President—Investment Management Operations and Director (directed all activities relating to mutual fund management)
Herbert Glaser	Executive Vice President—Real Estate and Director (directed the real estate operations and Liberty Savings and Loan)
Fred Levin	Executive Vice President—Insurance Operations and Marketing and Director
Samuel B. Lowell	Executive Vice President—Corporate Operations and Finance and Director (chief financial and accounting officer)
Marvin A. Lichtig	Executive Vice President—Administrative Service and Treasurer
R. W. Loeb	Executive Vice President—General Counsel and Secretary
James C. Smith	Vice President—Insurance Operations (reported to Fred Levin and served as his principal staff assistant)
Michael Sultan	Vice President and Corporate Controller (reported to Samuel Lowell and served as his principal staff assistant)

*Resigned as of January 31, 1973.

Of the foregoing, only Messrs. Glaser and Loeb served the company during the Trustee's administration.

II. EFCA'S PERIOD OF ACQUISITION, 1967–1972

The following chart details the acquisition program chronologically:

1967

October — Presidential Life Insurance Company of America, whose name was later changed to Equity Funding Life Insurance Company.

1968

January — Crown Savings and Loan Association, later merged into Liberty Savings and Loan.

September — Investment advisor and distributor of Republic Technology Fund, Incorporated, whose name was later changed to Equity Progress Fund, Inc.

1969

January — Investors Planning Corporation of America, a sales organization, subsidiaries of which served as the investment advisor and distributor of Fund of America, Inc.

January — Ankony Farms, cattle breeding operation.

May — Bishop's Bank and Trust Company Limited.

July — Bundy Development Corporation, whose name was later changed to Equity Funding Development Corporation, real estate activities.

August — Traserco, Inc., which held an interest in an oil and gas exploration concession offshore Eucador.

1970

June — Diversified Land Co. (rescinded in 1972).

August — Independent Securities Corporation, a sales organization.

Appendix

1971

April — Liberty Savings and Loan Association.
October — Bankers National Life Insurance Company, and its subsidiary, Palisades Life Insurance Company, whose name was later changed to Equity Funding Life Insurance Company of New York.

1972

June — Northern Life Insurance Company.

III. EFCA'S MAJOR FINANCING ACTIVITIES

Although EFCA ultimately issued 7,874,699 common stock shares in various transactions, its 1964 offering of 100,000 shares at $6 per share through New York Securities Company was its first and only publicly underwritten primary stock offering. EFCA incurred substantial debt in order to finance certain of its acquisitions and to provide it with necessary working capital.

Set forth below in chronological order is a synopsis of the known major borrowings of EFCA. It is possible that other borrowings may have been made and repaid without entries having been made in EFCA's records. Of the borrowings listed below, which total $229 million, approximately $204 million were still outstanding at April 5, 1973.

1965

March — Private placement of $400,000 5¾% Subordinated Promissory Note—Series A, due 1970, and $600,000 5¾% Subordinated Convertible Promissory Note, Series B, due 1975

December — Public offering of $2,000,000 5½% Capital Subordinated Notes due 1980 with common stock purchase warrants

1967

May — Public offering of $6,000,000 5½% Convertible Debentures due 1982

1968

June — Public offering of $15,000,000 5¼% Convertible Subordinated Debentures due 1983

1969

February — Eurodollar public offering by N.V. of $25,000,000 5¼% Guaranteed Subordinated Debentures due 1989, guaranteed Subordinated Debentures due 1989, guaranteed by EFCA

November — Eurodollar private placement by N.V., of $10,000,000 7½% Guaranteed Subordinated Notes due 1974, guaranteed by EFCA, with EFCA common stock purchase warrants

1970

December — Public offering of $22,000,000 9½% Debentures due 1990 with common stock purchase warrants

1971

June — Private placement by N.V. of Note due 1973 for 4,000,000 Swiss Francs, guaranteed by EFCA

December — Public offering of $38,500,000 5½% Convertible Subordinated Debentures due 1991

December — Private placement by N.V. of Notes due 1975 for 20,000,000 Swiss Francs guaranteed by EFCA

1972

February — Private placement by N.V. of Notes due 1974 through 1977 for 19,200,000 Swiss Francs, guaranteed by EFCA

June — Private placement of $8,000,000 7¼% Notes due 1973 through 1975

June — Revolving credit agreement for up to $75,000,000, under which $50,535,688 was outstanding as of April 5, 1973

APPENDIX

1963–1973

Private placement of notes to finance funding programs, of which notes totalling $40,264,754 were outstanding at April 5, 1973

IV. SUMMARY OF ADJUSTMENTS TO BALANCE SHEET

(millions)

Stockholders' Equity at December 31, 1972 as shown in 1972 Annual Report to Stockholders **$143.4**

Eliminations of Fictitious or Fraudulently Inflated Assets
Inflated funded loans receivable ....(62.3)
Inflated value attributed to EFLIC ....(35.4)
Note receivable recorded in connection with a fictitious sale of future commissions ....(12.7)
Non-existent investments in securities and commercial paper ....(10.6)
Bogus note receivable from a Liechtenstein corporation ....(9.1)
Fictitious commissions receivable and advances to sales agents ....(5.9)
Fictitious investment in Bishop's Bank ....(2.7)
Revenues from purported sale of future Casualty Agency profits ....(2.9)
Fictitious capitalized mineral exploration costs ....(1.8)
Total Eliminations ....($143.4)

Writedowns of Assets
Investments in presently unsuccessful oil and gas exploration ventures ....(10.8)
Goodwill recorded on acquisition of marketing and cattle subsidiaries ....(14.1)
Deferred costs of debt financings ....(5.7)
Investment in Bishop's Bank (to net realizable value) ....(3.7)
Furniture, equipment and leasehold improvements ...(2.4)
Securities (to market value) ....(1.1)
Deferred stock bonus costs ....(4.4)
Total Writedowns ....($ 42.2)

Other Adjustments
  Foreign exchange revaluation losses ....(2.3)
  Reserves for doubtful collectibility of receivables ....(7.3)
  Modification of accounting practices in real estate
    operations ....(3.6)
  Trade payables and vendors' claims ....(1.4)
  Other adjustments including results of operations of
    EFCA and certain subsidiaries for period from
    January 1, 1973 to April 5, 1973 ....(2.6)
  Total Other Adjustments ....(17.2)

TOTAL REDUCTIONS ....($202.8)

Deferred taxes previously provided on nonexistent profits 17.3

**TOTAL REDUCTION NET
OF TAX ADJUSTMENT** ....($185.5)

**STOCKHOLDER'S EQUITY (DEFICIENCY
IN ASSETS) AT APRIL 5, 1973
AFTER ADJUSTMENTS** ....($ 42.1)

V. HISTORICAL RECORD OF GROWTH AND DEVELOPMENT OF EQUITY FUNDING CORPORATION 1961–1972 INCLUSIVE*

Major Corporate Events	Total Assets	Gross Revenue
1961—Jan. Company organized in September, 1960, under name of Tongor Corporation of America. Adopted present name January, 1961.	3,157,032	1,765,947
Engaged in sale of life insurance as general agent for two insurance companies, and mutual funds through selling group agreements.		
Originated the "Funded Program" concept in 1960, and marketed it through a broker-dealer subsidiary.		
1962—Sales of Funded Programs suspended in June pending compliance with regulatory and administrative requirements for registration of the "Programs" as a security.	4,496,909	1,836,260
1963—July Concluded a General Agency and Financing Agreement with Pennsylvania Life Insurance Company for the exclusive sale of their insurance policies in the "Programs."	6,245,077	1,324,852
Oct. First Registration Statement covering the Funded Programs declared effective by the SEC.		
1964—Dec. First public offering of shares of EFCA common stock—100,000 shares offering price $6 per share.	9,373,116	2,869,199
1965—March Private Placement of $400,000 Principals Amount 5¾% Subordinated Promissory Note—Series A, due 1970, and $600,000 5¾% Subordinated Convertible Promissory Note—Series B—due 1975.	16,528,822	5,363,348
May Secondary Offering 70,148 shares EFCA Common Stock.		
Dec: Public Offering of $2,000,000—5½% Capital Subordinated Notes due 1980 with Common Stock Purchase Warrants.		
1966—Aug. First Public Offering of shares of Equity Growth Fund of America, EFCA's first proprietary mutual fund. Formation of EFC Management Co. and EFC Distributors Corporation to manage the Fund and distribute its shares. Total Fund assets at year end $2,800,000.	20,167,953	7,486,812
Nov. Original listing of EFCA Common Stock .30 par value on American Stock Exchange.		
1967—May Public Offering of $6,000,000 principal amount—5½% convertible debentures due 1982 and 147,000 shares of EFCA Common Stock.	43,779,803	11,178,943
Oct. Acquisition of Presidential Life Insurance Company and Presidential Life Insurance Agency, October, 1967. Name later changed to Equity Life Insurance Company.		

Appendix

Net Income	Earnings Per Share (note a)	Long Term Debt	Branch Offices	Sales Force	# of States Doing Business	New Programs Sold	Face Amount New Life Ins. Sold	Amount Mutual Funds Sold
124,630	.05	None	10	224	3	2,309	56,960,000	5,547,000
24,320	.10	None	12	217	3	2,180	49,195,000	7,029,000
52,758	.21	300,000	15	167	3	371	24,863,000	3,637,000
389,467	.16	301,000	20	587	3	682	69,692,000	8,363,000
795,944	.28	3,063,047	22	687	7	1,525	156,000,000	19,673,000
1,177,355	.41	3,004,166	47	1,060	14	2,763	226,000,000	29,865,000
2,530,380	.52	13,649,038	85	1,810	22	3,912	N/A	36,235,000

Major Corporate Events	Total Assets	Gross Revenue
1968—Jan. Acquisition of Crown Savings & Loan Association and Palm Escrow Company.	79,005,010	19,179,117
June Public Offering $15,000,000—5¼% Convertible Subordinated Debentures due 1983, and 34,366 shares of EFCA Common Stock.		
Sept. Acquisition of Investment Advisor & Distributor of Republic Technology Fund, Inc. Name later changed to Equity Progress Fund, Inc.		
Sept. Formation of Equitex Petroleum Corp. to enter into oil and gas exploration ventures overseas in Africa and the Middle East.		
Oct. Equity Resources Ltd. Partnership Public Offering—Oil & Gas Exploration Investment Program.		
1969—Jan. Equity Funding Capital Corp., N.V. Eurodollar Offering of $25,000,000—5¼% Guaranteed Subordinated Debentures due 1989.	66,147,359	48,033,408
Apr. Acquisition of domestic business and assets of Investors Planning Corporation of America, including the investment advisor and distributorship of Fund of America, Inc., the sponsorship of 5 Contractual Plans, and a sales force of 2,000. Twenty-nine sales offices and approx. 200,000 clients.		
May Acquisition of 50% interest in Bishop's Bank & Trust Company Ltd., Bahamas. Later capital contribution increased interest to 97%.		
June Public Offering $10,000,000 Equity Resources Ltd. Partnership Offering (Oil & Gas Exploration and Development Investment Program).		
July Acquisition of assets and business of Ankony Angus and affiliates, cattle breeding and feeding operation.		
July Acquisition of Bundy Development Corporation. Name later changed to Equity Funding Realty and Construction Corporation.		
Aug. Acquisition of Traserco, Inc.—interest in Oil & Gas Exploration concession offshore Equador.		
Sept. Acquisition of Bedec International, SA., a research and consulting firm for international development.		
Oct. Equity Resources Ltd. Partnership 1969 Offering—$5,000,000—year end.		
Nov. Eurodollar Placement by Equity Funding Capital (EFCC) Corporation, N.V., guaranteed by EFCA, $10,000,000		

Appendix

Net Income	Earnings Per Share (note a)	Long Term Debt	Branch Offices	Sales Force	# of States Doing Business	New Programs Sold	Face Amount New Life Ins. Sold	Amount Mutual Funds Sold
12,870,000	1.86	50,739,000	113	5,000	37	11,139	825,000,000	N/A
18,192,000	2.45	49,728,000	131	5,000	43	13,813	1,700,000,000	108,000,000

	Major Corporate Events	Total Assets	Gross Revenue

Dec. Public Offering of $38.5 million—5¼% Convertible Subordinated Debentures due 1991.

Dec. Public Offering of $5,000,000 of Limited Partnership Interests in Ankony Cattle Systems /1971.

1972—Apr. First unsecured revolving credit agreement with First National City Bank for $40,000,000.   737,511,000   152,601,000

June Second unsecured revolving credit agreement with First National City Bank for $75,000,000.

June Acquisition of 91.2% of Northern Life Company.

Aug. Public Offering of $6,000,000 of Limited Partnership Interests in Equity Property Ltd. /1972.

Dec. Public Offering of $5,700,000 of Limited Partnership Interests in Equity Properties Ltd. /1972—Series B—later changed to EPL/73—3,322,000 of Offering sold prior to bankruptcy. All interests in the partnership, including land, completed and uncompleted buildings were sold to EJM Development Corporation, the proceeds of sale of which were used for full refund of Limited Partners Investment.

Range of Common Stock Prices

1965	1966	1967	1968	1969
6⅝–10½	8½–20¼	12–17⅜	14⅜–64⅜	44⅝–80¾

*Sources: Registration Statements as filed with the SEC, Prospectuses, Annual Reports to Stockholders, and various Company records.

Note (a): Earnings per share adjusted for stock splits.

All figures shown are year-end.

Appendix

Net Income	Earnings Per Share (note a)	Long Term Debt	Branch Offices	Sales Force	# of States Doing Business	New Programs Sold	Face Amount New Life Ins. Sold	Amount Mutual Funds Sold
22,617,000	2.81	104,499,000	132	4,000	47	N/A	1,781,690,000	N/A

1970	1971	1972
12¾–57⅞	27¾–47	31¾–46½

INDEX

Abernathy, John, 253
Abraham, Marshall, 80–82
Ada Oil Company, 115
Aikin, Lorn, 207
Allied Crude Vegetable Oil Refining Corporation, 149
American National Bank & Trust Company, 154, 180–81
"American National Trust Company," 154, 180–81
American Stock Exchange, 261
Amicor Bank of Switzerland, 99
Amir, Dov, 111–12, 114–15
Anderson, Harry, 128
Ankony Corporation, 23, 292, 300, 304
Apatinska Tekstilna Industrija, 119
Arbitrage accounts, 106
Arkus-Duntov, Yura 28, 92–93, 100–12, 114, 177, 188, 195, 218, 220, 227, 240–50, 270
Armstrong, Christy P., 181–82, 187, 221
Ashley, Daniel J., 148–49
Assicurazione Generali Insurance Company, 95
Auditors, role of, 16, 19, 75, 138–39, 141–42, 145, 154, 172–73, 175, 181, 183, 198–99, 203–4, 227, 244, 252–55, 282
  indictments, 19–20
  procedures, 139, 141–42, 183, 199, 203, 253
Augustine, Paul, 26–27

Baker, Lawrence, 187, 221–22, 224–27, 237, 240, 241
Ball, Joseph, 85, 214
Balint, Michael, 198–99, 204–5, 243

Banco di Santo Spirito, of Rome, 101
Bank of America, 262
Bank of Fernando Po, 113
Bankers National Life Insurance Company, 22, 47, 66, 78, 82, 128, 131, 137, 156, 161–63, 172, 200, 224, 254, 259, 285, 293, 302
Bankers Trust Company of New York, 184–85, 188, 194
Bankruptcy, 120, 245, 260
Banks, James Howard, 16, 135, 200–1, 202, 207, 240, 256
Banque du Rhône, 106
Barger, Richards D., 181–83, 227, 241–56
Bayh, Senator Birch, 71
Beckerman, Gary S., 16, 154–55
BEDEC International, 22, 94–95, 115, 300
Beneficial Standard Life Insurance Company, 162, 189
Beverly Wilshire Hotel, 187, 189, 198
Beyer, Harry M., 46
"Big Three," The, 50, 240, 244, 255
Bishop's Bank & Trust Company, Ltd., 23, 87, 105–6, 110, 118–21, 123, 163, 292, 300
Bland, Stephanie, 200
Block, Solomon, 16, 45, 183
Blundell, William E., 185, 193–94, 197–98, 200–1, 207, 224, 228–29, 257
Board of Directors, 33, 215, 239, 241–56,
  last meeting, 239, 241–56
  post-funeral meeting, 34–36
Bolger, Ray, 30

307

Bolton, John, 181
Boltz, Gerald E., 197-98, 202, 207-8, 211, 227-28, 240, 241, 244, 257, 262
"Borrowing theory," 129-30
Boston Company, Inc., The, 180, 183, 184, 190, 196, 272-74
Bowie, Robert R., 177, 215, 223-24, 227, 240-56, 261
Bowman, Wallace, 196-97
Bradley, Mayor Thomas A., 34
Brazil, 163
Brewer, H. C. "Jerry," 197, 223, 230-37, 240
Bristol, John W. & Company, 196, 273-74
Brown, Governor Edmund G., 18, 85
Buchalter, Irwin, 238
Buchalter, Nemer, Fields & Savitch, 219, 227, 238, 250
Buchalter, Stuart, 224, 238-39, 241-56
"Bugging." *See* Electronic eavesdropping
Bundy Development Corporation, 292, 300
Buszin, John M., 184

Cady, Roberts Company, case, 266
California Insurance Commission, 21, 39, 53, 85, 152, 164, 170, 175, 177, 178, 181-82, 206, 208, 210, 221, 242, 261
  audit, 181-82, 187, 206
  seizure, 221-22, 225-27, 244
Campbell, Glen, 66
Capo, David Jack, 16, 17, 159-60
Capurso, Michael, 224
Century City, 125, 187, 200, 231, 236, 238, 285
Certificates of deposit, 221-22
Chapter 10 proceedings. *See* Bankruptcy
Chase Manhattan Bank, 118
Cifico-Leumi Banque of Geneva, 116, 118
Citibank. *See* First National City Bank of New York
Clapp, Gloria Martica, 104
Class action suits, 261, 287
Code "99," 134, 139
Code "R," 134
Code "Y," 134, 172-73, 189, 191

Coe, Roger, 87, 119-21
Coinsurers, 129
"Cold comfort," 183
Collateral, 86
Collins, Lawrence Grey, 16, 140, 200-1, 240, 256
Compañía de Estudios y Asuntos, 117
Compagnie Financière de Paris et de Pays Bas, 122
Computers, 133-49, 158-59, 176, 198, 203, 218, 221, 254
  codes, 134, 143-48, 203
  crimes aided by, 142-49, 176
  role in Equity Funding fraud, 136, 142, 176, 203, 221
  staff, 135-40, 198, 200, 203
Congressional Life Insurance Company, 173
Connecticut General Life Insurance Company, 134, 173
Consul-Generalship of Senegal, 72
Cornfeld, Bernard, 22, 50, 104, 116
Counterfeit securities, 154-55
Courtney, Thomas W., 180, 183
"Creative accounting," 163-64
Cressey, Donald R., 130-31
Crown Savings & Loan Association, 292, 300, 302
Curtis, Jesse W., 17, 90, 206
Cuthbertson, Eugene R., 40-41, 43

Day, Dennis, 30
Dayan, Moshe, 70-71
Delafield, Childs, Inc., 168, 173, 184
Delafield, Walter, 194
De Silva, Alfonso Perez, 118, 119-20
Dirks, Lee, 168
Dirks, Raymond, 165, 166-71, 172-75, 178-180, 183-85, 188, 190-93, 201, 267, 270, 272
  background, 167-68
  early rumors, 173-74, 178-79, 193-94, 198
  insider question, 166, 169, 180, 183-85, 196-97, 265-68, 270-72
  meeting with Goldblum, 186, 190-93
Dishy, Bernard, 105-6
Dishy, Easton & Company, 104-5, 122, 220, 262, 270, 281
Dow Banking Corporation, 122
Doyle, Jack, 180-81, 231
DuPage County Grand Jury, 14

INDEX

309

D'Urso, Allessandro, 98, 100-1

Easton, Stanley, 105-6
ECLIPSE Project, 159
Ecuador, 112
Edens, Lloyd Douglas, 16, 128, 134, 139, 154, 163, 180-81, 203, 231, 240, 256
EFC Management Corporation, 93
Efi Banca of Rome, 95
Electronic data processing department, 133-34, 145, 158-59, 203, 219
Electronic eavesdropping, 200-1, 205-7, 239, 243
Embezzlement, 131, 176, 253, 280
  "Mary X" case, 86
  phony death claims, 131, 253
Encyclopaedia Britannica case, 148
Enslen, Sanford William, 175, 200, 218-19
Equitex Petroleum Corporation, 112, 300
Equitex Resources Corporation, 22, 112, 300
Equitorial Guinea, 113
Equity Development Corporation, 22
Equity Funding Capital Corporation, N.V., 23, 118, 122, 202, 300
Equity Funding Corporation of America (EFCA), 20, 39-42, 49, 95, 151, 177, 230, 257, 285-86
  assets, 295-96
  collapse, 259-60, 286
  European operations, 22, 50, 91-123
  founding, 20-21, 40-42
  future, 285-88
  general organization, 44, 160, 289-91
  growth, 292-99, 301-3
  major borrowings, 293-95
  members of board, 177
  sales force, 23, 46, 116, 137, 151, 226-27, 246
  stock sales, 19-20, 48, 185, 188, 195-97, 220
Equity Funding Life Insurance Company (EFLIC), 12, 18, 151, 154, 160, 176, 207, 220, 231, 244, 252, 257, 259, 285, 293
  dismantling, 285
  growth records, 47, 220, 286
  history, 38, 50, 293
  program and concept, 38-39
  role in fraud, 18-19, 154, 207, 231, 244
  seizure, 221-22, 225-27, 244
Equity Growth Fund, 22
Equity Progress Fund, 22, 292
Erickson, Ralph H. 198, 202
Ernst & Ernst, 128
Estes, Billie Sol, 149
Etablissement Grandson, 117
Ethiopia, 112
Evans, Jerome H., 15, 18
Executive lunches, 56-57
Executive offices, 62-64
Executive protocol, 126-27, 160

Federal Bureau of Investigation, 219
Federal Grand Jury indictment, 14, 45-46, 134-35, 140-41, 154, 206-7, 258, 280, 283
Fernando Po, 113
Feuerstein, Donald, 273-74
Fidelity Corporation of Richmond, Virginia, 223, 234, 240-41
First Executive Corporation of Los Angeles, 181
First National City Bank of New York, 86, 99, 163, 178, 197, 211, 223, 230-31, 240, 242, 247, 258-59, 304
Foreign bank deposits, 106, 111, 116, 123-24, 280
Founders Life Insurance Company, 220, 225
Fowler, Jerry, 180
Fraud, 21, 44-46, 52, 124, 131, 142, 154, 160, 172, 188, 191, 197, 201, 212, 218, 227, 234, 244, 254, 275, 277-78, 285-87
Franklin National Bank of New York, 118, 230, 259
Freedman, Levy, Kroll & Simonds, 205
Freedman, Marlene, 105-11
Freeman, Neil, 253
Fund of America Corporation, 22, 292, 300
"Funded program" concept, 37-40, 298

Gardinier, Richard, 16
Garrett, Ray, Jr., 52
Germann, Edward J., 175, 178
"Give-ups," 104-9

Glaser, Herbert, 28, 43–44, 113, 183, 208–9, 210, 215–29, 238, 240, 241–56
Glore Forgan & Company, 41
Goff, Donald, 198, 201
Golan, Joseph, 92–95, 100–2, 112, 123
Goldblum, Leah, 58–60
Goldblum, Marlene, 60, 262, 279
Goldblum, Stanley, 11, 15, 33, 54–73, 83, 127, 154, 157–60, 177, 179, 181, 182, 190–93, 195–97, 203–4, 208–9, 210–11, 215–18, 220–26, 236, 240–50, 262–63, 279–83, 287
  Beverly Hills home, 31, 34, 61–62, 64–65, 67, 279–85
  childhood, 57–58
  early aspirations, 58
  interview with authors, 54–55, 64, 178, 279–83
  mathematical ability, 58
  personality, 32, 54–55, 66–67, 69–70, 83, 157, 283–84
  physical fitness, 58, 64–65
  possible role in fraud, 18, 49, 73, 119, 154, 181, 203–4, 210–11, 215–16, 280
  resignation, 72–73, 240, 250
  stock shares, 220, 269–70, 281
  Vatican meeting, 96
Goldman, Sachs & Company, 167, 186, 196
Goldstein, Samuelson swindle, 197
"Good faith" policy, 135
Good, William F., 83–84, 224
Goodman, Steven Michael, 207
Goodman, Theodore, 28
Gootnick, William, 17, 134, 141, 158–59, 198, 203–4, 223
Gorrelick, Allen, 173, 178, 184, 198
Great Southern Insurance Company, 254
Green, Alan Lewis, 16, 135–38, 145, 200
Growth standards set for company, 212

Hackett, Buddy, 65
Haskins & Sells, 75, 160, 198, 204, 243, 252
Haveson, Joe, 46
Herman, Edward S., 271–72
Hilsman, Roger, 69
Holloway, L. E., 232
Holmes, Gardis, 205–6, 219
Hopper, Patrick, 128, 161–64, 172, 174, 186, 189, 197, 200–2, 228,

Humphrey, Hubert, 69–70
Hyatt Corporation, 72, 113
Hyman, Frank, 141–42

Illinois Insurance Department, 21, 76, 152, 164, 170, 180–82, 206, 210, 222, 242, 261
  audit, 154, 180–82, 187, 206, 210, 219, 221, 243
"Impossible Dream," 30
Independent Securities Corporation, 161, 292, 302
Indonesian Development Corporation, 251
Insider trading, 166–71, 180, 184, 185, 196–97, 265–73
Institutional Capital of Chicago, 180, 185
Institutional Investor's Conference, 197
"Insurance Club," 131
Insurance industry regulation, 21
Internal Revenue Service, 50–51, 104–5, 108–09, 111, 121, 131
International Business Machines Corporation, 134, 147, 148–49, 159
Investors Diversified Services, 264
Investors Overseas Services, 22, 50, 51, 104, 116
Investors Planning Corporation of America, 116, 292, 300
Israel, 70–72, 94, 112, 163

Jacobson, Robert V., 146

Kalmbach, DeMarco, Knapp & Chillingworth, 181
Kaunda, Kenneth David, 112
Keller, Lester M., 16
Keller, William D., 14
Kentucky Central Insurance Company, 254
Keystone Custodian Funds, Inc., 39, 43, 104–5
Kramer, Vic, 183, 184, 194–95, 202–3, 208, 212
Kroll, Milton, 205, 209, 212, 216–17, 219, 240–56

Lawson, Herbert, 185, 193, 202
Lechler, Charles, 26
Levin, Carol, 78, 79, 83, 232
Levin, Fred, 15, 17, 49, 68, 74, 76–80, 83–85, 123, 127, 131, 154, 162–64,

INDEX

173, 181, 182, 190, 195, 197, 206, 209, 211–12, 223, 224, 230–37, 240–50, 281–83, 287
  background, 76
  certificate of deposit, 85, 222
  confrontations with authors, 78
  guilty plea, 17–18, 90, 206, 283
  Northern stock deal, 230–37
  personality, 74, 83, 223
  possible role in fraud, 164, 173, 181, 234, 236
Lewis, Arthur Stanley, 15, 128, 133–34, 136, 154, 174–75, 187, 191, 202, 210, 240, 256
Lewis, Mark Charles, 16, 138–39, 252
Liberté trip, 92
Liberty Savings and Loan Association, 23, 50, 259, 292, 293, 302
Lichtig, Marvin A., 16, 45
Liechtenstein, 117, 119
"Little Six," The, 240, 244, 247
Livingston, Gale, 241–56, 261
Loeb, Rhodes, 121
Loeb, Rodney, 55–56, 99, 188–89, 192–93, 200, 204–6, 209, 212–15, 218, 219–29, 238–56, 262–63, 285
Loeffler, Robert, 23, 260, 262–64, 275–77, 280, 285–87
  appointment as trustee, 263–64
  EFCA's future, 277, 285
Loews Corporation, 195–97
Logan, William A., 29
Lombardi, Vincent, 32
Lonn, Mary, 193
Los Angeles County Sheriff's Office, 148
Los Angeles *Times*, 129, 276
Loud, Nelson, 28, 177, 217, 241–56, 261, 270
Lowell, Barbara, 75, 79, 96
Lowell, Samuel, 15, 17, 50, 74–76, 85–90, 96, 118, 121, 123, 127, 151, 158, 209, 218, 220, 240–50, 270, 282, 287
  background, 50, 75–76
  "confession," 88–90, 250
  "Mary X," 86–88
  personality, 74, 218
Luna, Douglas, 222

Madagascar, 113
Majerus, Francis D., 17, 162, 189, 199–200, 202, 228
Maloney, William, 185–86, 189

"Manufacturing parties," 136–41, 162
"Maple Drive Gang," 133–50, 252
Maple Drive office, 138–50, 219, 227, 252
  atmosphere, 139–40
  personnel, 138
  phony insurance, 136, 227
Mass Marketing Division, 138
Mauck, Fred, 226
McClellan, Donald, 16
McCormick, Gordon C., 29, 37–42, 49, 59
  mutual funds and insurance, 38–40
  "squeezed out," 41
McGovern, George, 69
McIntyre, James Francis Cardinal, 29
McKesson & Robbins case, 149–50
McLeod, Edith, 105
Meir, Golda, 70–71
Memmo, Roberto, 101
Mercado, William, 16,17,51–53,158, 251
Merrill, Lynch, Pierce, Fenner & Smith case, 266
Miami Dolphins, 26
Middle management, 126, 136–42, 176
  role in fraud, 141
Minneapolis National Life Insurance Company, 127
Minnesota Insurance Commission, 46–47
Monkarsh, Eugene, 183, 251
Monkarsh, Jerry, 183, 202, 251
Morgan Guaranty Trust Company of New York, 144–45
Mutual Funds, 37–40, 298

National Association of Securities Dealers, 67
National Bank of North America, 230, 259
National Committee for the Reelection of a Democratic Congress, 71–72
Nemer, Jerry, 15, 238–39, 241–56, 258
New Jersey Insurance Commission, 163–64
New York Securities Company, 188, 194, 217
New York Society of Security Analysts, 157–58
New York State Insurance Commission, 175, 178, 188
New York Stock Exchange, 21, 104, 166, 169–70, 185, 188–89, 194,

197, 208, 220, 234, 243, 261, 268
New York *Times*, 167
Newman, John Marshall, 78, 123, 258
"Ninety-Nine Business," The, 134
Nixon, Richard M., 71, 276
Northern Life Insurance Company of Seattle, 22, 86, 137, 178, 230–32, 254, 259, 285, 293, 304
  stock certificates, 86, 231, 235–37

Ochoa, Robert, 17, 154–55
Offset by banks, 259
Ogg, Leslie L., 178, 202
Ohio Teacher's Retirement Fund, 275
Osborne, J. Carl, 285
Outside directors, 177, 215, 241–56, 261

Pacific Telephone Company case, 146–47
Palisades Life Insurance Company, 47, 293, 302
Panarites, Peter E., 209, 241–56
Pantenella pasta factory, 95–97, 114
Parker, Donn B., 142–44, 149
Pavia & Harcourt, 117
Payne, Gleeson, 181, 200, 220–22, 225–27, 240
Peat, Marwick, Mitchell & Company, 252
Pennsylvania Life Insurance Company of Los Angeles, 46, 129, 137, 173
"Phillips, Joseph S.," 180
Phoenix Mutual Life Insurance Company of Hartford, 134
Phony bonds, 137, 154, 180, 221, 224, 231, 244, 247
Phony insurance policies, 18–19, 46–48, 133, 137, 139, 162, 189, 198, 218, 221, 244, 251, 281
  manufacture of, 133, 137–39
  merger into system, 137–39
Phony reinsurance, 129, 137, 173, 236, 254
Pilella, Gianfranco, 101
Platt, Raymond J., 40–41, 43
"Policy parties," 136, 139–41, 162
Pollack, Irv, 207
Pregerson, Harold, 258, 260, 263, 285
Premium loans, 48
Presidential Life Insurance Company of America, 49, 77, 292
Price, Waterhouse & Company, 255

Public shareholders, 275–78

Quaalude, 140

Raff, William F., 177, 200, 218–19, 243
Ranger National Life Insurance Company of Dallas, 134, 137, 173–74, 252, 254
"Razzle," 31
Reagan, Ronald, 221
Receivership, 214, 244, 254
Reinsurance, 18–19, 134–35, 159, 173, 254
Republic Technology Fund, 107, 292, 300
Resignations, executive, 239–40, 242–50, 282
Richards, Harold, 223, 224, 233–34, 236, 240–41, 247
Riordan, Jacqueline, 26, 29
Riordan, Michael, 25–35, 40–42, 60, 72, 103, 108–10, 116, 230
  death and funeral, 27, 29–32
  founder of EFCA, 40–42
  role in early history of company, 49–50, 103, 111, 116
Riordan, Richard, 35–36
Ritter, Dr. Rupert, 117
Rothman, Frank, 211, 213–14, 250, 282
Rouble, Maurice D., 182, 187

St. Martin of Tours Church, 29
Sakaguchi, Kiyofumi, 176–77, 200, 218–19
Salaries and expense accounts, 66, 127–28, 191, 249, 255
Salik, Charles E., 107
Salik Bank of Basel, 106–7
Salomon Brothers, 196, 272–74
Sasse, Ginny, 204, 213
Sayre, Judson, 215, 241–56, 261
Schneider, John, 239–40, 242–56
Schoenfeld, Douglas, 83
Sears, Roebuck and Company Pension Fund, 180
Secrist, Ronald, 16, 87, 131–32, 141, 160–61, 164, 172–74, 177, 180, 183, 186, 267, 270
Securities and Exchange Commission, 12, 21, 51–53, 104, 107, 164, 166, 170, 178, 188, 197–98, 202, 205, 210, 219, 234, 235, 240, 244–48, 257–58, 265–66, 271

Index

Seidman and Seidman, 45, 138, 154, 180–81, 183, 198, 204, 209, 218–19, 227, 243, 244, 252–54
Seligman, Lorna, 50, 104–5
Seligman, Ralph, 50, 103–4
Senegal, 72, 113
Senghor, Léopold-Séder, 94
Shareholder claims, 275–76
Sheridan, Thomas, 270, 283
Slade, Jarvis, 188–89, 194
Smith, Barney & Company, 158, 177, 181
Smith, James Cyrus, Jr., 15, 17, 85, 127, 134–35, 154, 174, 176, 191, 203, 210, 222, 233, 240, 256
Smith, Page, 276–77
South American ventures, 87–88, 123
Spencer, Robert, 199, 201, 253
Sporkin, Stanley, 198, 202, 207
Stainbrook, Dr. Edward, 128–29, 132
Steen, James, 224
Steffens, Roswell case, 143–44
Standard & Poors Corporation stock report, 155–156
Stans, Maurice, 71
Stock bonuses, 253
Stock certificates, 230–35, 237
Sultan, Michael E., 15, 86, 99, 154, 160, 220
Supreme Meat Packing Company, 59
Swiss bank accounts, 118, 123–24, 280
Switzerland, 109–10, 118, 123, 280–81
Symonds, William E., 16, 129–30, 132, 139–40, 240, 256

Texas Gulf insider case, 266–67
"Tippee rule," 261, 266
Tisch, Laurence A., 195–96, 197
Tongor Corporation, 38–39, 298
Traserco Inc., 112, 115, 292, 300
Touche Ross & Company, 255
Tunney, John, 70
"Twisting," 39

Unione Bank of Milan, 99

United California Bank, 79, 107, 118, 154, 163
United Missouri Bank, 262
U.S. Court for the Southern District of New York, 196, 273
United States Justice Department, 116, 123, 219
University Computer Company case, 148

Vatican, 95–96, 100
Venouziou, Aaron, 17

Wall Street, 20, 30, 104, 125, 155, 166, 169, 180, 198, 265–67, 273
  initial impact of fraud, 198, 208
  lack of preventive measures, 169
Wall Street Journal, The, 12, 45, 50, 79, 169, 185, 193, 197, 201, 204, 228–29, 257, 260, 267–68, 271
"Wangerhof, Dr. Heinrich," 117, 119
Warshauer, Jack, 251
Watergate, 276–77
Weiner, Julian S. H., 16, 45
Wells Fargo Bank, 85, 222, 230–31, 232, 235, 259
Wild Whist Bridge Club, 74
Williams, Lawrence, 66–67, 188–89, 204–5, 208, 209–10, 219, 223, 240, 242–56
Winters, Jonathan, 30
Wolbach, William W., 273–74
Wolfson, Weiner, Ratoff and Lapin, 45, 138
Wyman, Bautzer, Rothman and Kuchel, 211, 262
Wyman, Eugene, 65, 70, 282

"X, Mary," 86–88

"Y Business," The, 134, 172, 189, 191
Yorty, Sam, 34
Yugoslavian transaction, 119

Zambia, 112, 114
Zukowski, Gerald S., 180